W9-BLT-289

Success seems to be largely a matter of hanging on after others have let go.

—William Feather

HOW TO
START &
OPERATE
A SMALL
BUSINESS

A GUIDE FOR THE YOUNG ENTREPRENEUR

Module 1: Basic and Intermediate
Module 2: Advanced

The National Foundation for Teaching Entrepreneurship

By Steve Mariotti with Tony Towle

Ninth Revised Edition

This module is dedicated to
Raymond Chambers, Elizabeth, Charles G. and David H. Koch,
and the Honorable John C. Whitehead

Special dedication to
Bernard A. Goldhirsh and Diana Davis Spencer

Special thanks to
Joanne Beyer of the Scaife Family Foundation
Barbara Bell Coleman of the
Newark Boys' and Girls' Clubs
Chris Podoll of the William Zimmerman Foundation
Stephanie Bell-Rose of the Goldman Sachs Foundation
The Shelby Cullom Davis Foundation
Tom Hartocollis, Jeff Raikes, and the Microsoft Corporation
Nasdaq Educational Foundation
Ronald McDonald House Children's Charities
Dr. Kathleen R. Allen, University of Southern California
and
Michael Caslin, Debra DeSalvo, Julie Silard Kantor
Leslie Pechman Koch, and Jack Mariotti

Curriculum development assistance from
Chris Meenan and Nancy Rosenbaum

Edited by
Debra DeSalvo

Design Consultation/Production by
WestGroup Communication, Inc.

Photography by
Mike Kuczera, and Krasner and Trebitz

Illustrations by
Maija Wilder
(Some illustrations were based on previous work by Jeff Faria, Meryl Hurwich,
Al Stern, and Daryl Joseph Moore.)

For further information regarding NFTE programs and products, or to discuss the
availability of programs in your area, contact (212) 232-3333; fax (212) 232-2244; www.nfte.com.

Office of the President
The National Foundation for
Teaching Entrepreneurship, Inc. (NFTE)
120 Wall Street, 29th Floor
New York, NY 10005

Dear Student:

This course has been designed to teach you everything you will need to start and maintain your own small business. We hope that what you learn here will help you achieve financial independence and personal satisfaction. Knowing how business works will be of great value in any future employment you may have.

Learning the principles of entrepreneurship will teach you about more than just business and money, however. In this module, for example, you will learn, among other things, how to negotiate, calculate return on investment, perform cost/benefit analysis, and keep track of your income and expenses. These are all skills that apply to your personal as well as your business life. Even if you don't become a lifelong entrepreneur, learning how to start and operate a small business will give you an understanding of the business world that will make it much easier for you to get jobs and create a fulfilling career for yourself.

The characteristics of the successful entrepreneur — a positive mental attitude, the ability to recognize opportunities where others only see problems, and openness to creative solutions — are qualities worth developing. They will help you perform better in any situation life throws at you.

This is not a difficult course and I hope you will enjoy it. Just take it one chapter at a time. If you have any questions or comments, please write to me at the above address. I also hope you will visit our website for NFTE graduates, http://alumni.nfte.com for information on how you can compete in our national business plan contests. Good luck!

Sincerely yours,

Steve Mariotti

Steve Mariotti
Founder and President, NFTE

Attention Students

NFTE wants to hear from you! Besides being the publishers of your textbook, we are a national organization that helps young people like you improve their academic performances and start their own small businesses. By completing this course, you may be eligible to become a member of the NFTE alumni network. As a NFTE alumnus, you can:

- Log on to our alumni website, where you will find information about small business financing, colleges, scholarships, internships, and much more: **http://alumni.nfte.com**
- Participate in our summer BizCamps
- Enter national and local business plan competitions
- Join a young entrepreneurship club in your community

And the best part is that you won't have to wait until you finish the course to join. Visit our alumni website (listed above) and start enjoying the benefits right now!

You can also contact us directly:

National Alumni Services
The National Foundation for Teaching Entrepreneurship (NFTE)
120 Wall Street, 29th Floor, New York, NY 10005
1-800-FOR-NFTE
Fax: 212-232-2244
E-Mail: alumni@nfte.com

Preface

The two Modules designated 1 and 2 that comprise *How to Start and Operate a Small Business: A Guide for the Young Entrepreneur* can be used as an independent introduction to entrepreneurship and basic business principles, or may be interwoven with other curricula. The course material meets academic standards, including the U.S. Department of Labor Secretary's Commission on Achieving Necessary Skills (SCANS), the National Council for the Teaching of Mathematics (NCTM) Curriculum and Evaluation Standards, and NCSS Curriculum Standards for Social Studies.

The two Modules are meant for use in conjunction with the corresponding Workbooks, also designated 1 and 2.

Entrepreneurship draws from a number of disciplines, so that many of the topics touched on in this course — such as economics and accounting — could not be explored in depth. We hope that students will be inspired to study in greater detail subjects that we can only introduce. Our purpose here is to provide the fundamentals of starting and operating a small business venture.

Our textbooks have been designed to correlate in a general way with our online learning program, NFTE BizTech™, which can be reached at www.nfte.biztech.com/nfte/biztech.

Below are the respective contents for both Modules 1 and 2 and BizTech.

Module 2	BizTech Chapters

Steve Mariotti

President & Founder
National Foundation for Teaching Entrepreneurship (NFTE)

Steve Mariotti received his undergraduate and M.B.A. degrees from the University of Michigan, Ann Arbor, and has studied at Harvard University, Stanford University, and Brooklyn College. His professional career began by serving as a Treasury Analyst for Ford Motor Company. He then founded Mason Import/Export Services in New York.

In 1982, Steve Mariotti made a significant career change and became a business teacher in the New York City public school system. It was at Jane Addams Vocational High School in the Bronx that Steve Mariotti developed the insight and inspiration to bring entrepreneurial education to youth. This led to founding the National Foundation for Teaching Entrepreneurship (NFTE) in 1987.

Since its founding, NFTE has become a major force in promoting and teaching entrepreneurial literacy and basic academic and business skills to young people both in the United States and abroad. To date, NFTE has served over 40,000 young people and trained more than 1,500 teachers and youth workers in 42 states and 14 countries.

Steve Mariotti has received many honors and awards for his work in the field of youth entrepreneurship including: Best Economics Teacher in New York State (1988); National Award for Teaching Economics, The Joint Council of Economic Education (1988); Best Teacher of the Year, National Federation of Independent Businesses (1988); Honorary Doctorate in Business and Entrepreneurship, Johnson & Wales University (1990); Entrepreneur of the Year Award, *Inc.* magazine, with Ernst & Young and Merrill Lynch (1992); The Appel Award, Price Institute for Entrepreneurial Studies (1994); and The University of Michigan Business School Entrepreneurship Award (1999).

Mr. Mariotti has co-authored sixteen books, including *How to Start and Operate a Small Business*, with Tony Towle, and *Entrepreneurs in Profile*, with Jenny Rosenbaum. A more advanced version of *How to Start and Operate a Small Business* was published by Times Books, a division of Random House, in 1996. Now in its second edition, this popular book, *A Young Entrepreneur's Guide to Starting and Running A Business*, has sold more than 75,000 copies.

Tony Towle

Tony Towle has worked for Steve Mariotti and NFTE since its inception. In addition, he has written about art and is a poet whose books include *North, Autobiography, Works On Paper, Some Musical Episodes* and, most recently, *A History of the Invitation (New & Selected Poems 1963–2000)*.

About NFTE

The National Foundation for Teaching Entrepreneurship, Inc. (NFTE, and pronounced "Nifty") is a national nonprofit organization founded to introduce youth to the world of business. Through special training programs, NFTE teaches the fundamentals of entrepreneurship, focusing on how to start and maintain a small business.

NFTE believes that young people have extraordinary potential for business achievement and possess many of the qualities of the successful entrepreneur, such as a willingness to take risks, and resiliency. By making business both interesting and comprehensible, NFTE seeks to encourage youth to participate economically in their communities, as well as in society at large.

NFTE's goal is to strengthen local communities through youth training, teacher education, curriculum research and development, as well as public education and information forums.

Acknowledgments

I would like to thank my writing partners, Tony Towle, who from NFTE's very beginning helped me organize my thoughts and experiences, and Debra DeSalvo, without whose gift for organization and rewriting, this book would never have been possible. I would also like to acknowledge the significant contribution of Pittsburgh Regional Director Chris Meenan, as well as other NFTE executives: Del Daniels, Margaret Dunn, Elsa Huaranca, Dorian Johnson, Julie Silard Kantor, Leslie Pechman Koch, Talia Nagar, Christine Poorman, Jane Walsh, Joel Warren, and particularly Nancy Rosenbaum and Leonora Snyder, who have made numerous helpful suggestions and have taught me the importance of sound process.

In addition, I would like to thank my brother, Jack, the best CPA I know, and my father, John, for financing much of NFTE's early work and for their continuing love and guidance. I'd also like to acknowledge my partner and colleague, Michael Caslin, for bringing order and discipline to our organization, and for invaluable counsel in helping me learn the finer points of vision and leadership. Mike has also made innumerable suggestions to refine our curriculum. Thanks are due, also, to Alaire Mitchell for her educational expertise; to Peter Eisen for helping me get the accounting sections "right"; and to all the other teachers, students, experts, and friends who were kind enough to review this book and help me improve it. Special thanks also go to Marvin Berk & Felicia Telsey at WestGroup Communication for their creativity and dedication.

In addition, I must express my gratitude to Jenny Rosenbaum for helping me write many of the entrepreneurial profiles included in the text (which are adapted from NFTE's *Entrepreneurs in Profile*). Thanks also, to Howard Stevenson, Jeffry Timmons, NFTE Board Member Stephen Spinelli, and William Bygrave for their academic and business expertise; my first three students — Vincent Wilkins, Josephine Reneau, and Howard Stubbs; and Lisa Hoffstein, Executive Director of the University Community Outreach Program, who gave us our first contract and has been instrumental in NFTE's development. The efforts of NFTE Board Chairman Tom Hartocollis of Microsoft, Richard Fink of Koch Industries, Michie Slaughter, Bob Rogers, and Michael Herman of the Ewing Marion Kauffman Foundation, and Mike Hennessy and John Hughes of the Coleman Foundation, have also been crucial to NFTE's development over the years.

I would also like to recognize the efforts and contributions of members of NFTE's National Board of Directors: Albert Abney, Patricia Annino, Bart Breighner, Jay Christopher, John Fullerton, Bernard Goldhirsh, Verne Harnish, Tom Hartocollis, Landon Hilliard, James Holden, Robert Hurst, Loida N. Lewis, James Lyle, Arthur Samberg, Andrew Sherman, Diana Davis Spencer, Kenneth Starr, and Peter Walker. I would also like to acknowledge the inspired guidance provided by our National Executive Committee: Howard Buffett, Lewis Eisenberg, Theodore Forstmann, Hon. Jack Kemp, Elizabeth Koch, Alan Patricof, Jeff Raikes, and Hon. John Whitehead. I also would like to express appreciation and deep gratitude to the many philanthropists who have supported our work. In addition, please see page xii for the list of NFTE's largest supporters over the years.

Finally, I want to thank my mother, Nancy, a wonderful special-education instructor who showed me that one great teacher can affect eternity; my friends and mentors, Ray Chambers and Hon. John Whitehead; Bernard Goldhirsh for twelve years of friendship and helping put entrepreneurship on the map with the founding of *Inc.* magazine; and the late Gloria Appel of the Price Institute for Entrepreneurial Studies, for funding NFTE teacher education and being a good friend.

In addition, I would like to thank Steve Alcock, Lena Bondue, Andrea Levitt Bonfils, Dawn Bowlus, Camy Calve, Shelly Chenoweth, Janet McKinstry Cort, Erik Dauwen, Clara Del Villar, Tom Flaherty, Christine Chambers Gilfillan, Andrew Hahn, Dolores Hirschmann, Kathleen Kirkwood, Cynthia Miree, David Nelson, Helene Robbins, Victor Salama, Carol Tully, Liza Vertinsky, Dilia Wood, and Elizabeth Wright, as well as Stephen Brenninkmeyer, Peter Cowie, Joseph Dominic, Paul DeF. Hicks, Jr., Ann Mahoney, David Roodberg, Phyllis Ross Schless, Remi Vermeir and Maija Wilder, who have all provided countless insights into providing entrepreneurial opportunities to young people.

STEVE MARIOTTI

Curriculum Reviewers

Elaine Allen
National Director
Not-for-Profit Services Group
Ernst & Young

Sunne Brandmeyer
Retired Lecturer/Advisor
Center for Economic Education
University of South Florida

Stanlee Brimberg
Teacher
Bank Street School for Children

Richard Chute
Partner
Hill & Barlow

Alan Dlugash, CPA
Partner
Dlugash & Kevelson

Peter Eisen
Business Department Director
Murry Bergtraum High School

Steve Frasene
Accounting and
    Entrepreneurship Teacher
Jane Addams Vocational
    High School

Deborah Hoffman
Audit Manager
Ernst & Young

Sanford Krieger, Esq.
Partner
Fried, Frank, Harris,
    Shriver & Jacobson

Dr. Jawanza Kunjufu
President
African American Images

Corey Kupfer, Esq.
Founding Partner
Kupfer, Rosen & Herz, LLP

Dr. Don Lavoie
David H. and Charles G. Koch
    Chair of Economics
The Institute of Public Policy
George Mason University

Alaire Mitchell
Former Assistant Director of
    Curriculum Research
New York City
    Board of Education

Seana Moran
Doctoral Candidate
Harvard Graduate School of
    Education

Eric Mulkowsky
Engagement Manager
McKinsey and Company, Inc.

Raffiq Nathoo
Senior Managing Director
The Blackstone Group, LLP

Ray E. Newton, III
Managing Director
Perseus Capital, LLC

William H. Painter
Retired Professor of Law
George Washington University

Alan Patricof
Founder and Chairman
Patricof & Company

Hilda Polanco, CPA
Managing Partner
Ellenbogen, Rubenstein
    Eisdorfer & Co.

Christopher P. Puto
Dean and Professor
    of Marketing
Georgetown University,
    McDonough School of Business

Ira Sacks, Esq.
Partner
Fried, Frank, Harris,
    Shriver & Jacobson

Dr. William Sahlman
Professor of Business
    Administration
Harvard Business School

Dr. Arnold Scheibel
Professor of Neurobiology
University of California
    at Los Angeles

Sandra Sowell-Scott
State Director,
Youth Entrepreneurship
    Education
Fox School of Business
    & Management
Temple University

Dr. Vernon Smith
Professor of Economics
University of Arizona

Liza Vertinsky, J.D., Ph.D.
Attorney
Hill & Barlow

Peter Walker
Managing Director
McKinsey and Company, Inc.

Dr. Donald Wells
Professor of Economics
University of Arizona

John C. Whitehead
Former Co-Chairman,
Goldman Sachs
Former Chairman,
The Brookings Institution

NFTE Supporters

NFTE deeply appreciates the generosity of its supporters. The following is a partial list of NFTE's major contributors.

Alliance Capital Management

Allied Capital Corporation

Argidius Foundation

Artistic Impressions

The Atlantic Philanthropies

The Barr Foundation

Arthur M. Blank Foundation

Bodman Foundation

Bruce W. Calvert

Castle Rock Foundation

Nathan Cummings Foundation

Shelby Cullom Davis Foundation

Dunn Family Foundation

Paul and Phyllis Fireman Foundation

First Republic Bank

Fleet Bank

Gap Foundation

Bernard A. Goldhirsh

Goldman Sachs & Co.

Goldman Sachs Foundation

Vira I. Heinz Endowment

Robert J. Hurst

JM Foundation

Robert Kaplan Foundation

Ewing Marion Kauffman Foundation

F.M. Kirby Foundation

Charles G. Koch Foundation

David H. Koch Foundation

Loida N. Lewis

MCJ Foundation

McKinsey & Co.

Merrill Lynch

Microsoft Corporation

Myers Family Foundation

Nasdaq Educational Foundation

The Pampered Chef

Pepsico Foundation

Jeffry and Barbara Picower Foundation

Philanthropic Collaborative

Pittsburgh Foundation

Price Institute for Entrepreneurial Studies

Princess House

Prudential Foundation

Putnam Investments

Ronald McDonald House Children's Charities

Arthur J. Samberg

Scaife Family Foundation

Diana Davis Spencer

Kimberly Spencer

U.S. Mint

Verizon Foundation

William Zimmerman Foundation

Contents

Module 2: Advanced

Advanced: What You Need to Know to Grow

Resources for the Young Entrepreneur

HOW TO START & OPERATE A SMALL BUSINESS

Basic: Starting Your Business
Includes: Chapters 1-14 and the Basic Business Plan

The Basic chapters of NFTE Module 1 will teach you what you need to know to start a simple business. Once you have completed these chapters, you will be able to prepare an income statement, understand marketing basics, perform cost/benefit analysis, and calculate return on investment. You will also learn what it means to be an entrepreneur and how you can use your unique skills and talents to start a small business venture.

After you have finished Chapter 14, you will be ready to apply what you have learned by preparing your Basic Business Plan. A complete version of the Basic Business Plan can be found in your NFTE Module 1 Workbook.

Intermediate: Running a Business Successfully
Includes: Chapters 15-28 and the Intermediate Business Plan

The Intermediate Chapters of NFTE Module 1 will teach you how to successfully manage and run your business. Once you have completed these chapters, you will be able to create a cash flow statement, identify your competitive advantage, and keep good records for your business.

After you have finished Chapter 28, you will be ready to apply what you have learned by preparing your Intermediate Business Plan. A complete version of the Intermediate Business Plan can be found in your NFTE Module 1 Workbook.

Advanced: What You Need to Know to Grow
Includes: Chapters 29-50 and the Advanced Business Plan

The Advanced Chapters of NFTE Module 2 will teach you how you can grow a small business venture you have already started. Once you have completed these chapters, you will be able to create a balance sheet, do break-even and financial ratio analysis, and select the best financing strategy for your business.

After you have finished Chapter 50, you will be ready to apply what you have learned by preparing your Advanced Business Plan. A complete version of the Advanced Business Plan can be found in your NFTE Module 2 Workbook.

KEY OBJECTIVES

**READING THIS CHAPTER AND DOING
THE EXERCISES WILL ENABLE YOU TO:**

- Explain the difference
  between an employee and
  an entrepreneur.

- Discuss how entrepreneurs
  create value from scarce
  resources, and why they
  love change.

- Evaluate the pros and cons of
  owning your own business.

WHAT IS AN ENTREPRENEUR?

The Difference Between an Employee and an Entrepreneur

Most Americans earn money by working in business. **Business** is the buying and selling of products or services in order to make money. Someone who earns a living by working for someone else's business is an **employee** of that business.

There are many different kinds of employees. At Ford Motor Company, for instance, some employees build the cars, some sell the cars, and some manage the company. But employees all have one thing in common — they do not own a business, they work for others who do.

Some people start their own businesses and work for themselves. They are called **entrepreneurs**. Entrepreneurs are both owners and employees. An entrepreneur is responsible for the success or failure of his or her business. A successful business sells products or services that customers need, at prices they are willing to pay. Of course, the prices must also be high enough for the entrepreneur to be able to cover all the costs of running the business.

Big and Small Business*

The public often thinks of business only in terms of "big" business — companies such as Ford, General Motors, IBM, McDonald's, and Nike. A "big" business has more than 100 employees and sells more than $1 million worth of products or services in a year.

Most of the world's businesses are small businesses, though. A baby-sitting service and a neighborhood restaurant are examples of small businesses. Surprisingly, the principles involved in running a large company like General Motors and a little restaurant are similar. In fact, most of the large businesses in this country started out as small, entrepreneurial **ventures**. Many of the biggest businesses in the world, like Microsoft or McDonald's, began as an idea thought up by one or two entrepreneurs.

Profit

No matter how big or small, a business must make a **profit** to stay "in business." A business makes a profit when the amount of money coming in from sales is greater than the amount of money required to pay the bills. Many businesses do operate "at a loss" when they are getting started because they have to spend money on setting up operations and on advertising to attract customers. But if a business continues to lose money, eventually the entrepreneur will run out of cash and be unable to pay the bills. If a business continues to lose money, the entrepreneur may have to close it.

Closing a business is nothing to be ashamed of; most successful entrepreneurs open and close more than one business during a lifetime. If your venture is not making a profit after you've gotten it up and running, that's a signal that you may be in the wrong business. Closing it may be the best decision.

Entrepreneurs Create Value

If your business is making a profit, you are clearly doing something right. Profit is a sign that an entrepreneur has added value to the "scarce" (limited) **resources** he or she is using. A scarce resource is something of value that can be used to make something else or to fill a need. Oil is a resource because it is used as fuel by cars. Wood is a resource, because it can be used to make a house, or a table, or paper.

---

* Source of definitions: Small Business Administration.

Debbi Fields, the founder of Mrs. Fields Cookies, took resources — eggs, butter, flour, sugar and chocolate chips — and turned them into cookies. People liked what she did with those resources so much that they were willing to pay her more for the cookies than it cost her to buy the ingredients. She earned a profit. The profit was her signal that she was doing something right — she was adding value to the resources she was using.

Debbi Fields added value to scarce resources by creating something out of them that people were willing to buy for a price that gave her a profit. This is how entrepreneurs create value.

The Free-Enterprise System

This is also how the American **economy** works. An economy is a country's financial structure. It is the system that produces and distributes wealth in a country. The United States economy is a **free-enterprise system**, meaning that anyone is free to start a business. You do not have to get permission from the government to start a business, although you do have to obey laws and regulations.

We all benefit from this system because it discourages entrepreneurs who waste resources. It encourages entrepreneurs who use resources efficiently to satisfy consumer needs. We also benefit because it encourages competition between entrepreneurs. Someone who can make cookies that taste as good as Mrs. Fields Cookies, and can afford to sell them at a lower price, will eventually attract Mrs. Fields Cookies customers. This may force Mrs. Fields Cookies to lower its prices to stay competitive.

To lower prices and still make a profit, the entrepreneur has to figure out how to use resources even more efficiently. Consumers benefit because they get to buy cookies at a lower price.

Entrepreneurs are motivated by competition to find ways to use resources more efficiently. When the countries that sell oil to the United States raised prices dramatically in the 1970s, for example, American automobile manufacturers were motivated to develop smaller cars that used oil more efficiently.

> :) **"Entrepreneurship is a way of thinking, reasoning, and acting that is opportunity-obsessed, holistic in approach, and leadership balanced."**
> —Jeffry A. Timmons, Entrepreneurship Professor

Entrepreneurs Love Change

Automobile manufacturers had to make smaller cars because consumers didn't want to buy big cars anymore that used lots of expensive gasoline. Giant corporations like

automobile manufacturers can find it difficult to respond to change. They tend to move slowly because so many people and so much money is involved in any change they make. Entrepreneurs, in contrast, love change because they can move quickly to take advantage of it. They understand that change creates opportunities to start new businesses.

Debbi Fields is a millionaire today not because she had a great chocolate chip cookie recipe, but because she noticed that families were changing. Fifty years ago many women did not work full-time outside the home. But in the 1970s more women entered the workforce. Very few had time to bake. Mrs. Fields took advantage of this change. Fields created cookies that tasted home-baked. The name Mrs. Fields Cookies reminded the consumer of coming home to Mom and a plate of freshly baked cookies. Her business probably would not have succeeded if women had not begun working away from home.

The Pros and Cons of Being an Entrepreneur*

This text, along with classroom instruction, will show you how to start and run your own business. Most people never even consider going into business for themselves. In thinking about this option, you will learn a lot about your own character. Perhaps you will figure out what you would like to do with your life. You will be learning basic business skills. You will learn how the free-enterprise system works. Even if you don't decide to become an entrepreneur, having started even one small business will make you a much more valuable employee when working for others. Employers are always more interested in hiring someone who understands business.

* With thanks to The National Federation of Independent Businesses, *The Entrepreneurs Series*, 1983.

There Are Advantages and Disadvantages to Being an Entrepreneur

Some advantages are:

INDEPENDENCE: Business owners do not have to follow orders or observe working hours set by someone else. They must please their customers in order to succeed, but how they structure their work day is up to them.

SATISFACTION: Turning a skill, hobby, or other interest into your own business can be much more satisfying than working at a job you don't enjoy.

FINANCIAL REWARD: Through hard work, the sky can be the limit. In addition, you can't be laid off or fired from your own enterprise. Most of the great fortunes of this country were built by entrepreneurs.

SELF-ESTEEM: Knowing you created something valuable can give you a strong sense of accomplishment.

Some disadvantages are:

BUSINESS FAILURE: Many small businesses fail. You risk losing not only your money but also money invested in your business by others.

OBSTACLES: You will run into unexpected problems that you will have to solve. In addition, the entrepreneur may face discouragement from family and friends.

LONELINESS: It can be lonely and even a little scary to be completely responsible for the success or failure of your business.

FINANCIAL INSECURITY: Your earnings may rise or fall depending upon how your business is doing. You may not always have enough money to pay yourself.

LONG HOURS/HARD WORK: You will have to work long hours to get your business off the ground. Some entrepreneurs work six, or even seven, days a week.

The advantages and disadvantages of owning your own business can be seen as two sides of the same coin:

- Your hard work can reap great rewards.

- Facing loneliness, financial insecurity and other obstacles can build inner strength.

- The challenges and risks that come with being a business owner will help you uncover and develop new talents and abilities.

If your business fails, the time and experience will not have been wasted. Early failures can lead to later success. Many, if not most, successful entrepreneurs failed a number of times before they finally succeeded.

Chapter 1 Review

NOTE: The exercises printed below can be found in the corresponding chapter of the NFTE MODULE 1 WORKBOOK that came with your textbook. Please write your answers there. If you do not have a workbook, write your answers on a separate sheet of paper.

Critical Thinking about ... Entrepreneurship

1. What would be the best thing about owning your own business?

2. What would be the worst?

3. Would you rather be an employee or an entrepreneur? Why?

4. Do you think the number of businesses owned by women and minorities is increasing? Give the reasons for your answer. How could you explore this further?

5. Go on the Internet and do research on entrepreneurship. What was the most interesting site you found?

Getting the Facts

1. What is one thing all employees have in common?

2. Define "small business."

3. Even if your enterprise fails, what will you have gained?

Using New Words

business
economy
employee
entrepreneur
free-enterprise system
profit
resource
venture

Write five sentences, using one or more of the vocabulary terms in each. Write about your family or your neighborhood.

Example: *My father is an employee of Baxter Shipping Company.*

Review

Chapter 1 Review

Exploring Your Community

1) Bring a newspaper or magazine article about a small business to class.

2) Interview an entrepreneur in your neighborhood — the owner of the corner deli, or a local bookstore or record store, for example. Write up your interview as a one-page report that includes the answers to these questions:

1. When did you start your own business?

2. Why did you decide to become an entrepreneur?

3. What resources do you use and how do you add value to them to create profit?

4. Was there an opportunity you noticed in the neighborhood that you decided to meet?

5. What has been the hardest part of running your own business?

6. What do you like best about being a business owner?

Review

Chapter Summary

I. Business is the buying and selling of products and services for profit.

A. An employee works for a business.

B. An entrepreneur owns a business and often employs people.

II. Entrepreneurs add value to resources and take advantage of change.

A. Profit is the signal that an entrepreneur is adding value to resources.

B. Entrepreneurs see changes in our society as opportunities to start new businesses.

III. Being an entrepreneur has its pros and cons.

A. Advantages: control of your life, satisfaction, potential for financial reward, self-esteem.

B. Disadvantages: business failure, obstacles and discouragement, loneliness, financial insecurity, long hours.

C. Early failures and struggles can teach you how to succeed.

*Inch by inch,
everything's a cinch.*

— Unknown

KEY OBJECTIVES

READING THIS CHAPTER AND DOING
THE EXERCISES WILL ENABLE YOU TO:

■ Recognize entrepreneurial
opportunities.

■ Distinguish between an idea
and an opportunity.

■ Understand the importance
of putting together a team
to take advantage of
opportunities.

OPPORTUNITY RECOGNITION

Where Others See Problems,
Entrepreneurs Recognize Opportunities

Many famous businesses have been started because an entrepreneur solved a problem by turning it into a successful business. Entrepreneurs recognize that problems can be opportunities.

Georgette Klinger founded her skin-care company because she had acne. Anita Roddick started The Body Shop — a cosmetics company that uses only natural ingredients in its products — because she was tired of paying for fancy packaging when she bought makeup. Bill Gates is another problem solver. Before he started Microsoft, most software was complicated and confusing — even scary! — for the average person to use. Gates solved this problem by creating software that would be fun and easy. He became one of the richest men in the world.

Remember what we said about change in the last chapter? Entrepreneurs love change because it presents them with new opportunities. Look at the Internet! Most experts believed that telephone companies were going to dominate the Internet, but entrepreneurs like Jerry Yang, who started Yahoo! and Steve Case, who founded AOL, have been the real winners. The phone companies were like dinosaurs — too big and slow to deal with the new technology. It can take a large corporation six years to create a new business. Entrepreneurs are more like roadrunners — lean and fast. Entrepreneurial companies like Earthlink and Netscape beat AT&T and MCI in getting online.

To become an entrepreneur who can recognize business opportunities, ask yourself such questions as:

> What frustrates me the most when I go to buy something?
>
> What product or service would really improve my life?
>
> What really annoys me?
>
> What product or service would eliminate that annoyance?

Voluntary Exchange

Voluntary exchange is a transaction between two people who agree to trade money for a product or service. No one is forced to trade. Both parties do so because they benefit from the trade. In contrast, a robbery is an *involuntary* trade.

Entrepreneurs Imagine What They Want and Then Create It

Businesses are also created when entrepreneurs fantasize about products or services they wish existed. You can jump-start your imagination by asking yourself (or your friends) questions like the following:

> What is the one thing you would like to have more than anything else?
>
> What does it look like?
>
> Or taste like?
>
> What does it do?

An Idea Is Not Necessarily an Opportunity*

There is one crucial difference, however, between an idea and an opportunity. An opportunity is based on what consumers want. A business can fail because an entrepreneur

---

* With special thanks to Jeffry Timmons, Howard Stevenson, and William Bygrave for the ideas they contributed to this chapter.

didn't understand that it had to meet a consumer need. You can have a good idea for a business, but if what you're selling doesn't meet anyone else's needs, it will fail.

A business opportunity is an idea that also has these qualities:

- It is attractive to customers.

- It will work in your business environment.

- It can be executed in the "window of opportunity" that already exists.

- You have the resources and skills to create the business, or you know someone who does and who could start the business with you.

- You can supply the product or service at a price that will be attractive to customers yet will be high enough to earn you a profit.

A "window of opportunity" is the time you have to bring a business possibility to the marketplace. You might have a great idea, but if competitors have had the same thought and brought the product or service to the consumer first, your window of opportunity will have been slammed shut.

The Roots of Opportunity in the Marketplace

Problems are just one example of opportunities that entrepreneurs need to be able to recognize. A changing situation or trend is another.

In the late 1980s, for example, Russell Simmons was promoting rap concerts at the City College of New York. At the time, rap was considered a passing fad. Simmons had a hunch, though, that music consumers were getting bored with rock. He formed Def Jam Records with fellow student Rick Rubin for $5,000. They produced hit records by Run DMC and LL Cool J. Today Simmons is a multimedia mogul worth over $60 million. He has businesses based on opportunities he saw in the hip-hop culture he loves — everything from television shows like Def Jam Comedy to clothing lines like Phat Farm.

Simmons applied one simple principle: If you personally know ten people who are eager to buy a product or service, there are probably ten million who would buy it if they knew about it.

There are five roots of opportunity in the marketplace:[*]

1.   **PROBLEMS** that your business could solve.

2.   **CHANGES** in laws, situations, or trends.

3.   **INVENTIONS** of totally new products or services.

4.   **COMPETITION** — If you can find a way to beat the competition based on price, location, quality, reputation, reliability, or hours, you can operate a very successful business with an already existing product or service.

5.   **TECHNOLOGICAL ADVANCES** — Scientists may invent new technology, but entrepreneurs must figure out how to market it.

The Eight Rules of Building a Successful Business

Simmons applied the eight basic rules of building a successful business:

1.   **RECOGNIZE AN OPPORTUNITY** — Simmons believed rap music was an untapped business opportunity.

2.   **EVALUATE IT WITH CRITICAL THINKING** — He tested his idea by promoting concerts and observing consumer reaction.

3.   **WRITE A BUSINESS PLAN** — Simmons planned his operations.

4.   **BUILD A TEAM** — Simmons added Rick Rubin to his team.

5.   **GATHER RESOURCES** — He and Rubin pooled $5,000.

6.   **DECIDE OWNERSHIP** — Simmons and Rubin formed their business as a partnership.

7.   **CREATE WEALTH** — Simmons is now (as of 2000) worth over $50 million.

8.   **EXECUTE YOUR PLAN AND SATISFY CONSUMER NEEDS** — Simmons understood his customers and he used this knowledge to grow his business.

---

[*] Adapted from *Master Curriculum Guide: Economics and Entrepreneurship*. Edited by John Clow, et al., Joint Council on Economic Education, 1991.

The Team Approach to Opportunity

Simmons and Rubin turned Def Jam into a huge success because they made a good team. Alone, neither of them had enough money to launch a record label, but together they were able to do it. Their business was also helped by the fact that they each knew different artists and had different contacts in the record industry.

Everyone you know is a potential business-formation opportunity. Your friends or family members may have skills, equipment, or contacts that would make them valuable business partners.

Let's say you would like to start a T-shirt business, but you're not an artist. If you have a friend who is, the two of you could start the venture together. Or maybe you'd like to form a DJ business, but you only have one turntable. If you formed the business with a friend, you could pool equipment and records.

When putting together a business team, organize it so that everyone involved shares in the ownership and profits. People often work harder when they are working for themselves.

Broaden Your Mind

Successful entrepreneurs are constantly coming up with business ideas and evaluating them as opportunities. The best way to train your mind to think like an entrepreneur is to broaden it with many new experiences. Practice staying alert for problems and consumer needs no matter what you are doing.

Some good ways to broaden your mind include:

- Travel.
- Making new friends.
- Learning a new language.
- Reading outside your current interests.
- Listening to others.
- Developing new hobbies.
- Watching the news, reading newspapers and magazines.
- Discussing current events with friends and mentors.
- Internships.

Remember, not every idea is an opportunity. For an idea also to be an opportunity, it must lead to the development of a product or service that would be of value to consumers.

The Four Parts of Business

Each business is basically composed of four parts. An entrepreneur, though, might initially have to handle all four parts alone. These are:

1) **Production** — Making or obtaining the product.

2) **Financing** — Securing and efficiently using money to develop the business.

3) **Marketing** — Developing strategies for getting the consumer interested in the product or service.

4) **Customer Service** — Maintaining and servicing a product or service once it has been sold; the act of keeping customers happy and loyal to the business.

Chapter 2 Review

NOTE: The exercises printed below can be found in the corresponding chapter of the NFTE MODULE 1 WORKBOOK that came with your textbook. Please write your answers there. If you do not have a workbook, write your answers on a separate sheet of paper.

Critical Thinking about ... Recognizing Opportunities

1. Explain how a business opportunity differs from a business idea.

2. Give an example of a change that has occurred or is about to occur in your neighborhood and discuss any business opportunities this change might create.

3. Do you have artistic ability? How might you turn your talent into a business?

Getting the Facts

1. Why did Georgette Klinger start a cosmetics company?

2. Who was Russell Simmons' business partner when he started Def Jam? How much money did they use to start the company?

3. Give an example of a product or service that you think failed because it missed its "window of opportunity."

4. Why is it a good idea to give members of your business team a share in the profits of the business?

Exploring Your Community

1) Have a conversation with a parent or other adult relative. Ask this person to tell you about things that he or she finds frustrating in the neighborhood. Write down their complaints.

2) Generate at least three business opportunities from this conversation.

3) Evaluate each of these opportunities using the "Business Opportunities" questions in Chapter 2 of the Module 1 Workbook.

4) On a separate sheet of paper, list your hobbies, skills, resources, and interests and those of two friends. Then come up with some businesses you think you could form alone, or with one or both of them.

5) On a separate sheet of paper, fill in the blanks below to come up with more business opportunities.

I wish there were more _____ in my neighborhood.

I could make _____ (product or service) better by doing or offering _____ .

_____ is a trend that I think I could turn into a business opportunity.

Review

17

Chapter 2 Review

Analyzing Business Opportunities

"SWOT" Analysis — another way to evaluate a business opportunity — is to look at its Strengths, Weaknesses, Opportunities, and Threats.

Strengths — The entrepreneur's abilities and contacts.

Weaknesses — The problems the entrepreneur faces, from lack of money or training to lack of time or experience.

Opportunities — Lucky breaks or creative advantages the entrepreneur can use to get ahead of the competition.

Threats — Anything that might be bad for the business, from competitors to legal problems.

Exercise: Write a SWOT analysis of one of the business opportunities you came up with in this chapter.

Exploring Your Community

1. List three problems and a business solution for each.

2. Think about where you live. List five business opportunities in your neighborhood and the need they would satisfy.

The Entrepreneur as Problem Solver

Given these hypothetical situations, what business would you consider starting or investing in?

1. A 100% increase in the price of gasoline.

2. A going-out-of-business sign in the window of a local grocery store.

3. A new airport being built near your home.

4. An increase in the percentage of women entering the workforce.

5. Local government decides to privatize garbage collection and impose recycling on households.

6. The state government allows parents to receive a sum of money that they can spend as they wish on education for their children.

Chapter Summary

I. Where others see problems entrepreneurs recognize opportunities.

    A. Others might fear change, but entrepreneurs understand that change generates opportunities.

    B. Entrepreneurs find business opportunities by trying to solve problems.

    C. Entrepreneurs also use their imaginations to think of products they (and others) might want.

II. An idea is not necessarily a business opportunity. To be an opportunity, an idea must:

    A. Be attractive to customers.

    B. Work in the entrepreneur's environment.

    C. Be possible to execute in the existing window of opportunity.

III. For an entrepreneur to successfully turn an opportunity into a business, he or she must:

    A. Have the skills and resources to create the business, or know someone who does.

    B. Be able to supply the product or service at a price that attracts customers yet is high enough to earn the entrepreneur a profit.

IV. The five roots of opportunity are:

    A. Problems your business could solve.

    B. Changes in laws, situations, or trends.

    C. Inventions.

    D. Competition.

    E. Technological advances.

V. The eight rules of business formation are:

    A. Recognize an opportunity.

    B. Evaluate it with critical thinking.

    C. Write a business plan.

    D. Build a team.

    E. Gather resources.

    F. Determine ownership.

    G. Create wealth.

    H. Execute your plan and satisfy consumer needs.

VII. Activities that broaden your mind will sharpen your ability to recognize business opportunities.

KEY OBJECTIVES

READING THIS CHAPTER AND DOING THE EXERCISES WILL ENABLE YOU TO:

- List characteristics of successful entrepreneurs.
- Identify your own traits.
- Explore your entrepreneurial potential.
- Focus your energy.

CHARACTERISTICS OF THE SUCCESSFUL ENTREPRENEUR

What Kind of People Become Entrepreneurs?

Many successful entrepreneurs have started life with very little money or education. Often, they come from families that have little financial wealth but are rich in their ability to dream and turn those dreams into reality. Growing up in a difficult environment helped make them tough-minded and competitive. These are some of the characteristics an entrepreneur needs to succeed.

Many **immigrants** have become entrepreneurs. Immigrants are people who leave their homeland to settle in a new country. Many such immigrants have started businesses in the United States. These businesses usually serve the needs of the community where the entrepreneurs themselves live.

The Entrepreneur Needs Energy

An entrepreneur can be defined as "a person who has created — out of nothing — an ongoing enterprise."[*] To imagine your business, set it up and make it succeed, is going to take a tremendous amount of energy.

The energy required to succeed as an entrepreneur can only come from sensible mental and physical habits. Young people naturally have lots of energy, but don't always know what to do with it.

If you can direct some of your energy toward something constructive (such as your own business) you will reap both financial and emotional rewards. Many students who have completed this course have started their own companies. Some have achieved significant success.

Characteristics of the Successful Entrepreneur

Many successful entrepreneurs were enterprising as children. At an early age they exhibited some of the characteristics entrepreneurs need to be successful. No one is born with *all* the characteristics needed for success. If you have drive and motivation, though, the other traits can be developed. Take a look at the list below. Notice the characteristics you already possess and those you think you could develop.

ADAPTABILITY — the ability to cope with new situations and find creative solutions to problems.

COMPETITIVENESS — a willingness to compete with and test oneself against others.

CONFIDENCE — the belief that you can accomplish what you set out to do.

DRIVE — the desire to work hard to achieve one's goals.

HONESTY — a commitment to refrain from lying; to be truthful and sincere in dealings with other people.

ORGANIZATION — the ability to structure one's life and keep tasks and information in order.

PERSUASIVENESS — the knack for convincing people to see one's point of view and to get them interested in one's ideas.

---

[*] Collins, O. and Moore, D. (1970). *The Organization Makers: A Behavioral Study of Independent Entrepreneurs.* Englewood Cliffs, NJ: Prentice Hall.

DISCIPLINE — the ability to stay focused and adhere to a schedule and deadlines.

PERSEVERANCE — the refusal to quit; willingness to keep goals in sight and work toward them, despite obstacles.

RISK-TAKING — the courage to expose oneself to possible losses.

UNDERSTANDING — an ability to listen to and empathize with other people.

VISION — the ability to see the end results of one's goals while working to achieve them.

Entrepreneurs Are Optimists

The kind of person you are can determine how successful you will become. It is important that you recognize both your strengths and your weaknesses. Try to improve a little each day.

You may have noticed that your time at school or at home goes better when you feel good about yourself and the world. This is an *optimistic* or *positive* attitude. Entrepreneurs tend to be **optimists**. They have to be — in order to see **opportunities** where others only see problems.

In Chapter 9 we'll talk more about the importance of cultivating a positive mental attitude. For now, just start paying attention to your own thoughts. Are they mostly negative? positive? Are you critical of yourself and of other people? When you catch yourself thinking negatively about yourself or another person, try to be more positive. Practice observing your thoughts and noticing how they affect you. You will probably begin to notice that negative thinking makes you feel powerless and depressed, while positive thoughts make you feel happy and full of energy. Negativity is a bad habit but like any bad habit, it can be changed through a little conscious effort. Give it a try.

Entrepreneurs Are Salespeople

Entrepreneurs are salespeople, first and foremost. If you've ever bought anything from anyone, you already know that you are a lot more likely to buy from a happy, positive person than from a grouch. Many great entrepreneurs who built multi-million-dollar businesses started as salespeople. Ray Kroc, who created the McDonald's empire, was a traveling milkshake-machine salesman, for example. Good salespeople can make great entrepreneurs because they talk to customers all day long. Salespeople learn firsthand what customers need. That's why even though you won't study selling in detail until Chapter 27, you'll begin practicing selling early in this course. Selling is a skill you can't practice too much. It will help you develop a positive attitude and the ability to listen for the valuable information customers have to offer.

Chapter 3 Review

NOTE: The exercises printed below can be found in the corresponding chapter of the NFTE MODULE 1 WORKBOOK that came with your textbook. Please write your answers there. If you do not have a workbook, write your answers on a separate sheet of paper.

Critical Thinking about . . . Your Potential

Your *potential* is the chance of becoming something or doing something, based on who you are. In your own words describe what you think your entrepreneurial potential is, based on the results of the "characteristics" survey in your NFTE Module 1 Workbook. Discuss what type(s) of business you think you could start.

Getting the Facts

True or False?

1. Entrepreneurs should come from wealthy families.

2. Students have started their own companies.

3. Discipline is a characteristic of the successful entrepreneur.

4. Problems can actually be business opportunities.

Using New Words

immigrant
optimist
opportunity

Answer the following questions with complete sentences using the vocabulary words.

1. Why do you think immigrants start businesses in their own communities?

2. Do you think you are an optimist? Why or why not?

3. Write about a time when you were tempted to give up on something but didn't, or about a time when you did. What difference can perseverance make?

4. Which subjects in school motivate you? Why? Why is motivation important in starting a business?

In Your Opinion

Discuss with a group:

1. Can growing up in a tough neighborhood make someone more successful in life? Or can the stress make it harder to succeed? Do any examples come to mind?

2. Do you have too much energy? Not enough? What could you do to become more positive and productive? Write a memo answering these questions that includes a plan for becoming a more positive and productive person.

Review

Chapter Summary

I. Entrepreneurial ability is often shaped by challenging life experiences.

A. Many immigrants start their own businesses.

B. Growing up in a difficult environment may help someone become strong and tough enough to be a good entrepreneur.

II. Entrepreneurs need lots of energy.

A. To create a successful business out of nothing takes drive, determination, and perseverance.

B. You can increase your energy through sensible habits.

C. Try directing your energy toward something constructive, such as starting your own business.

III. The kind of person you are determines your success.

A. Success traits can be developed.

B. Successful entrepreneurs are optimistic.

1. Optimism helps you see problems as opportunities.

2. An optimistic attitude makes your day go better.

C. Successful people have positive mental attitudes.

1. With practice you can develop a positive mental attitude.

2. Consciously replace negative thoughts about yourself or others with positive ones.

A Business for the Young Entrepreneur: T-Shirts

How many T-shirts do you own with something printed or painted on them? What about your friends? Decorated T-shirts are very popular. It's easy and fun to make colorful T-shirts that other people will want to buy from you.

There are two easy ways to turn a plain T-shirt into a profitable creation:

- Silkscreening
- Fabric painting

Silkscreening

Silkscreening is a stencil method of printing. Place the silkscreen, which has your design cut into it, on top of the T-shirt. Next, use a wedge to push the ink through the screen. The ink only comes through where your design has been cut into it.

Supplies	Where to Find Them
silkscreen	arts & crafts store
wedge	arts & crafts store
ink	arts & crafts store
plain T-shirts	wholesaler

Fabric Painting

Fabric painting is a good method to use if you want each of your T-shirts to have a unique design. You paint directly onto each shirt. Experiment with gluing decorative jewelry to shirts, too.

Supplies	Where to Find Them
fabric paint	arts & crafts store
plain T-shirts	wholesaler

Market Research

Before making your T-shirts, conduct some market research. Ask your friends and other potential customers what size T-shirts they wear. Ask them what designs they might like. Ask what price they might be willing to pay for your shirts.

Tips

- Wear one of your creations to school to promote your business.
- Offer to silkscreen T-shirts for a school sports team or a local rock band to sell at concerts. They supply the design, you make the T-shirts.

KEY OBJECTIVES

READING THIS CHAPTER AND DOING THE EXERCISES WILL ENABLE YOU TO:

- Prepare a monthly income statement.
- Calculate net profit or loss.
- Analyze line items as a percentage of revenue.

INCOME STATEMENTS: THE ENTREPRENEUR'S SCORECARD

The essence of small business success is this principle: *Create value, meet consumer needs, and keep good records.* In this chapter, we will discuss keeping good records in more detail. All successful entrepreneurs use their financial records to prepare monthly income statements. This **income statement** is also called a **profit and loss statement**.

The Income Statement

Monthly income statements show the state of your business. They show the sales and costs that took place during the month. If sales are greater than costs, the income statement balance will be positive, showing that the business was profitable. If sales are less than costs, the balance will be negative, showing a loss.

The income statement is also a good short-term road map for the business owner. If the company is not making a profit, examining the income statement can tell the entrepreneur what may be causing the loss. Then he or she can take steps to correct the problems before net losses force the business into bankruptcy. As you've already learned, profit is the reward for using resources efficiently.

It is important to keep your ledger accurately, as you will use it to prepare your income statement at the end of each month.

Income statements for a retail business are made up of the following seven parts:

(A) SALES — how much money the company receives for selling a product.

(B) TOTAL COST OF GOODS OR SERVICES SOLD — The Cost of Goods Sold for one unit times the number of units sold. Never disclose your Cost of Goods Sold. You want to keep secret how much you are paying for your product so you can sell it for a profit.

(C) GROSS PROFIT — Sales minus Cost of Goods Sold. It is not the final, or "**net,**" profit because Operating Costs and Taxes must be subtracted.

(D) OPERATING COSTS* — Items that must be paid to operate a business. These items are usually Utilities, Salaries, Advertising, Insurance, Interest, Rent, and Depreciation (referred to as USAIIRD).

    (D1) FIXED COSTS — All Operating Costs that stay the same within a range of sales.

    (D2) VARIABLE COSTS — All Operating Costs that vary with sales.

---

* This concept will be explained in chapter 10: The Costs of Starting and Operating a Business.

(E) PROFIT BEFORE TAXES — This is a business' profit before paying taxes and after all costs have been paid.

(F) TAXES — A business must pay income and other business taxes.

(G) NET PROFIT/(LOSS) — This is the business' profit or loss after taxes have been paid.

The power of the income statement is that it tells you whether you are succeeding at meeting customer needs, creating value, and keeping good records. Let's say David buys 25 ties at $2 each and sells them all at $4 each, for revenue of $100. He also spent $24 on flyers to advertise his ties. The income statement quickly shows whether or not he is making a profit.

DAVID'S INCOME STATEMENT:		THE MATH:
(A) Sales	$100	(A) 25 ties x $4/tie = $100
(B) Less Total Cost of Goods Sold	50	(B) 25 ties x $2/tie = $50
(C) Gross Profit	50	(C) A – B = C
		$100 – $50 = $50
(D) Less Operating Costs		
(D1) Fixed Costs	$ 24	
(D2) Variable Costs	0	
	24	(D) D1 + D2 = D
(E) Profit before Taxes	26	(E) C – D = E
		$50 – $24 = $26
(F) Taxes	6	(F) Taxes = $6
(G) Net Profit (Loss)	$ 20	(G) E – F = G
		$26 – $6 = $20
David's business is profitable!		

Percentages

To analyze an income statement, divide sales into each line item. Now you can express each item as a **percentage** of sales.

"Percentage" literally means "a given part of every hundred." Percentages express numbers as part of a whole, with the whole represented as 100%.

Let's say you have 100 pennies. Because *percentage* means "out of a hundred," if you take 18 pennies out, you have removed 18% of the pennies

Example:

100   80   20

Similarly:
20 pennies out of 100 = 20%

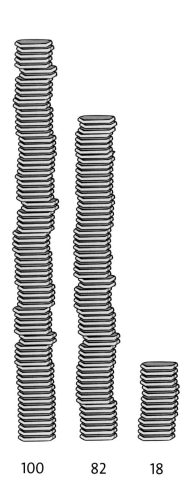

100   82   18

18 pennies out of 100 = 18%

100   65   35

Similarly:
35 pennies out of 100 = 35%

Use this formula:

$$\frac{\textbf{Part}}{\textbf{Total}} \text{ x } \textbf{100} = \textbf{Percentage}$$

$$\frac{18}{60} \text{ x } 100 = 30\%$$

You probably know that 1/2 of something can be expressed as 50%, but here's how that percentage is actually figured:

1) Divide the *numerator* (top) by the *denominator* (bottom) of the fraction:
   1/2 = 1 ÷ 2 = .50

2) Multiply the divided fraction by 100 to express it as a percentage:
   .50 x 100 = 50%

RULE OF THUMB: If you have trouble with percentages, let your teacher know so you can get special assistance.

Financial Ratio Analysis

Expressing each item on an income statement as a percentage of sales makes it easier to see the relationship between the items. In the example below, for every dollar of sales, 40 cents was spent on cost of goods sold. The **gross profit** per dollar was 60 cents. The net profits, after 30 cents were spent on operating costs, and 10 cents on taxes, was 20 cents.

Looking at the income statement this way makes business decisions easier. To increase gross profit, for instance, you could try cutting the cost of goods sold or raise your sales. Analyzing the income-statement items as percentages of sales makes clear the relationship between the items and how each affects net profit. The percentage created by dividing sales into net profit/(loss) is called "return on sales," or "profit margin."

ANALYZING AN INCOME STATEMENT			
	Dollars	**Math**	**Financial Analysis (% of Sales)**
Sales	$10	$\frac{\$10}{10} = 1 \times 100 = 100\%$	100%
Total Cost of Goods Sold	4	$\frac{4}{10} = .40 \times 100 = 40\%$	40%
Gross Profit	6	$\frac{6}{10} = .60 \times 100 = 60\%$	60%
Less Operating Costs	3	$\frac{3}{10} = .30 \times 100 = 30\%$	30%
Fixed Costs	3	$\frac{3}{10} = .30 \times 100 = 30\%$	30%
Variable Costs	0	0	0%
Profit	3	$\frac{3}{10} = .30 \times 100 = 30\%$	30%
Taxes	1	$\frac{1}{10} = .10 \times 100 = 10\%$	10%
Net Profit/(Loss)	$ 2	$\frac{2}{10} = .20 \times 100 = 20\%$	20%

Creating Wealth

The income statement is the "scorecard" of the business. If your venture is successful, your income statements will prove it by showing net profits. Normally, a successful small business can usually be sold for between three and five times yearly net profit because the buyer expects the business to continue generating that profit. If your net profit for one year is $10,000, for example, you should be able to sell your business for at least 3 x $10,000 = $30,000.

This is how entrepreneurs create great fortunes. They establish a successful business, sell it, and use the resulting wealth to create new enterprises and more wealth. Entrepreneurs can also use their wealth to support political, environmental, and social causes, and to help others.

Henry Ford: Cutting costs to make cars affordable

One of the most important reasons for a monthly income statement is to keep an eye on a business' costs and how these are affecting net profit. An entrepreneur's ability to find creative ways to cut costs can often mean the difference between having a struggling business and a thriving one.

In the early 1900s, Henry Ford was determined to create an automobile that most people could afford. To do this, he had to search for ways to cut costs. In those days, cars were manufactured one at a time. It was a slow, expensive process.

To cut production costs, Ford developed the assembly line. The cars were assembled, or built, as they rolled past the workers on a conveyer belt.

In this way, Ford cut costs enough to be able to offer an affordable automobile to the consumer and still make a net profit. He also revolutionized industry by introducing the concept of mass production on a grand scale.

Chapter 4 Review

NOTE: The exercises printed below can be found in the corresponding chapter of the NFTE MODULE 1 WORKBOOK that came with your textbook. Please write your answers there. If you do not have a workbook, write your answers on a separate sheet of paper.

Critical Thinking about ... Income Statements

Suppose you have a business selling caps to friends and classmates. This month you bought 12 caps at $5 each and sold them all for $10 each. You also spent $30 on posters and flyers and paid $12 in taxes. Prepare your income statement.

Analyzing an Income Statement

Now, prepare a financial analysis of the income statement for the cap business.

Using New Words

gross profit
income statement
net
percentage
profit and loss statement

On a separate sheet of paper, identify the vocabulary term that completes each sentence.

1) An income statement is also referred to as a _____.

2) _____ profit is the profit after taxes have been deducted.

3) You can use _____, which expresses numbers as parts of one hundred, to analyze your income statement.

4) When the total cost of goods sold is subtracted from sales, the resulting difference is called _____.

Review

Chapter 4 Review

Getting the Facts

1. When are income statements prepared?

2. For what do the letters in "USAIIRD" stand?

3. When will an income statement show a profit?

4. What is the difference between gross profit and profit before taxes? Between profit before taxes and net profit?

5. What is a good way to analyze an income statement?

6. Which cost does the wise entrepreneur always keep secret? Why?

Exploration: Creation of Wealth

Assuming each of these businesses could be sold for three times annual net profit, figure the sale price for each.

Example: Annual Net Profit of Business A: $20,000

Sale Price for Business A: $60,000 ($20,000 x 3 = $60,000)

Exploration: Converting Fractions to Percentages

To convert any fraction to a percentage, divide the denominator (bottom) into the numerator (top) and multiply by 100.

$$\frac{numerator}{denominator} \times 100$$

Example: $\frac{9}{10} \times 100 = 90\%$

In Your Opinion

Using the McDonald's one-year income statement in your NFTE Module 1 Workbook, answer these questions:

a. What would the profit before taxes be if the owner finds a paper supplier who only charges $100,000 for the year?

b. What would the profit margin be for the year in that case?

c. Suppose you wanted to raise profits by $5,000 a month. What would you do and why?

d. How much do you think the business could be sold for? Why?

e. Do you have a business? If so, compare your income statement with that of McDonald's.

Review

Chapter Summary

I. The income statement is a short-term road map for the business.

A. The income statement shows whether or not the business is profitable.

B. The income statement can help a business owner figure out why a business is losing money.

II. The income statement is made up of seven items:

A. Sales

B. Total Cost of Goods Sold

C. Gross Profit

D. Operating Costs (Fixed and Variable)

E. Profit Before Taxes

F. Taxes

G. Net Profit/(Loss)

III. Income statements show the balance between income and expenses over a month.

A. If income is greater than expenses, the business made a net profit.

B. If income is less than expenses, the business took a net loss.

C. The power of the income statement is to tell you whether you are succeeding at creating value, meeting consumer needs, and keeping good records.

IV. To analyze an income statement, divide each line item by sales to express it as a percentage of sales.

A. Expressing each item as a percentage of sales makes it easier to analyze the relationship between the items.

B. Such financial analysis helps the business owner see where he or she can cut costs to improve net profit.

A Business for the Young Entrepreneur: Party D.J.

If you're the kind of person who keeps up with the latest musical trends, you could make a great party D.J. A party D. J. is hired to play records during a party. This is a more expensive business to start than some — unless you already own one or two turntables and lots of records.

Some D.J.'s join or form record pools. These are clubs that let D.J.'s rotate or share records, so they always have new ones to play. Ask at your local record store about D.J. clubs. D.J.'s also get records by getting on mailing lists for recording labels. Do you know any local labels trying to get attention for their artists? Call and ask about getting free records in return for exposing the artist to a wider audience by playing the records at your parties.

What You'll Need to Get Started

- One or two turntables — if you use two turntables, you'll also need a mixer.
- Speakers and amplifier.
- Records.
- Flyers — advertise your service by handing out flyers at parties and school events.

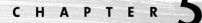

KEY OBJECTIVES

READING THIS CHAPTER AND DOING THE EXERCISES WILL ENABLE YOU TO:

- Calculate return on investment.
- Explore the relationship between risk and return.
- Define liquidity.

RETURN ON INVESTMENT

"To invest" means to put money, time and energy into something with the expectation of gaining financial profit or personal satisfaction in the future. The decision to attend college is an **investment** in education. An investment is something you put time, energy or money into because you expect to receive money or satisfaction in return. You stay in school instead of going to work because you believe the investment in college will pay off later. You believe college will help you obtain better career opportunities and achieve financial profit and personal satisfaction.

Rate of Return

When you start your own business, you are investing time, energy and money. You do this because you believe that someday your business will earn you more than the value of the time, energy and money you put into it. Without realizing it, you have calculated the **rate of return** on your investment and have found it to be acceptable.

Businesspeople need to know what the rate of return will be on their investments. Rate of return is often called **Return on Investment** (ROI). It is expressed as a percentage of the original investment.

Return on Investment (ROI)

Let's say your little brother asks you for $1.00 to buy lemonade mix because it's a hot day and he wants to sell lemonade on the street. You tell him okay, but that you want half the profits. At the end of the day he's sold all the lemonade and gives you $2.00 back. You have just received a 100% rate of return on your investment of $1.00. If he had given you $1.50, the rate of return would have been 50%, because your profit of 50 cents is 50% of the dollar you invested.

How to calculate return on investment:

1) Take the amount you possess at the close of a business period. Call this your end-of-period wealth (A).

2) Subtract the amount of your original investment. Call this investment your beginning-of-period wealth (B).

3) Divide the resulting number by your beginning-of-period wealth.

4) Multiply the results by 100. This will give you the percentage of the return on your investment.

The formula is:
$$\frac{A - B}{B} \times 100 = \text{ROI (Return on Investment)}$$

In the lemonade example:
$$\frac{\$2.00 - \$1.00}{\$1.00} \times 100 = 100\%$$

This saying is an easy way to remember this formula:
"What you made over what you paid, times a hundred."[*]

$$\frac{\text{What you made}}{\text{What you paid}} \times 100 = \text{ROI}$$

RULE OF THUMB: In business formulas, "on" means "divided by." Return on Investment means Return (A – B) divided by Investment (B).

---

[*] With thanks to Frank Kennedy.

Example of Return on Investment:

RETURN ON INVESTMENT (ROI)		
End-of-Period Wealth	Beginning-of-Period Wealth	Rate of Return
$2	$1	100%*
$30	$15	100%
$90	$30	200%
$10	$9	11.1%
$100	$200	−50%
$80	$60	33%
$1,000	$2,000	−50%
$9	$10	−10%

$$* \frac{2-1}{1} = \frac{1}{1} \times 100 = 100\%$$

Risk, Time, and Liquidity

Risk means the chance of losing your money. When you buy $50 worth of assorted jewelry wholesale to resell at $100, you *risk* not being able to sell it. You could lose your $50.

When an investor, such as a bank, lends money (the loan amount is called the **principal**) it charges **interest** — expressed as an **interest rate**. The interest rate is a percentage of the principal. When someone borrows money from a bank, he or she pays back the principal *and* the interest.

Banks lend money to businesses at different interest rates, depending on the degree of risk involved. A large and successful company that has been in business many years will receive a lower interest rate than a small or new business that the bank perceives as more risky.

A successful business that has been in existence for ten years might be able to borrow money from a bank at an interest rate of 11%. A newly established business might have to pay an interest rate of, say, 14%.

Similarly, the greater the time factor, the greater the rate of return should be. The longer someone has your money, the greater the chance that your investment could somehow be lost.

Finally, an investor has to consider *liquidity*. Liquidity refers to the ease of getting cash in and out of an investment. How "liquid" is the investment? Can you call the business in which you have invested and get your money back if you suddenly have need for it? If so, the investment is *liquid*, or easily converted into cash.

In general, the longer you have to wait for the payback on your investment, the greater the return should be. The easier your money is to retrieve, the lower your return will probably be.

The lower the risk of the investment, the lower the required rate of return. The higher the risk of the investment, the higher the required rate of return.

Small-Business Risk and Returns Are High

The rate of return on a small business can be very high. The risk of failure for most small businesses is also very high. *The higher the risk of the investment, the higher the required rate of return.*

Some businesses that young people start, however, face a lower risk of failure than the small businesses started by adults. The young entrepreneur usually has fewer fixed costs, such as rent or insurance. For this reason, businesses started by young people can be quite profitable, when compared to the time and money invested.

The rate of return on a young person's business can also be quite high because the original investment, or start-up costs, are very low. Savings banks typically offer 4% over a year; a small business usually earns a much higher rate of return, as in the chart on the next page.

 RULE OF THUMB: The higher the risk of investment, the greater its return should be.

GREATER RISK EQUALS GREATER REWARD

	End-of-Period Wealth (A)	Beginning-of-Period Wealth (B)	Rate of Return
Savings Account	$104	$100	4%*
Small Business	$500	$100	400%

$$\frac{^*A - B}{B} \times 100$$

$$\frac{^*104 - 100}{100} = \frac{4}{100} \times 100 = 4\%$$

The Time Value of Money*

It's a great idea to start saving and investing when you're young, because you have time on your side. It's pretty easy to make sure you'll have money for your old age, if you start saving now. The government allows you to set up tax-free retirement accounts called IRAs (Individual Retirement Accounts). Tax-free means you don't have to pay any taxes on any returns your investment earns as long as you keep the money in your IRA until you retire. If you take it out, you will have to pay a penalty.

One type of IRA, the Roth IRA, can be a good choice for a young person, because it allows you to make a one-time withdrawal of money from the IRA to buy a house. So with the Roth IRA you can save not only for your retirement, but for buying a house someday! Two thousand dollars is the maximum you are allowed to invest in a Roth IRA per year.

Let's look at two people who invest in Roth-IRAs. Let's assume that they both invest the money in their IRAs in investments that return 12% per year.

PERSON A: Invests $2,000 a year for six years at a rate of return of 12%, then stops.

PERSON B: Spends $2,000 a year on him/herself for six years. Then invests $2,000 a year for the next 35 years at a rate of return of 12%.

---

* Adapted by Jack Hemphill from *Common Sense: A Simple Plan for Financial Independence* (10th Edition), by Art Williams (Park Lake Publishers, Inc., 1991).

PERSON A: Only invested a total of $12,000: $2,000 per year x 6 years = $12,000.

PERSON B: Invested a total of $70,000: $2,000 per year x 35 years = $70,000.

The chart on the next page shows how each person's investment is growing over time.

At "age 62": Person A, who only invested $12,000, has earned nearly as much on the investment as Person B, who invested $70,000!

Moral: Start investing early. Let time work for you!

TIME VALUE OF MONEY CHART

	PERSON A		PERSON B	
Age	Payment	Growth at End of Year *	Payment	Growth at End of Year *
22	$ 2,000	$ 2,240	$ 0	$ 0
23	2,000	4,479	0	0
24	2,000	7,559	0	0
25	2,000	10,706	0	0
26	2,000	14,230	0	0
27	2,000	18,178	0	0
28	0	20,359	2,000	2,240
29	0	22,803	2,000	4,749
30	0	25,539	2,000	7,559
31	0	28,603	2,000	10,706
32	0	32,036	2,000	14,230
33	0	35,880	2,000	18,178
34	0	40,186	2,000	22,559
35	0	45,008	2,000	27,551
36	0	50,409	2,000	33,097
37	0	56,458	2,000	39,309
38	0	63,233	2,000	46,266
39	0	70,821	2,000	54,058
40	0	79,320	2,000	62,785
41	0	88,838	2,000	72,559
42	0	99,499	2,000	83,507
43	0	111,438	2,000	95,767
44	0	124,811	2,000	109,499
45	0	139,788	2,000	124,879
46	0	156,563	2,000	142,105
47	0	175,351	2,000	161,397
48	0	196,393	2,000	183,005
49	0	219,960	2,000	207,206
50	0	246,355	2,000	234,310
51	0	275,917	2,000	264,668
52	0	309,028	2,000	298,668
53	0	346,111	2,000	336,748
54	0	387,644	2,000	379,398
55	0	434,161	2,000	427,166
56	0	486,261	2,000	480,665
57	0	544,612	2,000	540,585
58	0	609,966	2,000	607,695
59	0	683,162	2,000	682,859
60	0	765,141	2,000	787,042
61	0	856,958	2,000	861,327
62	0	959,793	2,000	966,926

Total Contributions:	**$12,000**		**$70,000**	
Total at age 62:		**$959,793**		**$966,926**

* assuming a 12% interest rate

Chapter 5 Review

NOTE: The exercises printed below can be found in the corresponding chapter of the **NFTE MODULE 1 WORKBOOK** that came with your textbook. Please write your answers there. If you do not have a workbook, write your answers on a separate sheet of paper.

Critical Thinking about . . . Return on Investment (ROI)

Formula: ROI =

$$\frac{\text{End-of-Period Wealth} - \text{Beginning-of-Period Wealth}}{\text{Beginning-of-Period Wealth}} \times 100$$

Assume a one-year investment period and calculate the Return on Investment.

Example:

End-of-Period Wealth = $1.00
Beginning-of-Period Wealth = $0.50

$$\frac{\$1.00 - \$0.50}{\$0.50} \times 100 = 100\% \text{ ROI}$$

Using New Words

risk
rate of return
principal
interest
interest rate
investment
return on investment

Use each vocabulary term in a sentence.

Getting the Facts

1. What is another phrase for "rate of return"?

2. Will a bank charge a higher interest rate for a five-year loan or a three-year loan? Why?

3. Why do businesses started by young people face a lower risk of failure than adult businesses?

4. What else can be invested besides money?

5. Define "end-of-period wealth."

In Your Opinion

What would be the acceptable return to you for investing your time, energy or money in the following situations? (Note: Your return does not have to be financial.)

1. Baby-sit a neighbor's child for two hours.

2. Help your mother with the laundry.

3. Do an hour of volunteer work at a hospital.

4. Loan a friend $20 to start a candy business.

Review

Chapter Summary

I. To invest is to put time, money or energy into something in hopes of gaining financial profit or personal satisfaction.

A. An investment should generate an acceptable rate of return.

B. Rate of return is also called return on investment.

II. The formula for ROI (Return on Investment expressed as a percentage) is:

$$\frac{\text{End-of-Period Wealth} - \text{Beginning-of-Period Wealth}}{\text{Beginning-of-Period Wealth}} \times 100 = \text{ROI}$$

III. Risk is the chance of losing money on an investment.

A. The amount of risk determines the interest rate on a loan.

B. Time and liquidity affect risk and, therefore, rate of return.

C. The greater the risk, the greater the return should be.

IV. Small businesses are high-risk, high-return investments.

KEY OBJECTIVES

READING THIS CHAPTER AND DOING THE EXERCISES WILL ENABLE YOU TO:

- Increase your creativity.
- Challenge assumptions and practice lateral thinking.
- Use "practical daydreaming" to invent new products.
- Analyze how businesses solve problems and meet needs.

INVENTIONS AND PRODUCT DEVELOPMENT

The Entrepreneur as Market-Minded Artist

Entrepreneurs can be thought of as the *artists* of the economy. They create businesses from ideas, visions, or dreams.

Companies such as Ford Motor Company and Apple Computer were founded by extremely creative and resourceful people (see the stories of Henry Ford and Apple co-founder Stephen Wozniak in NFTE's *Entrepreneurs in Profile* *). The difference between artists and entrepreneurs is not creativity — both are creative. The difference lies in how that creativity is used:

- Artists create in response to an inner need to express themselves.
- The entrepreneur tries to create something consumers will want to buy because it meets their needs.

---

* This book, by Steve Mariotti and Michael Caslin, can be ordered from NFTE.

Some artists are also successful entrepreneurs. Madonna changes her look and music frequently, to keep her audience fascinated. Oprah Winfrey is a shrewd business-woman as well as a talented actress and talk-show host.

Creativity Can Be Developed

Creativity is the ability to invent or make something using your imagination. You may think of this as something you must be born with, but that's not accurate. People are born with talent. *Anyone* can develop creativity.

The secret of developing creativity is the willingness to entertain new ideas and change or throw away old ones. This is called being *open-minded*.

Creative people are also not afraid to make mistakes or to be different. Henry Ford tinkered with a "horse-less carriage" in his backyard, even though neighbors made fun of him. The American artist, Andy Warhol, silkscreened images of Campbell's soup cans on giant canvases. At first, people thought his paintings were ridiculous, but Warhol become rich and famous. Today, these paintings are very much in demand and hang in museums.

It is a rare artist, though, who can experiment with new ideas early in his or her career and succeed. One can break the rules only after one understands them. Many painters, for example, start their careers copying great paintings of the past.

Likewise, an entrepreneur should read biographies of successful entrepreneurs and study business skills and techniques. An entrepreneur does not necessarily need an advanced degree in business, but should have some knowledge in many different subjects, including current events.

Lateral Thinking *

Author Edward de Bono argues in his books that creativity can be developed through **lateral thinking**. Lateral thinking looks for alternative ways of thinking about a problem or obstacle. Most of us use **vertical thinking**, which stacks one idea on top of the next. In math, for instance, you learn how to add, then you learn how to multiply.

The problem with always using vertical thinking, de Bono says, is that it builds "concept prisons of old ideas." Vertical thinking encourages you to try to fit new information into patterns you've already learned. You may even unconsciously throw away new information because it doesn't fit into your mind's patterns.

For example, this is how people hang onto racist or sexist stereotypes. They ignore anything good they see or hear about people different from themselves. They focus instead on negative images that fit into their "concept prison."

Challenge Assumptions

You can develop lateral thinking by challenging *assumptions*. An assumption is anything you assume or believe to be true. Challenging an assumption, however, might lead to the creative solution of a problem. To experience this yourself, use lateral thinking to solve this problem:

On a separate sheet of paper, link up the nine dots below using only four straight lines and without raising the pencil from the paper.

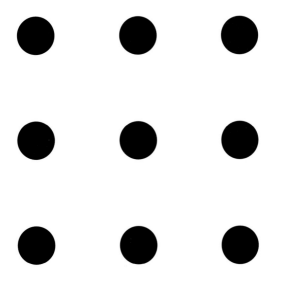

---

* Material in this chapter is adapted from *Lateral Thinking, Creativity Step by Step*, by Edward de Bono (Harper & Row, 1970).

New Research Suggests Intelligence Can Be Improved

Scientists used to believe that every person was born with a level of intelligence that never changed. They believed that physical exercise could help muscles grow, but that nothing helped the brain grow.

Recent research indicates, though, that stimulating the mind with mental exercise may actually cause brain cells, called *neurons*, to send out branches of *dendrites*. Dendrites connect brain cells. More dendrites means more brain cells can be used.

Dendrites can be encouraged to grow by doing many things that you probably enjoy. Dr. Arnold Scheibel, Professor of Neurobiology at the University of California-Los Angeles School of Medicine, suggests the following activities:

- Solve puzzles.
- Play a musical instrument.
- Fix something — learn to repair cars or electrical equipment.
- Make art — paint, sculpt, write poetry.
- Dance.
- Make friends with people who challenge you to think about new things; have conversations that make you think about new subjects.

Since both your intelligence and your creativity may be stimulated and improved, *you should never feel that you are not good enough, creative enough, or smart enough to succeed.* Always remember, there are different types of intelligence, many of which are not measured by standardized, multiple-choice tests.

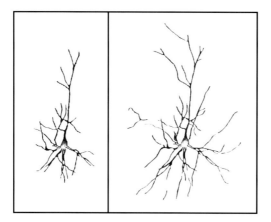

On the left is a brain cell from a rat raised without mental exercise. The dendrites are the branch-like lines.

On the right, the brain cell of a rat that was given toys. Note the increased number of dendrites.

 RULE OF THUMB: It's not how smart you are, it's how you are smart.

You Have Unique Knowledge*

Not only can you develop your creativity and intelligence by using them, but you have unique knowledge that no one else has. You know your neighborhood better than someone from another neighborhood ever could, for example. You have had life experiences that no one else has had.

These experiences make up your knowledge of the world. You can use that knowledge, along with your creativity and intelligence, to become a successful entrepreneur.

Your Market

The difference between an artist and an entrepreneur is that artists create for themselves and entrepreneurs create for a *market*.

A market is a group of people who might buy your product or service. Think of your neighborhood and school as your market. You know this market very well. Think creatively for a moment about what your classmates and neighbors might wish they could purchase at school or in the neighborhood. What would they really want to buy? What kind of service would save them time? Are there any problems you could solve for them by creating a business?

Practical Daydreaming . . . about Inventions!

Everyone daydreams, but entrepreneurs daydream with a *market* in mind. Some entrepreneurial daydreams have become inventions that have changed the world.

Computer scientist and entrepreneur An Wang, who founded Wang Laboratories, patented forty inventions in his lifetime. He said his best ideas were "presented to me by my subconscious almost as a gift."

Wang immigrated to the United States from China in 1945 when he was 25. While at the Harvard Computation Laboratory, he invented the "magnetic memory core." This invention, which Wang patented, made computer memory possible. At 28, Wang gave up his job and, with a few hundred dollars, started Wang Laboratories in a small loft above a garage.

Sometimes Wang and his wife encountered discrimination. He said this made him more determined to succeed: "A small part of the reason I founded Wang Laboratories," he said, "was to show that Chinese could excel at things other than running laundries and restaurants."

---

* Special thanks to Charles Koch for demonstrating the importance of this concept.

Eventually, IBM purchased the rights to the magnetic core he had invented. Wang used the money from the sale to start marketing some of the new devices he had patented in the meantime, including desk-top calculators. The calculators led to a growth in sales for Wang Laboratories to $39 million by 1972. In 1984, Wang was the fifth richest American, with a net worth of $1.6 billion.

Product Development

You can use your creativity and your unique knowledge of your market to develop new products (or improve existing ones). Just follow these steps:

Step 1: Play with possibilities.*

- Ideas don't cost anything. Just write them down.
- To jump-start your imagination, complete this sentence on a separate sheet of paper:
  "I wish someone would make a _____ that _____."

Step 2: Think of possible solutions to problems in your neighborhood, community, or the world.

- Pretend anything is possible.
- Write and/or sketch your solutions.

Step 3: Make a model of the product.

- This model can be rough. Use inexpensive materials such as paper, wood, paint, cloth or plaster of paris, as you may go through many models.
- Does it work? How could it work better?
- Conduct some market research by showing the model to friends, acquaintances, store keepers. Collect ideas and suggestions.
- Revise your design. Don't be afraid to experiment.

Step 4: Find out who might manufacture your product; have a prototype made.

- A **prototype** is an exact model of the product made by the manufacturing process that would be used in actual production.
- This can be expensive; prototypes cost many times the final production cost per item.

---

* Special thanks to Sylvia Stein for the ideas she contributed to this chapter.

- Check the *Thomas Register*, which lists all U.S. manufacturers, to find one you might contact about your invention.

The twenty-six volumes of the *Thomas Register* are broken into three categories:

GROUP ONE — Volumes 1-16 are a list of types of products and services arranged alphabetically. Within each category, you can look up companies alphabetically by state and city. Use Group One to locate manufacturers in your area that make products similar to your invention.

GROUP TWO — Volumes 17 and 18 hold profiles of different companies, listed alphabetically by company name. After you find a manufacturer in Group One that looks interesting, find its profile in Group Two. This will include the manufacturer's address, telephone numbers, office locations, and the names of company officials.

GROUP THREE — Volumes 19-26 offer catalogs arranged alphabetically by company name. These will include product information, such as drawings, photos, and statistics.

Step 5: Reality check

- Does your invention solve a problem that is big enough — that is, faced by many people?
- Can you reach these people (this market) easily?
- Is the manufacturing cost too high?
- Is there competition? Is someone else selling a similar product? How is yours better or different?
- Try test marketing. Place a display with the product in a store and see how it sells.

Patents

Once you have developed a good invention, you can either go into business for yourself or sell the idea to a manufacturer. Before taking either step, however, you must protect your rights as the inventor by patenting the invention.

A **patent** grants to the inventor the exclusive privilege of making, using, and selling, and authorizing others to make, use, and sell his/her invention. A patent can be obtained for any original and useful device or process and is valid for twenty years. After that time, anyone may sell the invention without paying the inventor.

Thomas Jefferson wrote: "The issue of patents for new discoveries has given a spring to invention beyond my conception." Later, Abraham Lincoln noted, "The Patent System added the fuel of interest to the fire of genius." The first patent and copyright law was passed in 1790. The United States Patent Office was established in 1836.

We will go into the details of filing for a patent in Chapter 28. For now, you just need to know that a patent application will have to include the following:

1. An in-depth description of the invention.

2. A drawing of the invention.

3. A completed "Declaration for Patent Application."

4. A notarized statement from the inventor to the effect that he or she is the original inventor of the subject of the application. ("Notarized" means the statement has been witnessed by a notary. Most banks have notaries who will witness statements for a small fee.)

5. The filing fee ($345–$690.)

Public Domain

If an invention is put into use by the inventor for more than one year without obtaining a patent, the invention is considered **public domain** and a patent will no longer be granted.

An unfortunate example of this is the case of Louis Temple, an African American from New Bedford, Massachusetts, who invented the toggle harpoon in the 19th century. This invention greatly increased the efficiency of whaling at a time when whale oil was extremely valuable — it was used for lighting lamps and making candles.

Temple gave prototypes of the harpoon to several New Bedford ship captains to test the design. In those days whaling voyages took about two years. By the time the ships returned and reported the harpoon's great success, Temple's invention had become public domain. Temple was never able to profit from his invention and died in poverty.

Remember, however, that you don't need to go to the trouble and expense of obtaining a patent unless your invention is unique and you intend to sell it.

Trademarks

Trademarks are "any word, name, symbol, or device, or any combination thereof adopted and used by a manufacturer or merchant to identify his goods and distinguish them from those manufactured or sold by others," according to the United States Patent and Trademark Office. If you have registered your trademark, you should put an ® next to your product name. If you are claiming a trademark, but have not registered it with the United States Patent and Trademark Office, use ™. To indicate a service mark, you should use ᔆᴹ with your service name.

Unsung Inventors

Many inventors have made important contributions to American businesses that were not attributed to them at the time. Nobody knows how many inventions were thought up by slaves before the Civil War, for example, because the credit was taken by others. There were probably quite a few, because ideas for making a job easier or faster often come from those who have to do the actual work.

In 1895, an African-American Congressman, **George Washington Murray**, read into the *Congressional Record* a list of ninety-two patents that had been issued to African Americans. Murray wanted the general public to know that African Americans had made important contributions to the industrial revolution. Murray himself received eight patents for improvements to farm machinery.

The first known patent granted to an African American was in 1821 to **Thomas L. Jennings** of New York for a dry-cleaning device. The second went to Henry Blair in 1834, for his improved seed planter. In 1842, **Norbert Rillieux** received a patent for inventing a process for refining sugar.

Elijah McCoy invented a device for the self-oiling of railroad locomotives in 1872. This invention saved a great deal of time and money. Before it was available, the train's fireman had to get out of the cab and oil the parts by hand so they would not wear out prematurely. McCoy was inspired to invent this device because, while working for the Michigan Central Railroad, he had often been assigned to perform this tiresome job.

Jan E. Matzeliger invented an automatic shoe-stitching device, a "lasting" machine, in 1883. It could stitch 700 pairs of shoes a day, instead of the few pairs that could be sewn by hand. This invention revolutionized the shoe industry and greatly reduced the price of the average pair of shoes.

Almost everyone knows the name of **Thomas Edison**, but few people know that an African American named **Lewis H. Latimer** invented the incandescent light bulb that made the practical application of Edison's electric-light system possible. Latimer worked closely with Edison and installed the first municipal electric-light systems in New York, Philadelphia, London, and Montreal.

From Inventions to Fame and Fortune

Many early African-American inventors died in poverty and obscurity, but there were some fortunate exceptions.

When Elijah McCoy died in 1929, he was both financially secure and respected by the engineering community. Jan Matzeliger died prematurely at age 37, but his ten percent ownership of the company that manufactured his invention would have made him very wealthy.

Although not strictly an inventor, **Madame C.J. Walker** pioneered the mail-order marketing of beauty products for women of color and became the first African-American millionaire.

Dr. George Washington Carver is the one African-American inventor who was internationally known in his lifetime. Born at the end of the Civil War, Carver completely transformed farming in the South by developing and popularizing ways to use the peanut, the sweet potato, and the soybean. Because of his efforts, the South's dependency on cotton as the only exportable cash crop ended. Although Dr. Carver did not become rich from his work, he did receive honor and fame.

More Recent Success Stories

In the 1900s, African-American inventors were better able to realize some reasonable financial return on their inventions.

When **Garret A. Morgan** invented a gas mask in 1914, he already had a very profitable business based on a hair-straightening cream he had accidentally discovered and successfully marketed. Although his gas mask was originally meant for use in mines and tunnels, the U.S. Army bought it for the troops in World War I.

In 1923, Morgan also invented the first three-way traffic signal, the forerunner of today's traffic light. General Electric paid him $40,000 for the rights to his invention, a considerable sum at the time.

In the 1960s, **Dr. Meredith Gourdine** developed a million-dollar company based on inventions in the field of "electrogas dynamics" — converting gas into electricity. Even though Dr. Gourdine became blind in 1973, he remained active in the company he founded.

The bulletproof glass used to protect bank tellers was invented by **Emanuel L. Logan, Jr.**, who was prompted by the growing number of bank robberies that seemed to be occurring throughout the country.

African-American contributors to the United States' space program include **Dr. Robert E. Shurney**, who designed effective tires for the Moon Buggy after the landing of 1969, and **Dr. George Carruthers**, who invented a special ultraviolet camera used aboard Apollo 16's 1972 moon landing.

Women Inventors

Nuclear fission, solar heating, bras, drip coffee, the ice cream cone, the Barbie doll, dishwashers, rolling pins, windshield wipers, medical syringes — these are just some of the products invented by women. The stories of women inventors are finally coming to light with the increasing interest in women's history.

Many early women inventors thought up products to help them where they spent most of their time — in the home: cooking, cleaning, and sewing. **Mary Kies** became the first woman patentee in 1809. She invented a process for weaving straw with silk or cotton thread that was instrumental in boosting New England's hat-making industry. When the War of 1812 cut off supplies of hats from Europe, New England hat makers used Kies's process to take over the market.

As women began to work outside the home as secretaries, they invented helpful office products. **Bette Graham** invented "Liquid Paper," or "whiteout," to save secretaries the trouble of typing over an entire page when they made an error.

For some time, women have been moving into traditionally male fields, such as medicine and science, and their inventions in these areas have been correspondingly increasing. In 1988, for example, **Gertrude Elion** became the first woman inducted into the inventors' Hall of Fame. During the 39 years she worked for a drug company, Burroughs-Wellcome, Elion patented 45 medical compounds. She shared the 1988 Nobel Prize for medicine with her colleague, **George H. Hitchings**. They invented a compound that prevents transplant patients' immune systems from rejecting donor organs.

An earlier important medical breakthrough was the invention of Nystatin fungicide by **Elizabeth Hazen** and **Rachel Brown** in the early 1950s. Hazen and Brown's invention was stimulated by the need to find a cure for the fungus infections that many U.S. servicemen suffered from during World War II. The two women studied countless soil samples before finally discovering the substance they developed into Nystatin. It took six years to convince the government to give them a patent for what turned out to be a very important medicine. The patent generated $13 million in royalties, most of which Hazen and Brown used to establish scholarships for college students pursuing the biological sciences.

Ann Moore's invention of the child-carrying Snugli™ illustrates that successful inventions often draw on personal experience and careful observation. The Snugli can be seen on almost every American street, but Moore got the idea during her service in the Peace Corps in West Africa in the 1960s. In Togo, mothers carried their babies around with them all day in fabric harnesses. Moore developed this concept into a pouch-like child carrier that is both comfortable and washable. She began selling the Snugli in 1979. By 1984, annual sales reached $6 million. Moore has used the Snugli technology to develop the Airlift™ — a padded, portable oxygen-tank carrier for people who need a steady supply of oxygen.

Hispanic-American Inventors

The ranks of Hispanic-American inventors include **Dr. Eloy Rodriguez**, who has developed some important drugs from tropical and desert plants that are being tested on viruses and cancers. He was drawn to these discoveries by noting that monkeys and other primates eat certain plants when they are sick. Dr. Rodriguez established a new biology field called Zoopharmacognosy — the study of self-medication by primates.

Another medical breakthrough by a Hispanic-American is the invention of the process of harvesting insulin from bacterial cells. **Dr. Lydia Villa-Komaroff** was a key member of the team that developed this process.

These stories illustrate the diverse backgrounds and situations from which great inventors — and wonderful new businesses — come.

Chapter 6 Review

N O T E : The exercises printed below can be found in the corresponding chapter of the **NFTE MODULE 1 WORKBOOK** that came with your textbook. Please write your answers there. If you do not have a workbook, write your answers on a separate sheet of paper.

Critical Thinking about . . . Inventions

Prepare for the class Invention Contest by developing a new invention or a product improvement. Describe your invention in a memo that includes a drawing. Be sure to describe how your invention will meet a consumer need.

Using New Words

creativity
lateral thinking
patent
prototype
public domain
vertical thinking

On a separate sheet of paper, identify the vocabulary term that completes each sentence.

1) creativity
   a) ability to be imaginative and inventive
   b) ability to imitate
   c) ability to think vertically

2) lateral thinking
   a) thought that stacks ideas
   b) thought that challenges assumptions and provokes new ideas
   c) thought that develops "concept prisons"

3) vertical thinking
   a) creative way of thinking
   b) thought that discourages "concept prisons"
   c) thought that stacks ideas

4) prototype
   a) a rough product model
   b) an exact product model
   c) a type of product

5) patent
   a) exclusive right to an invention
   b) exclusive right to a work of art
   c) exclusive right to invent new products

6) public domain
   a) free from copyright or patent
   b) patented
   c) open for business

Review

Chapter 6 Review

Getting the Facts

1) What is a prototype?

2) Why can entrepreneurs be called the "artists" of the economy?

3) Do you have to be born with creativity?

4) When was the first copyright and patent law passed?

5) How can you find a company to make a prototype of your invention?

6) Who invented the incandescent light bulb?

Exploration

Write a two-page research report on a minority or woman inventor. If you have access to the Internet, research the report online. If not, use library resources such as an encyclopedia.

In Your Opinion

Discuss with a partner:

1. Write a list of businesses you could imagine starting. Ask your partner about his or her interests or hobbies. Now write a list of businesses you could imagine your partner starting based on what you've learned. Compare and discuss your lists with your partner.

2. Think of a recording artist you and your partner both like. Discuss: Is this person a good entrepreneur? Is he or she setting or following trends? Is this artist aware enough of the market to stay on top? Report your findings to the class.

Chapter Summary

I. Entrepreneurs are the driving, creative force of the business world.

    A. Problems, inconveniences or obstacles inspire new businesses.

    B. Hobbies, interests or skills can become new businesses.

II. Creativity can be developed.

    A. Try being open-minded.

    B. Don't be afraid to make mistakes.

    C. Challenge assumptions and use lateral thinking.

III. Intelligence can be developed.

    A. Research shows mental exercise causes the brain to grow dendrites.

    B. More dendrites reach more brain cells, creating more brain power.

IV. You have a unique knowledge of your market.

    A. Studying the needs of your market can give you business ideas.

    B. Your business must fill a need for people in your market.

V. An invention goes through four steps to become a real product:

    A. Model

    B. Prototype

    C. Test marketing

    D. Patent

VI. A patent grants the inventor exclusive rights to the invention for twenty years.

    A. A patent takes about two years to obtain.

    B. An invention that has been in use for more than a year cannot be patented.

In the midst of difficulty lies opportunity.

— Albert Einstein,
physicist who formulated the
Theory of Relativity

KEY OBJECTIVES

READING THIS CHAPTER AND DOING THE EXERCISES WILL ENABLE YOU TO:

- Compare debt and equity financing.
- Calculate debt-to-equity ratios and debt ratios.
- Open a bank account.

FINANCING STRATEGY: BORROW OR SELL?

Financing

Financing is the use and manipulation of money. Raising money to start a business is one aspect of financing. This money is called *start-up capital*.

If an entrepreneur cannot raise all the money he/she needs for the business, another option is "Other People's Money" (OPM). There are two ways to raise OPM; each affects the future organization and earning power of the business differently. These are:

DEBT — The business borrows the money and pays it back over a set period of time at a set rate of interest. The entrepreneur signs a **promissory note**, promising to repay the sum borrowed, with interest.

EQUITY — The business gives up a percentage of ownership for money. The investor receives a percentage of future profits from the business based upon the percentage of ownership.

Debt

To finance through **debt**, the entrepreneur goes to a person or an institution that has money and borrows it, signing a promise to repay the sum with interest. That promise is called a promissory note.

One advantage of debt is that the lender has no say in the future or direction of the business as long as the loan payments are made. Another is that the payments are predictable.

Interest is figured by multiplying the principal by the interest rate. If $1,200 is borrowed at ten percent to be paid back over one year, the interest on the loan is $1,200 x .10 = $120.

The disadvantage of debt is that if the loan payments are not made, the lender can force the entrepreneur into *bankruptcy*. To do this, the lender must go to court and prove that the business owner cannot pay his or her debts. The court can then force the owner to close the business and sell its *assets* (anything of value that it owns) to raise the cash to pay its debts. The lender can even go after the home and possessions of the owner of a sole proprietorship or the partners in a partnership.

This disadvantage of debt should be carefully considered by the beginning entrepreneur because it often takes time for a new business to show a profit. *The risk of debt is that failure to make loan payments can destroy the business before it gets the chance to prove itself.*

Equity

Equity means that, in return for money, the investor receives a percentage of ownership in the company. For the $1,200 investment we discussed above, an equity investor might want ten percent ownership of the company, which would give him or her ten percent of the business' profits. The investor is hoping ten percent of the profits will provide a high rate of return over time on the initial investment of $1,200.

However, the equity investor assumes greater risk than the debt lender. If the business does not make a profit, neither does the investor. The equity investor cannot force the business into bankruptcy to get back the original investment. If a business is forced into bankruptcy, debt investors get paid off first from the sale of the business assets. Equity investors have a claim on whatever is left over after debt investors have been paid.

The equity investor's risk is higher than that of the debt lender, but so is the potential for return. The equity investor could make an investment back many times over if the business prospers. He or she accepts a higher level of risk than the debt lender, whose risk of losing the investment is lower.

The advantage of equity financing is that the money doesn't have to be paid back unless the business is successful. The disadvantage is that, through giving up ownership, the entrepreneur can lose control of the business to the equity holders.

Debt and Equity

Many companies, including small businesses and large corporations, are usually financed by both debt and equity. A *corporation* is a company owned by people who have invested in it. A corporation is considered a legal "person" and can borrow money by issuing bonds. A **bond** is an interest-bearing certificate representing the corporation's promise to pay back the bondholder the amount he or she has lent the corporation, plus interest. Corporations may also sell **stock**, to raise equity financing. A person who buys stock then owns a percentage of that corporation. Stockholders are paid *dividends* when the corporation is profitable.

Both stocks and bonds are traded openly on the financial markets. The prices of stocks and bonds on the market change as the fortunes of the companies and general economic trends change.

Ratios

The financial strategy of a company is expressed by its **debt-to-equity ratio**. If a company has a debt-to-equity ratio of one-to-one (expressed as 1:1), this means that for every one dollar of debt the company has one dollar of equity.

$$\frac{\textbf{debt}}{\textbf{equity}} = \textbf{debt-to-equity ratio}$$

Another ratio that gives a picture of financial strategy is the **debt ratio**. This is the ratio of debt to assets. A debt ratio of one means that every one dollar of assets is financed by one dollar of debt and one dollar of equity.

$$\frac{\textbf{Amount of debt}}{\textbf{Amount of assets}} = \textbf{debt ratio}$$

Example: $\frac{0.50}{1.00} = 0.50$

Donald Trump's Debt Financing Strategy

Companies that rely heavily on debt financing are described as highly *leveraged*. Leveraged means financed with debt. This financial strategy works well only when business is very good. When business is slow, debt payments are more difficult to meet.

This is a very dangerous position for a company to be in, because lenders of debt can force a company into bankruptcy or take company property.

Businesses sometimes find themselves in this position because the business owner is unwilling to give up any control by issuing equity and relies too heavily on debt financing.

In the 1980s, Donald Trump chose a debt financing strategy for his properties. Trump did not want to give up any control by selling stock (equity) when he needed money. Because of his reputation, banks were willing to lend him a great deal of money (debt). The banks took several important assets and properties of Trump's when the economy took a downturn in the late 1980s and he couldn't make his loan payments. In the '90s, Trump made a comeback and is now once again highly successful.

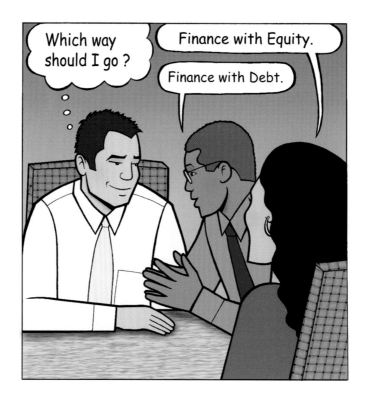

James Ling: Equity Financing Pioneer

James Ling was an entrepreneur who made equity financing into an art. Not only did he finance his own company by selling shares, but he developed the strategy of using one company's equity to buy another company.

In the 1950s, Ling was trying to secure financing for his company, Ling Electric, which provided electrical wiring for homes in Dallas. Although he had over $1 million in sales, the Texas investment banks were unwilling to help him expand.

Fed up with the banks, Ling offered 50% of his company (400,000 shares) directly to the public. He sold all the shares in three months by going door-to-door and by selling over the phone. The banks were astonished. Ling had raised $900,000 in equity capital by himself.

Ling used the rising stock market to make even more money. He would issue more stock, wait for its price to go up, and then trade it for ownership (equity) in other businesses. In this way he bought four major electronics firms by the early 1960s.

Throughout the 60s Ling built the L-T-V empire with this method. Unfortunately, his financing strategy required a rising stock market. The market's downturn in 1969-70 caught him completely off guard. His fortune collapsed as the price of L-T-V shares fell from $135 per share to only $9. His personal net worth fell from $100 million to under $10 million.

Despite the collapse of L-T-V, Ling is considered a pioneer in equity financing.

Anita Roddick: Using Equity

Anita Roddick didn't expect The Body Shop, which she founded in England, to change the cosmetics industry, be a force for social awareness, and make millions of dollars too—but it has. The Body Shop would have never gotten that far, though, if Roddick hadn't sold half the business to her friend Ian McGlinn in exchange for equity financing of £4,000 (around $7,000). Local banks refused to lend her money because she had only been in business for a few months.

McGlinn's investment came to be worth over £140 million (around $240 million). Roddick says she has no regrets, because without McGlinn's equity financing, she would not have been able to grow her company.

The Banking Relationship

As Roddick's story illustrates, some of the most successful entrepreneurs didn't finance their businesses with bank loans at first—because they couldn't get them. Even though it may be awhile before you will be ready to turn to bank financing for your business, it's never too early to begin cultivating a good relationship with a bank. You can start by opening a bank account.

When you have a bank account, you have a safe place to store your money. People who do not have bank accounts have to carry their money with them or hide it. Both of these options are risky and dangerous. Your money is safer in a bank, where it is insured by the federal government. Most banks have their deposits insured by the Federal Deposit Insurance Corporation (FDIC) up to $100,000. Even if the bank goes out of business, your money is protected up to $100,000.

Banks offer two basic accounts — savings and checking:

Savings Accounts

When you put money in a savings account, not only is the money safe, but the bank pays you interest. It is a low rate of return compared to some other investments, but there is virtually no risk that you will lose your money. A savings account is a "low-risk, low-yield" investment.

Banks make their profits by taking the money of the individual depositors and lending it. The banks receive a higher interest rate on the money they lend out than they pay on the deposits.

Checking Accounts

Paying by check, not cash, is the professional way to do business. It is safer, and the cancelled checks provide proof that you paid your bill. When you write a check, you are authorizing the bank to pay someone from your account.

Shop around before you decide where to keep your checking account. Different banks have different fees and requirements. With some accounts it is necessary to maintain a minimum balance. Others require a minimum balance for you to write checks for free. If your balance is lower, the bank charges you for each check you write. Look into what different banks offer. *Choose the checking account that best suits your needs.*

Technology Tip: 24-Hour Banking and Online Banking

Banks are using technology to make themselves available to customers 24 hours a day—good news for busy entrepreneurs! You can use your ATM (Automatic Teller Machine) card anytime. More banks are issuing debit cards that you can use at the ATM and that allow you to make purchases from your checking account without the hassle of writing a check and presenting identification. You can also arrange to have payment of monthly utility bills made automatically.

Online banking is also easy and convenient. Financial record-keeping software like Microsoft Money even lets you input information from your online bank statement directly into the financial records on your computer.

Alternative Financing

There are many alternatives to bank financing available to young entrepreneurs. Like Anita Roddick, you can start by offering an equity stake in your company to friends and family members. Another option is micro-loan financing. The federal government is supporting a growing number of micro-loan programs for entrepreneurs that make loans ranging from $100 to $25,000. The loan is made based on the entrepreneur's character and business plan. The money can be used to buy machinery, furniture, and supplies but may not be used to pay existing debt. A micro-loan can be a terrific financing option for a very small businesses.

A small business with a solid business plan might be able to attract "angel" financing. Angels are private investors who are typically worth over $1 million and are interested in financing a start-up business for a variety of reasons—from friendship to a desire to encourage entrepreneurship in a given field. Bill Gates has been an angel for several biotech startups, for example, because he is interested in the field of biotechnology. Angel financing typically ranges from $100,000 to $500,000. One network that is a good source of angel financing information is ACE-Net. You can learn more at www.sba.gov/advo/acenet.html.

Finally, there's always "bootstrap" financing. Plenty of successful entrepreneurs got their businesses off the ground for under $10,000 by doing things like:

- Hiring as few employees as possible.
- Borrowing, instead of buying equipment.
- Using personal savings.
- Arranging small loans from friends and relatives.
- Where there's a will, there's a way!

Chapter 7 Review

NOTE: The exercises printed below can be found in the corresponding chapter of the **NFTE MODULE 1 WORKBOOK** that came with your textbook. Please write your answers there. If you do not have a workbook, write your answers on a separate sheet of paper.

Critical Thinking about . . . Debt vs. Equity

1) List the advantages and disadvantages of each type of financing:

   Debt: loans, bonds

   Equity: stocks

2) Given your personality, do you think you would be more likely to choose Donald Trump's financing strategy or James Ling's? Explain.

Using New Words

bond
debt
debt ratio
debt-to-equity ratio
equity
financing
promissory note
stock

On a separate sheet of paper, identify the vocabulary term that completes each sentence.

1) If you raise money by selling stock, you are giving up _____

2) A highly leveraged company is financed primarily by _____

3) Holders of _____ receive dividends and annual corporate reports.

4) If you borrow money from a bank, you will have to sign a _____

5) The ratio of debt to assets is called a _____

6) When a corporation issues _____ it is raising money through debt.

7) _____ is really using other people's money to increase business profits or earn an acceptable return.

8) The financial strategy of a company is expressed by its _____

Getting the Facts

True or false?

1. Savings accounts offer low return for low risk.

2. Your bank account is protected by government insurance.

3. Banks are required by law to offer all consumers the same rates and balance requirements.

Review

Chapter 7 Review

Exploration: Planning Your Start-up Strategy

1) What are the estimated costs of starting your business?

2) How do you plan to finance the business? List your sources of financing, identifying whether each source is equity, debt or a gift. Indicate the amount and type of each source.

3) What is your debt/equity ratio?

4) What percentage of ownership would you give up to secure equity financing?

Review

Chapter Summary

I. Raising money for a business is called financing.

    A. Debt financing — the business borrows money.

        • Advantage — lender has no say in the business.

        • Disadvantage — lender can force business into bankruptcy.

    B. Equity financing — the business sells ownership.

        • Advantage — money raised does not have to be paid back.

        • Disadvantage — gives control of business to shareholders.

II. Large corporations use both debt and equity financing.

    A. Debt-to-equity ratio expresses financing strategy.

$$\frac{\text{debt}}{\text{equity}} = \text{debt-to-equity ratio}$$

    B. Debt ratio shows ratio of debt to assets.

$$\frac{\text{Amount of debt}}{\text{Amount of assets}} = \text{debt ratio}$$

III. Donald Trump relied too much on debt and lost assets when he couldn't make loan payments.

IV. James Ling relied too heavily on equity and lost control when stock prices collapsed.

V. Put your money in a bank account where it will be safe and earn interest.

VI. Banks pay interest on savings accounts because they profit by lending the deposits out at a higher interest rate.

    A. Paying by check, not cash, is more professional. Cancelled checks provide proof of payment.

    B. Checks are safer to carry than cash.

    C. Shop around for the best deal before choosing a bank for your checking account.

The propensity to truck, barter, and exchange one thing for another is common to all men.

—Adam Smith,
Scottish economist

KEY OBJECTIVES

READING THIS CHAPTER AND DOING THE EXERCISES WILL ENABLE YOU TO:

- Identify your skills and hobbies.
- Select your own business.
- Come up with the best name for your business.

SELECTING YOUR BUSINESS*

Things to Consider

Imagine yourself for a moment in the business of your choice. Is it a "good fit"? Are you going to stay interested in it and enthusiastic about it for a long time?

Consider keeping your business simple. This is going to be your very first enterprise, so don't bite off more than you can chew. Many successful entrepreneurs start more than one business over the course of a lifetime. Start with something simple that you know you can do well. You will have the rest of your life to move on to greater and more complex challenges.

For now, if you choose a simple business and follow these three rules, you can't lose:

1. Satisfy a consumer need.
2. Create value.
3. Keep good records.

---

* See Bonnie Drew's *Fast Cash for Kids* (Career Press, Inc., 1995) for an excellent source of 101 business ideas for young people.

The successful entrepreneur listens to what people in the community are saying. What do the people you know like? What do they want? What do they need? Could you fill one of their needs? Remember, you have unique knowledge of your market. Use it to come up with a great business idea.

Four Basic Business Types

All businesses, large or small, can be divided into four basic types:

1. **MANUFACTURING** — makes a tangible product.

2. **WHOLESALE** — buys in quantity from the manufacturer and sells to the retailer.

3. **RETAIL** — sells to the consumer.

4. **SERVICE** — sells an intangible good to the consumer.

Product or Service?

A business sells a **product** or a **service** (some businesses sell both). A product is something that exists in nature or is made by human beings. It is *tangible*, meaning that it can be touched. A *service* is work that provides time, skills or expertise in exchange for money. It is *intangible*. You can't literally touch it.

You could base your business on a product or a service (or both!). Are there any products you could make yourself? Are there any products you know that you can buy for less money than you could sell them for to your market?

Is there a service you could perform for your market? Do you have any special skills or expertise to offer?

Turning Hobbies, Skills and Interests into Businesses

As you will see from the following list of business ideas, the possibilities for young people starting businesses are almost limitless.

What you enjoy doing in your spare time might be turned into a profitable business. Making money through doing what you enjoy is a winning combination.

Competitive Advantage:
Your Strategy for Beating the Competition

For your business to be successful, you will need a **competitive advantage**. Your competitive advantage is your strategy for beating the competition. It's whatever you can do better than the competition that will attract customers to your business. Can you supply your product at a lower price than other businesses serving your market? Or can you attract more customers than your competitors can by offering something extra? If you are running a video game rental business, for example, maybe you could deliver the games, so the customers don't have to come to the store. There's your competitive advantage!

By now you may have several business ideas and can't decide which one would be best. Try writing down several possibilities, and then eliminate them one by one until you end up with the business you like best. This will be the subject of your business plan, which you will prepare for this class.

Possible Businesses for Young Entrepreneurs

Some of the businesses started by young people who have taken this course include:

- Candy wholesaling
- Carpentry
- Car repair for remote-control cars
- Computer repair
- Dating newsletter
- Delivery service
- Dressmaking
- Entertaining — magic shows, clown acts
- Greeting-card design
- House/office cleaning
- Jewelry-making
- Messenger service
- Music lessons
- Music-recording studio
- Pet care
- Plant care
- Music management agency
- The sale of all kinds of products: perfume, headbands, jewelry, ties, watches, etc.

- Software installation
- Songwriting
- Tutoring
- T-shirt designs
- Typing or word-processing service
- Wake-up service
- Website design

What kind of business do you think you could start? Again, consider what your friends, family, and schoolmates might want and need. They are your market.

Below are some business ideas you might consider. Remember, a youth business should be:

- Simple.
- Highly unlikely to injure anyone.

Arts and Crafts

If you like children, consider teaching your specialty (such as crafts, cooking, or exercise) to children one or two afternoons a week, or just have a special playtime with puppets, storytelling, or other activities.

Baby-Sitting Service

Are you reliable and responsible? Do you like children? Provide a baby-sitting service.

Baking

Do you like to bake? You can sell freshly made bread, cookies, cakes and other pastries. This is a business where "word of mouth" is truly the best advertising!

Bicycle/Auto/Appliance Repair

Are you mechanically inclined? Fix bicycles, cars, appliances or other machinery.

Books

Start a business selling books, concentrating on those you like to read yourself. You can start by selling your own, and once you start making money you can buy in quantity (wholesale) from the publishers at a discount (smaller publishers will sell small quantities).

Bumper Stickers

Offbeat or inspiring bumper stickers are very popular. Create your own and have them printed.

Calligraphy

Calligraphy is the art of handwriting in an elegant or unusual style. This service is in demand for wedding invitations, menus, birth announcements, and other special occasions. You can also hand-letter poems or lyrics on fine paper, frame them, and sell them as gift-shop items

Candle-making

Candles don't only have to be for Christmas. A crafts store has everything you need for making your own decorative candles. You can buy wax or melt down old candles and crayons. Empty milk cartons are among the household items that can be used as molds.

Car Washing

A car washing business can be a steady source of income if you put some effort into it. Consider working with a team of friends and advertise speedy service for busy people. Also, learn how to wax and detail cars so you can offer these extra services.

Catering

Do you like to cook? Start a catering business and supply whole menus for parties and other occasions.

Collectables

If you collect things like baseball cards, sports caps or other items of interest that are easily and cheaply available now, but could take on value in the future, this is a field that might be of interest. Collect things that you genuinely like because you will have them for a while.

Computer and Software Installation

If you are competent with computers, you can assist others in becoming familiar with them.

Delivery Service

Offer to run errands and make deliveries for small businesspeople and others who don't have the time to do so. Make yourself indispensable and you will soon have a growing business.

Desktop Publishing

You will need access to a computer, laser printer, and a good word-processing program. You also need design skills. With these resources, you can design menus and programs, print personal stationery, create and maintain mailing lists, etc.

Distributing Flyers

Do stores in your neighborhood need people to hand out flyers? These can be distributed on the street, put on car windshields, or given out at social functions. This is a service that could be offered to shopkeepers on a regular basis.

Entertaining

Are you a natural performer who enjoys being in front of an audience? Do you know any magic tricks or have any theater experience? You might like being a magician or a clown and entertaining at birthday parties and other events. If you have musical talent, you could get a band together and play at weddings and parties.

Fish/Aquarium Care

If fish are a hobby of yours, why not turn it into income? You will need to know how to care for both fresh and saltwater tanks. Offer your services to local businesses and restaurants, as well as to individuals.

Gardening/Lawn Cutting

Do you like working outdoors? From the street, you can often spot lawns and gardens that are not being kept up by their owners as well as they should be. You could also shovel snow in the winter.

Gift Baskets

Every holiday is an opportunity to create a different gift basket that you can sell for profit. You can also offer a custom service and make baskets based on the special interests of the persons receiving them.

Greeting Cards

With silkscreen equipment, rubber stamps and/or your own artistic talents, design and print greeting cards.

Growing Plants

Is there a room in your house or apartment that gets a lot of sunlight? You can grow herbs, flowers or other plants for sale. This can be a good "second" business because plants don't have to be watched every minute of the day.

Handicrafts

Do you like to make jewelry, leather goods or other handicrafts? Sell your own work and perhaps, for a percentage, that of your friends as well (if they don't want to be involved in the selling process).

Holiday Selling

Do you have spare time during the holidays? Try selling seasonal specialties, such as Christmas decorations or Valentine's Day candy, which have short but intense sales seasons. If you are willing to put in the time, you can make a lot of money in a relatively short period.

House/Office Cleaning

Do you like to see things clean and neat? Houses and offices need to be cleaned. Many people and businesses do not have the time to do it.

Ironing Service

Ironing is another chore that many people don't have the time for and which could be combined with another job, such as child care.

Jewelry-Making

Making and selling your own jewelry can be both fun, profitable, and can develop your creative talents, too.

 RULE OF THUMB: When selecting your business, choose something you enjoy doing.

Laundry Service

Do you have access to a good washer and dryer? Doing laundry (like dog-walking and house cleaning) is another chore many people do not have time for.

Messenger Service

Do you enjoy running around? Try a messenger/small-package delivery service. It is a business with low start-up costs. The service can expand rapidly as you build up a reputation for reliability.

Music Lessons

Do you play an instrument well enough to teach someone else? Even if you have only intermediate knowledge of an instrument, you could probably teach young beginners.

Painting/Furniture Refinishing

Do you like to paint? Paint rooms and apartments; repaint or refinish old furniture.

Pet Care/Grooming

Do you like animals? Dog-walking or taking care of pets are possibilities. Also, people who love their pets might not have the time to wash and groom them. Patience and a real love of animals will be necessary, however.

Photography/Videotaping

Do you have a good camera or camcorder? More and more, people are having their weddings, birthdays, parties and other events photographed or videotaped (or both). You'll need samples of your work to show to prospective clients.

Plant Care

Offices sometimes hire a service to come in once a week or so to water, clean and fertilize plants. As more and more people work outside the home, there is more demand for household plant care, too.

Stickers and Buttons

Rock and rap artists use stickers and buttons imprinted with their logos to promote themselves. So do stores and sports teams. Why not save them the trouble of contracting with a sticker or button manufacturer? If you establish a relationship with a manufacturer yourself, you can probably get a good price because you will be bringing that manufacturer new jobs. Turn that price advantage into profit.

Translating

Are you bilingual? Translate ads, flyers, signs, etc., for local shopkeepers who want to reach customers who speak different languages.

T-shirts

Are you artistically inclined? Design and print a line of customized T-shirts.

Tutoring

Do you know how to dance, act, sing, draw, or play a musical instrument well enough to teach it to young children? Or do you know one of your school subjects well enough to teach other students? Giving lessons (tutoring) requires patience, but you will discover the rewards and satisfaction of teaching.

Typing or Word-Processing Service

Are you a fast and accurate typist? If you can type well and/or use a word processor, there is a wide variety of services you can offer: typing up papers for other students, organizing and printing out mailing lists, or making up brochures, newsletters or flyers.

Wake-Up Service

Are you an early riser? Start a wake-up service for your fellow students.

Website Design

If you are computer literate and comfortable on the Internet, assist others in designing their "home pages" on the World Wide Web.

Naming Your Business

The name of a business soon comes to symbolize the character of the enterprise to customers, investors, and advisors.

It is common for entrepreneurs to name their businesses after themselves. Using your first name to identify your business — showing the pride you take in it — can be a good idea (Joe's Pizza). Using your last (family) name may not be such a good idea.

If you use your last name for your business, there are several risks:

- If the business fails, you will suffer the embarrassment of having your name associated with the failure. This can hurt you if you decide to start a new business and potential investors associate you with the old one.

- If the business succeeds, you might decide to sell it for a profit. But what if you hate what the new owner does with it? What if he or she engages in dishonest business practices? Your name is still on the door. Also, if you open up another business in the same field using your name again, old customers can be confused as to which is yours.

The best name is one that tells customers what the company does, sells or makes.

As Joe Mancuso says in his best-selling book, *Have You Got What It Takes? How To Tell If You Should Start Your Own Business* (1981), "Naming the company is the first move of many in which you should keep the customer's needs first and foremost in mind."

Possible Businesses for the Young Entrepreneur

Appliance repair

Art gallery

Artist

Auto repair

Baby-sitting

Baking

Bicycle repair

Board-game invention

Book selling

Bumper stickers

Band stickers and posters

Calligraphy

Candle-making

Car washing

Catering

Clothing design

Clown

Collectables

Computer and software
installation

Consignment store

Cosmetics

Dance lessons

D.J. service

Delivery service

Desktop publishing

Distributing flyers
and brochures

Entertaining

Exercise classes

Fish/Aquarium care

Flower delivery

Gardening/Lawn care

Gift baskets

Greeting cards

Growing plants

Handicrafts

Holiday selling

House/office cleaning

House painting

Internet service provider

Ironing service

Jewelry making

Laundry service

Magazine

Magician

Messenger service

Music lessons

Musical instruments

Newspaper

Painting/Furniture
refinishing

Pasta — fresh pasta and
sauces

Party performer

Pet care

Pet grooming

Photography

Plant care

Stickers and buttons

Teaching children arts
and crafts

Translating

T-shirts

Toys

Tutoring

Videotaping weddings,
concerts, etc.

Vintage clothing

Vinyl records

Wake-up service

Website design

Word processing

Chapter 8 Review

NOTE: The exercises printed below can be found in the corresponding chapter of the NFTE MODULE 1 WORKBOOK that came with your textbook. Please write your answers there. If you do not have a workbook, write your answers on a separate sheet of paper.

Critical Thinking about . . . Turning Your Hobbies, Interests, and Skills into Businesses

Match up business opportunities with your hobbies, interests, and skills.

Using New Words

competitive advantage
product
service

On a separate sheet of paper, answer the following questions:

1. What is the basic difference between a product and a service?

2. Is your business idea based on a product or service? Why?

3. What is the competitive advantage of your business idea?

Getting the Facts

1. List three rules for running your own business.

2. Why is it not wise to use your family name in naming your business?

3. Whose needs should come first when naming a business?

4. Who are the people who make up your unique market?

In Your Opinion

Discuss with a partner.

1. List five ideas for businesses you would be interested in starting. Discuss them with a partner. Ask him or her to help you evaluate your ideas by asking questions like:

   - Does the idea satisfy a consumer need?

   - Do you have the skills and resources to create this business?

   - What would be the competitive advantage of the business?

   Switch roles and help your partner evaluate his or her ideas. At the end of the discussion, you should each have chosen one business idea to pursue.

2. Write about your business idea. Describe it, and explain how you came up with it. Why do you think your idea will be a success? What is the name of your business?

Review

Chapter Summary

I. Choose a simple business and follow three rules:

A. Satisfy a consumer need.

B. Buy low, sell high.

C. Keep good records.

II. Many young people have successfully turned their interests into businesses.

A. Let your own interests inspire your business idea.

B. Consider what people you know like, want, or need.

III. The name of your business is very important.

A. Don't use your family name.

B. The name should tell customers what the company does.

In order to succeed we must first believe that we can.

— Michael Korda, author, editor-in chief of Simon & Schuster publishing house

KEY OBJECTIVES

READING THIS CHAPTER AND DOING THE EXERCISES WILL ENABLE YOU TO:

- Unlock the power of your thoughts.
- Discuss Clement Stone's "positive mental attitude."
- Begin training yourself to think positively.
- Strengthen your character.
- Set goals.

THE POWER OF POSITIVE THINKING

Character is Destiny

As discussed in Chapter 3, a hallmark of successful entrepreneurs is optimism. Entrepreneurs view problems as *opportunities* turned inside out. Few people are born optimistic, however. Most optimistic people are that way because they have decided to be so. They know that a positive mental **attitude** is the key to success.

The power of your thoughts lies in their ability to transform you. The few programs that have helped overweight people become thinner, for instance, focus on improving **self-esteem**. Self-esteem is having a positive attitude about oneself. Scientific devices used to monitor involuntary body functions, such as heartbeat or sweating, have proved that negative thoughts, anxiety and **stress** hurt the body.

Over the years successful entrepreneurs have described their "positive mental attitude," their "belief in themselves" or "faith" as crucial to their success. No matter how it is said, the common thread running through the history of entrepreneurship is the idea that thoughts have power. Who you decide you are determines who you will become.

Clement Stone and the Power of Positive Thinking

The father of "Positive Mental Attitude" was Clement Stone. He used it to get through the anxiety that would attack him when he set out each day to sell insurance policies for his mother's small insurance office in Detroit.

Stone was only fifteen years old, and was so scared about going into the large office building to find customers that he made up self-motivating phrases, such as "Do It Now," and "When there's nothing to lose and much to gain by trying, try."

That first day he literally ran from office to office to keep his fear of rejection from overwhelming him. He repeated his phrases to himself over and over. Soon his sales and his confidence improved dramatically. Stone became a master salesman using his method, which he called Positive Mental Attitude. He taught his philosophy to his sales force when he started his own company. He later wrote two best-selling books about training the mind to think positively.

Thoughts Have Power

Your thoughts are not neutral. What you are thinking acts like software in the brain. If you are thinking positively, you generate good ideas and see opportunities. If you are thinking negatively, you generate bad moods that blind you to opportunities.

That's why you should maintain a positive attitude, especially when you are faced with challenges.

Even a dog can tell when someone is afraid, and is more inclined to bite that person. The best way to pass a dog that frightens you is to put out strong, fearless vibes that will make the dog back down. This is the best way to go through life, too.

A positive mental attitude is easy to maintain when it's a warm sunny day and you have money in your pocket. It's harder to maintain when your life is stressful.

Think of it this way: To improve your body's appearance and strength you have to stress it — by running, or weightlifting, or some other exercise. Your mind improves and strengthens in the same way — when you think positively in spite of stress in your life.

Napoleon Hill, who interviewed some 500 wealthy men and wrote about the secret of their success in Think and Grow Rich, said it best: "Every adversity, every failure and every heartache carries with it the seed of an equivalent or a greater benefit."*

Goal Setting and Positivity

"Inch by inch, anything's a cinch!" is an inspirational quote that is good to remember whenever you set out to accomplish a goal — from getting an education to starting a business. Very few great things are accomplished quickly. Usually it's persistence that enables a person to create a successful business or discover a cure for a disease — or earn a degree. Persistence and positive thinking, of course.

Because it takes time and persistence to achieve goals, it's a good idea to get in the habit of writing them down. This is called *goal setting* and it's a great way to train the brain to stay focused on the big picture and not get stuck in the little frustrations of every day. What would you like to accomplish this week, this month, this year, or during your lifetime? Start writing these goals down. Having them written programs your brain to work on them. Goal setting combined with a positive mental attitude and persistence will help you achieve any dream you can dream.

Fifty Positive Quotes to Help You Develop a Positive Mental Attitude

Wealth Is Thoughts, Not Things . . . You Are What You Think

1. Nothing in the world can take the place of persistence. Talent will not; nothing is more common than unsuccessful men with talent. Genius will not; the world is full of educated derelicts. Persistence and determination alone are omnipotent. The slogan "press on" has solved and always will solve the problems of the human race.

    — *Calvin Coolidge*

2. All virtue lies in individual action, in inward energy, in self-determination. There is no moral worth in being swept away by a crowd, even toward the best objective.

    — *William Channing*

---

* Napoleon Hill. *Think and Grow Rich* (Fawcett Publications, Inc., 1965).

3. There are two ways of meeting difficulties. You alter the difficulties or you alter yourself to meet them.

    — *Phyllis Bottome*

4. The world turns aside to let any man pass who knows whither he is going.

    — *David S. Jordan*

5. Our aspirations are our possibilities.

    — *Robert Browning*

6. The secret of getting ahead is getting started.

    — *Sally Berger*

7. A minute's success pays the failure of years.

    — *Robert Browning*

8. Let him who wants to move and convince others be first moved and convinced himself.

    — *Thomas Carlyle*

9. Do unto others as you would have them do unto you.

    — *The Golden Rule*

10. Keep away from people who try to belittle your ambition. Small people always do that, but the really great make you feel that you, too, can become great.

    — *Mark Twain*

11. Success seems to be largely a matter of hanging on after others have let go.

    — *William Feather*

12. There is a tide in the affairs of men, which, taken at the flood, leads on to fortune; omitted, all the voyage of their life is bound in shallows and in miseries.

    — *William Shakespeare*

13. There's no such thing as a self-made man. I've had much help and have found that if you are willing to work, many people are willing to help you.

    — *O. Wayne Rollins*

14. Just don't give up trying to do what you really want to do. Where there is love and inspiration, I don't think you can go wrong.

    — *Ella Fitzgerald*

15. Leadership is knowing what you want and making it happen.

    —*Miriam Colon*

16. History records the successes of men with objectives and a sense of direction. Oblivion is the position of small men overwhelmed by obstacles.

    — *William H. Danforth*

17. It is not the critic who counts; not the man who points out how the strong man stumbled, or where the doer of deeds could have done them better. The credit belongs to the man who is actually in the arena, whose face is marred by dust and sweat and blood; who strives valiantly; who errs and comes short again and again; who knows the great enthusiasms, the great devotions; who spends himself in a worthy cause; who, at the best, knows in the end the triumph of high achievement, and who, at the worst, if he fails, at least fails while daring greatly, so that his place shall never be with those timid souls who know neither victory nor defeat.

    — *Theodore Roosevelt*

18. Sometimes I think creativity is magic, it's not a matter of finding an idea, but allowing the idea to find you.

    — *Maya Lin*

19. Someday I hope to enjoy enough of what the world calls success so that someone will ask me, "What's the secret of it?" I shall say simply this: "I get up when I fall down."

    — *Paul Harvey*

20. Don't let the opinions of the average man sway you. Dream, and he thinks you're crazy. Succeed, and he thinks you're lucky. Acquire wealth, and he thinks you're greedy. Pay no attention. He simply doesn't understand.

    — *Robert G. Allen*

21. Courage is resistance to fear, mastery of fear — not absence of fear.

    — *Mark Twain*

22. Wealth is when small efforts produce big results. Poverty is when big efforts produce small results.

    — *George David*

23. Service is the very purpose of life. It is the rent we pay for living on this planet.

    — *Marian Wright-Edelman*

24. The winners in life think constantly in terms of I can, I will and I am. Losers, on the other hand, concentrate their waking thoughts on what they should have or would have done, or what they can't do.

    — *Dennis Waitley*

25. The more you do of what you've done, the more you'll have of what you've got.

    — *Anonymous*

26. The life which is unexamined is not worth living.

    — *Plato*

27. One man with courage makes a majority.

    — *Andrew Jackson*

28. Money is the seed of money and the first franc is sometimes more difficult to acquire than the second million.

    — *Jean-Jacques Rousseau*

29. Ultimately we know deeply that the other side of every fear is freedom.

    — *Marilyn Ferguson*

30. Progress always involves risk. You can't steal second base and keep your foot on first.

    — *Frederick B. Wilcox*

31. I shall be telling this with a sigh, somewhere ages and ages hence: Two roads diverged in a wood, and I — I took the one less traveled by, and that has made all the difference.

    — *Robert Frost*

32. I always test the limits of my abilities and do the best job I can while remaining true to myself.

    — *Mae C. Jemison*

33. If money is your hope for independence you will never have it. The only real security that a man can have in this world is a reserve of knowledge, experience and ability.

    — *Emile Coué*

34. My life seems like one long obstacle course, with me as the chief obstacle.

    — *Jack Paar*

35. You must do the thing you think you cannot do.

    — *Eleanor Roosevelt*

36. I would rather see a crooked furrow than a field unplowed.

    — *Paul Jewkes*

37. The way to develop decisiveness is to start right where you are, with the very next question you face.

    — *Napoleon Hill*

38. Have the courage and the daring to think that you can make a difference. That's what being young is all about.

    — *Ruby Dee*

39. No person is your friend who demands your silence, or denies your right to grow.

    — *Alice Walker*

40. You can get everything in life that you want . . . if you'll just help enough other people get what they want.

    — *Zig Ziglar*

41. We know too much, and are convinced of too little.

    — *T.S. Eliot*

42. Do not follow where the path may lead. Go instead where there is no path and leave a trail.

    — *Muriel Strode*

43. No man is free who is not master of himself.

    — *Epictetus*

44. Some men have thousands of reasons why they cannot do what they want to, when all they need is one reason why they can.

    — *Willis R. Whitney*

45. Nothing in life is to be feared. It is only to be understood.

    — *Marie Curie*

46. Goals are as essential to success as air is to life.

    — *David Schwartz*

47. Come to the edge, he said. They said, we are afraid. Come to the edge, he said. They came. He pushed them . . . and they flew.

    — *Guillaume Apollinaire*

48. Unjust criticism is usually a disguised compliment. It often means that you have aroused jealousy and envy. Remember that no one ever kicks a dead dog.

    — *Dale Carnegie*

49. The man who does not work for the love of work but only for money is not likely to make money or to find much fun in life.

    — *Charles M. Schwab*

50. If you have knowledge, let others light their candles in it.

    — *Margaret Fuller*

Entrepreneurs and Philanthropy: Doing Something Positive for Your Community

The positive business ethics most entrepreneurs develop often carry over into how they conduct their personal lives. There is a long, proud connection in the United States between entrepreneurs and philanthropy.

Philanthropy is when people express their concern for social issues by giving money, time, or advice to charities that they support. Philanthropists often give their money through foundations. A *foundation* is a nonprofit organization that passes on donated money, through grants, to other nonprofit organizations that help people and social causes.

Many philanthropic foundations in this country were established by entrepreneurs. The Annenberg Foundation, the Annie E. Casey Foundation, the John D. and Catherine T. MacArthur Foundation, the Pew Charitable Trust, and the Robert W. Woodruff Foundation are all notable charitable institutions that have helped millions of people worldwide.

Use your imagination — if you could solve any problem in the world, what would it be? How could you use your business and the money you make from it to help others?

Training the Brain to Think Positively

By the age of 28, Clement Stone was a multimillionaire and had a thousand salespeople working for him selling insurance. He taught that the key ingredient of the successful sales call was the attitude of the salesperson. Stone authored two books on the subject of positive mental attitude:

- *The Success System That Never Fails*
- *Success Through a Positive Mental Attitude*

Both books are two of the all-time best sellers in the field of business.

Stone believed the mind could be trained to think positively and creatively. He recommended that people "set aside a half–hour each day for creative thinking time." Stone liked to say that "Thought is a power that grows with use."

Chapter 9 Review

NOTE: The exercises printed below can be found in the corresponding chapter of the NFTE MODULE 1 WORKBOOK that came with your textbook. Please write your answers there. If you do not have a workbook, write your answers on a separate sheet of paper.

Critical Thinking about . . . The Power of Positive Thinking

1) What does it mean to have self-esteem?

2) What attitude is most important for the entrepreneur and why?

3) What are three practical things you can do to make your dreams come true? Write an essay about a time you successfully used these three techniques to make a dream come true. Or, write about a time that you couldn't accomplish something you wanted to accomplish — what would you do differently today?

Using New Words

attitude
self-esteem
stress

Use each of the vocabulary words in a sentence about yourself.

Getting the Facts

1. What did Napoleon Hill say about adversity, failure and heartache?

2. How do your thoughts affect your mood?

3. What did Clement Stone call his sales method?

4. How old was Stone when he started selling insurance?

5. What do many entrepreneurs believe is the key to success?

Exploration: Positive Mental Attitude

1. Choose a saying or quotation as your motto for this class. Write it on a sign using magic markers, spray paint, glitter or other materials.

2. Collect at least three positive quotes or sayings from your parents or other adults. Share them with the class.

In Your Opinion

Discuss with a partner:

1. What is your attitude about money?

2. Does money solve problems? How important is it?

3. Tell the class what you've learned about your partner's attitude toward money and whether it differs from yours.

Review

Chapter Summary

I. Character is destiny.

  A. Your thoughts shape your character.

  B. Negative thoughts can even hurt your body.

  C. Positive thoughts are the key to success.

II. Clement Stone coined the phrase "positive mental attitude."

  A. He used positive mental attitude to overcome his fear of rejection.

  B. Through his method he became a great salesman.

III. Try to think positively.

  A. What you are thinking affects how well your brain works.

    1. Positive thoughts generate good ideas.

    2. Negative thoughts generate bad ideas.

  B. Like your body, your mind can be strengthened through effort.

IV. Writing your goals down and investing them with positive mental energy can help you achieve them.

A Business for the Young Entrepreneur: Music Production*

Do you like composing new music? This hobby could become a profitable business by creating instrumental music for individuals and companies in the music industry. If you have a love for music and a sense of business, then here are some opportunities for a music producer:

SONGWRITERS — People who write lyrics for popular songs need to have music to put the words to.

MUSIC PUBLISHERS — These companies need "instrumentals" to assign to songwriters to create "hit songs," which can then be licensed.

RECORD COMPANIES — These companies need music producers to create songs and put together musical groups to promote new music to the ever-changing tastes of the public.

Tips

- Secure an internship at either a recording studio or record company in your area. You will gain the knowledge, experience and clientele that will bring you more opportunities.
- Create a "demo" (demonstration) package. Put together a compact disc of your music, a one-page bio of yourself, and contact information that you can give to key individuals to promote your service.
- Post flyers and hand out your business cards at every opportunity. Go to nightclubs and performances to get acquainted with up-and-coming performers that can use your service. This will build up your resume. Attend meetings at your local ASCAP, BMI, and SESAC offices in order to increase your list of contacts and clients.

---

* Special thanks to Charles Smith III, of Urban Legends Muzik.

I see something I like, I buy it; then I try to sell it.

— Lord Grade,
British film and television
entrepreneur

KEY OBJECTIVES

READING THIS CHAPTER AND DOING THE EXERCISES WILL ENABLE YOU TO:

- Determine start-up costs, cost of goods sold, and operating costs.
- Explain the difference between fixed and variable costs.
- Figure gross profit.
- Calculate profit and profit per unit.

THE COSTS OF STARTING AND OPERATING A BUSINESS

Businesses make money by selling products or services. Making sales also generates costs, however. Only if sales are greater than costs does a business make a profit. In this chapter you'll learn about the costs of starting and operating a business.

The **costs**, or expenses, of starting and operating a business are divided into the following three categories:

1) **Start-up costs**

2) **Cost of goods sold**

3) **Operating costs, including fixed and variable costs**

Start-up Costs

Start-up costs are the one-time expenses of starting a business. Start-up costs are also called the "original investment" or "seed money." In a restaurant, for example, start-up costs would include stoves, food processors, tables, chairs, silverware and other items that are not replaced on a regular basis. Also included might be the one-time cost of buying land and constructing a building.

For a hot dog stand, start-up costs might look like this:

• Hot dog cart:	$1,500
• License from the city:	200
• Starting supply of hot dogs, buns, sauerkraut, mustard:	300
• Business cards and flyers (advertising):	50
• Telephone answering machine:	100
Total start-up costs	**$2,150**

Define a Unit of Sale

Next, a business owner must define the "unit of sale." Your unit of sale is the building block of your business. It can be whatever you define it to be. Entrepreneurs commonly define the unit of sale as:

1. one example of the product

2. one hour of service time, or

3. the average sale per customer (if the business sells more than one product)

   • If you are selling a service, the unit of sale is what you charge a customer for one hour of the service, or to complete one job.

   • If you are selling more than one product, the unit of sale is the average sale per customer. The average would be total sales divided by the number of customers:

$$\frac{\text{Total sales}}{\text{Number of customers}} = \textbf{Average unit of sale}$$

Cost of Goods Sold for One Unit

The **cost of goods sold** can be thought of as the cost of selling *one additional unit*. The cost of goods sold in a restaurant is the cost of the food served to the customer. The *total* cost of goods sold increases as the number of customers served increases. Once you know your cost of goods sold, you can calculate **gross profit**.

Suppose you have a business selling watches. You buy the watches for $3 each wholesale. You sell them for $10 each. Let's say you buy and sell ten watches.

Total Revenue   =   10 watches x $10 selling price   = $100

Total Cost of Goods Sold   =   10 watches x $3 selling price   = $ 30

Total Gross Profit   =   100 revenue - $30 C.O.G.S.   = $ 70

Total Revenue – Total Cost of Goods Sold = Total Gross Profit

The revenue, cost of goods sold, and gross profit can also be calculated for a single unit, such as a turkey sandwich:

ANALYSIS OF THE COST OF GOODS SOLD FOR A TURKEY SANDWICH

Item	Analysis	Cost per Sandwich
Turkey (4 oz.)	$2.60 per pound* ÷ 4	$0.65
Bread (large roll)	$1.92 per dozen ÷ 12	$0.16
Mayonnaise (1 oz.)	$1.60 per 32-oz jar ÷ 32	$0.05
Lettuce (1 oz.)	$0.80 per pound ÷ 16	$0.05
Tomato (1/4)	$1.12 per tomato ÷ 4	$0.28
Pickle (1/4)	$0.20 per pickle ÷ 4	$0.05
Wrapper	$10.00 per 1000 ÷ 1000	$0.01
Cost of goods sold per unit:		**$1.25**

* Reminder: 1 pound = 16 oz.

The cost of goods sold of the sandwich, subtracted from the price customers pay for the sandwich equals the *gross profit per unit*.

Selling Price – Cost of Goods Sold = Gross Profit per Unit

In this case:

Price of sandwich:	$4.00
Cost of goods sold:	–1.25
Gross profit per sandwich:	$2.75

Cost of Service Sold

For a service business, the cost of selling one additional unit is the *cost of service sold*.

A service business is selling labor; therefore the cost of labor should be included in the cost of the service sold. During the labor, the business may use supplies. A writer, for instance, is selling labor, but is also using paper for each job. The cost of supplies must also be included in the cost of service sold.

Below is an example of the cost of service sold for one completed writing job:

Labor

Value of writer's time per hour	$ 7.00
How long does it take writer to complete job?	x 4 hours
Labor cost per unit = $7.00 per hour x 4 hours	$28.00

Supplies

paper	+ 1.00
Cost of Services Sold per Unit = Labor + Supplies	**$29. 00**

The cost of service sold, subtracted from the price the customer pays for the writing job (unit), equals the gross profit for the service business.

Selling Price – Cost of Service Sold = Gross Profit

Operating Costs

The **operating costs** of a business are those costs necessary to operate it, not including cost of goods sold. Operating costs can almost always be divided into seven categories, although each business may have unique operating costs. An easy way to remember the seven operating costs that most businesses will have is USAIIRD:

Utilities (gas, electric, telephone)
Salaries
Advertising
Insurance
Interest
Rent
Depreciation

Depreciation is the reduction in value, calculated annually, of a long-term asset.

Fixed Costs and Variable Costs

As you learned in Chapter 4, operating costs are divided into two types: fixed costs and variable costs. To review, **fixed costs** are operating costs that stay the same over the range of sales the business is making. Rent can be an example of a fixed cost. Whether a shoe store sells 200 or 300 pairs of shoes in a month, it still pays the same rent on the store, so rent is considered a fixed cost.

Variable costs are operating costs that change (and are therefore variable) depending on the volume of sales, but cannot be assigned directly to the unit of sale. Let's say you own a shoe store and you pay each salesperson a commission. Whenever a salesperson sells a pair of shoes, he or she gets a dollar, for example. The commission is a variable cost because it varies with sales. If you sell a hundred pairs of shoes in one week, you will pay your staff $100 in commissions. If you sell fifty pairs, you will pay $50 in commissions.

Operating costs that stay constant are fixed costs and those operating costs that fluctuate with sales, but cannot be assigned to a specific unit of sale, should be viewed as variable.

Overhead

The term **overhead** is an informal term for fixed costs. "Overhead" derives from the literal "over head," that is, the roof over the business. Business owners strive for "low overhead" or low fixed costs because the less money they have to pay for overhead, the more they'll have to cover other costs, as profit, or to reinvest in the business.

Profit

Gross profit only subtracts Cost of Goods Sold (for a "product" business) or Cost of Service Sold (for a "service" business). It does not take into account the operating costs/expenses of running a business.

After calculating gross profit, therefore, the next step is to calculate **profit**. Profit is Gross Profit minus Operating Costs.

$$\textbf{Gross Profit – Operating Costs = Profit}$$

Profit per Unit

Sometimes an entrepreneur wants to know how much of the sale of each unit is profit. An easy way to calculate Profit per Unit is to divide the total Units Sold into Profit.

$$\frac{\textbf{Profit}}{\textbf{Units Sold}} = \textbf{Profit per Unit}$$

Chapter 10 Review

NOTE: The exercises printed below can be found in the corresponding chapter of the NFTE MODULE 1 WORKBOOK that came with your textbook. Please write your answers there. If you do not have a workbook, write your answers on a separate sheet of paper.

Critical Thinking about ... Economics of One Unit

For the following businesses, define the unit of sale and determine the gross profit per unit using this formula:

Unit Price - Cost Per Unit = Gross Profit Per Unit.

1. Pete, the owner of The Funky DJ, provides DJ service to parties and other social events in his neighborhood. He charges $40 per hour. He rents a double turntable from his older brother for $10 per hour every time he DJ's. What is Pete's gross profit per unit?

2. Sue's Sandwich Shoppe. Sue, the owner of the shop, sells sandwiches and soda out of a sidewalk cart in a popular park near her house. She sets up her cart in the summers to raise money for college. Last month she sold $600 worth of product (sandwiches and sodas) to 100 customers. She spent $200 on the sandwich ingredients and buying the sodas wholesale. What is Sue's gross profit per unit?

Using New Words

costs
cost of goods sold
depreciation
fixed costs
gross profit
profit
operating costs
overhead
start-up costs
variable costs

Imagine a business you would like to own and write an essay about its costs and profits. Use all the vocabulary words.

Getting the Facts

1. Name three operating costs.

2. What is another phrase for "start-up costs"?

3. How does one calculate profit per unit?

4. Gross profit is the business's profit before what other costs are subtracted?

5. What's the difference between a fixed and a variable cost?

Review

Chapter 10 Review

Analyzing . . . Cost of Goods Sold

Cost of Goods Sold is the cost of producing "one additional unit."

Let's break apart a sandwich and find the cost of goods sold and gross profit per sandwich.

Item	Cost
Ham (4 oz.)	$2.60 per pound
Bread (2 slices)	12 slices per $1.20 loaf
Cheese (1 oz.)	$3.20 per pound
Lettuce (1 oz.)	$0.80 per pound
Tomato (1/4)	$1.12 per tomato
Mustard (4 oz.)	$1.60 per 32 oz. jar
Wrapper	$10.00 per 1000
Retail Price of the Sandwich:	$4.00

Review

Chapter Summary

I. There are three types of costs.

A. Start-up costs are one-time business expenses.

B. Operating costs are overhead expenses, in particular utilities, salaries, advertising, insurance, interest on loans and rent (USAIIRD).

   1. Some operating costs are fixed. Fixed costs stay the same no matter how many sales the business makes.

   2. Some operating costs are variable. Variable costs vary, or change, depending on the volume of sales.

C. The cost of goods sold is the cost of selling one additional unit of a product.

D. The cost of service sold is the cost of selling "one additional unit" of service.

II. Selling Price – Cost of Goods Sold = Gross Profit

A. Gross profit does not take into account operating costs.

B. A business owner must figure both operating costs and cost of goods sold to know how to price products or services to make a profit.

III. To determine Profit per Unit, divide units sold into Profit.

$$\frac{\text{Profit}}{\text{Units Sold}} = \text{Profit per Unit}$$

A Business for the Young Entrepreneur: Mother's Helper

A mother's helper keeps children occupied so busy mothers can devote their time and attention to something else. The mother will still be in the house, but your job will be to take care of the children. This is a safe way to get some baby-sitting experience if you have never taken care of children before.

Suggestions

- Bring some games or art supplies. The best way to keep children happy is to keep them interested in something.

- Try not to interrupt the mother with questions. Ask all your questions before she leaves the children with you. Some good ones to ask are:

    What can I give the children to eat or drink?
    Where is the bathroom?
    Should I answer the phone?
    Can I take the children outside to play?

- Discuss with the mother before you come to work how much you will be paid and how long she will expect you to be there.

KEY OBJECTIVES

READING THIS CHAPTER AND DOING THE EXERCISES WILL ENABLE YOU TO:

- Contrast selling and marketing.
- Develop a marketing orientation.
- Apply the four elements of a marketing plan.
- Create a marketing plan for your business.
- Understand brand recognition.

WHAT IS MARKETING?

Marketing is the delivery of customer satisfaction at a profit. As an entrepreneur, your primary focus should always be on your current and future customers.* Together, this group of people is your market, and the process of matching these customers' needs with your product or service is called marketing. By making sure that customers' priorities are met, and that they are satisfied with your product, you can attract new customers and build a loyal customer base.

A good example of product marketing can be found in the cosmetics industry. Cosmetics companies such as Revlon and Maybelline not only sell the powders and creams they manufacture; but market the idea of beauty, which customers are eager to buy. These companies sell the idea that their products can and will meet a customer's need for fuller lips, more dramatic eyes, or smoother skin. They also use packaging that appeals to a customer's need to feel elegant and fashionable. In buying products with black and gold cases, pastel colored compacts and elegant shapes, customers feel as though they are purchasing luxury products at affordable prices. Through a strategy that combines visually and emotionally appealing factors, the cosmetic company meets its customers' need to feel special, pampered and beautiful.

---

* See Kotler, P. and Armstrong, G. *Principles of Marketing*. Prentice Hall, Upper Saddle River, N.J., 2001.

Your Marketing Strategy

A customer who goes to a hardware store to buy a drill does not need a drill — he needs a hole. The customer is buying the drill to make a hole. If he could go to the hardware store and buy the hole, he wouldn't bother to buy the drill. So, if you are marketing drills, you should emphasize what good holes your drills make!*

To "think marketing," first decide what benefits the customers in your market will get from your product or service. All your marketing and advertising choices should stem from that vision. That is your "marketing strategy," and it should affect all your future business decisions. Successful businesses always think about marketing. Every step they take is to strengthen the consumer's perception that their product or service is the best provider of the benefits he or she is seeking.

A single marketing insight can make a fortune. Ray Kroc of McDonald's did not invent or even improve the hamburger — he invented a new way of marketing hamburgers. When he visited the small burger restaurant in San Bernardino, California, run by the McDonald brothers, he saw that customers were buying the hamburgers because they were of consistent quality and were made fast in a clean environment.

Kroc realized that the customers flocking to the McDonald brothers' restaurant were not seeking the ultimate hamburger. They liked the fast, clean, efficient service and the low price.

These were the benefits that brought them to the product. By marketing those benefits, Kroc made McDonald's the huge success it is today.

Location, Location, Location

Place is particularly important. *Where* do you go to bring your product or service to the attention of your market? This is just as important as the selling process itself. If Revlon is selling cosmetics that are above average in price, they would not market them in stores visited by consumers who could not afford them. There is a humorous but accurate saying that the three most important factors in real estate are: *Location, location, location.* It can be true in marketing as well.

Marketing Strategy

Another aspect of marketing "strategy" is how you sell to your market. There are many ways to sell, including:

---

* From *Have You Got What It Takes? How To Tell If You Should Start Your Own Business,* by Joseph Mancuso (Prentice-Hall, 1982) .

By appointment (sales call)

Trade fairs (Flea markets) or street fairs

Direct mail (sending out product or service offers through mailing lists)

Door to door

Through classmates at school

Through community, school, religious, or Boy Scout/Girl Scout functions

"Cold calling"

By telephone

Through listings in a catalog

From home

From your own store

Through other stores

Through outside salespeople on commission

Through your own sales team

Through newspaper, radio, or television advertising

What Is Marketing?

"The Four P's"

Marketing is the overall strategic plan for bringing a product to market. The four essential elements of a marketing plan are called "The Four P's":

1. Product

2. Price

3. Place

4. Promotion

Your marketing goal is to bring the right product to the right place at the right price with the right promotion.

As you choose the four essential elements of your marketing plan, always keep in mind your overall marketing vision: what is the benefit you want to convince customers that your product or service will provide?

PRODUCT: The product should meet or create a consumer need.

PRICE: The product has to be priced low enough so the public will buy it, and high enough for the business to make a profit.

PLACE: The entrepreneur has to place the product where there will be a demand for it. Selling bathing suits in Alaska in February would be unprofitable.

PROMOTION: Advertising and publicity.

Advertising must be purchased, but **publicity** is free. If your business is providing a needed or unusual service to the community, for instance, you might be able to get publicity from local newspapers or radio stations willing to write or talk about your product or service.

Another valuable promotion is the **business card**. A business card includes the name, address and phone number of your business as well as your own name and title. Carry some cards with you wherever you go, to give to potential clients and contacts. Other common promotional devices are T-shirts or caps bearing the name of your product. These provide your business with "walking advertisements."

Cause-Related Marketing

Cause-related marketing is marketing inspired by a commitment to a social, environmental, or political cause. A business might get involved in cause-related marketing by donating a fixed percentage of its revenue (say, one or two percent) to a particular charity and then promoting this in its marketing materials.

As a young entrepreneur, you might consider donating one dollar out of every 50 sales to a school club or some outside charitable organization you support. This is a way of "doing the right thing" and gaining favorable publicity at the same time. Always remember that getting involved in your community is not only the right thing to do but will also be good for your business.

Technology Tip: Computerize Your Visuals

Your marketing efforts will have a stronger impact if your business materials are tied together with an image that clearly represents your company. Desktop publishing and word-processing software can help you create a logo and an overall "look." Logo is short for "logotype." It is a distinctive company sign — like the McDonald's golden arches or the Nike "swoosh." You can use a computer to create a logo and put it on all your business materials. See if you can create some of the items below on your computer:

- Business cards
- Stationery
- Flyers
- Brochures
- Press releases
- Mailing cards/coupons
- Posters

Russell Simmons: Marketing Hip-Hop Culture

Many business fortunes have been based on a single marketing insight. Russell Simmons was one of the first rap promoters to realize that this music could be marketed to both black and white audiences. From this realization, he created an entertainment empire that includes Def Jam Records (which had hits with Run DMC and LL Cool J), a film-production company, and even a line of hip-hop fashion.

In an interview in *Worth* magazine in 1992, Simmons said, "We don't make records, music or television for black people, but for people who consume black culture."

Simmons has used his talent for promotion and image-making to push hip-hop culture so far into the mainstream that his artists have sold millions of records.

In 1990, Simmons turned his attention to television, as he had once again noticed an exciting subculture that no one else was promoting. On his nightly trips out to see new musical talent, Simmons saw that many discos and rap clubs had comedy nights, which were always sold out.

He teamed up with Hollywood producers Bernie Brillstein and Brad Grey to produce *Russell Simmons' Def Comedy Jam*, a series of eight half-hour comedy specials for HBO. The show was HBO's most popular late-night comedy program ever.

Simmons' company, *Rush Communications*, keeps growing as Simmons finds new ways to market hip-hop culture to the world.

Your Brand Represents *You*

The logo is part of the total "branding" of your business. A *brand* is a name, symbol or trademark that represents and defines your business. It is very important that you pick a name that is easy to remember, describes your business, and helps to gain *mind share* with a customer. "Mind share" is the degree to which your business comes to mind when a consumer thinks of the need that your product or service could fulfill.

Brand Recognition

One of the most important aspects of business is developing a reputation. It is important that people have a positive association when they think of your brand or hear it mentioned. In the automotive world, for example, Mercedes is associated with high-quality engineering. Volvo is associated with safety. These are the benefits each company chose to emphasize in its marketing.

Always present yourself and your business in such a way that people will have confidence in your product or service. Anything that harms your reputation will have a damaging effect on your sales and profits. Anything that reinforces your reputation will have a positive impact on your business. Here are seven things you can do to build and maintain your brand and its reputation.

1. Provide a high-quality product or service.

2. Maintain the highest ethical standards.

3. Define your product or service clearly.

4. Treat your employees well.

5. Make all your ads positive and informative — whether they are simple posters and flyers or television commercials.

6. Associate your company with a charity.

7. Become actively involved in your community.

The last two items on the list have to do with *philanthropy*, which is giving your money, time or skills to help others. Philanthropy is an important part of entrepreneurship. Many of our greatest museums, libraries, and charities have been created with money given by entrepreneurs.

Remember, you want your product or service to be associated with positive words and thoughts in the customer's mind. That is the end result of successful marketing.

Chapter 11 Review

NOTE: The exercises printed below can be found in the corresponding chapter of the **NFTE MODULE 1 WORKBOOK** that came with your textbook. Please write your answers there. If you do not have a workbook, write your answers on a separate sheet of paper.

Critical Thinking about ... Finding Your Market

The first step of marketing is to determine who is likely to want your product or service. Does it appeal to men? Women? Children? What ages? What income levels? You won't be very successful if you try to market skateboards to senior citizens or ties to women. Make a list of the groups below that you think are in your market and describe each in a few sentences.

Friends

Classmates

Relatives

Young children

Adult women

Adult men

Elderly adults

Local business people

Other

Analyzing Your Market

1. What is the business you hope to start? What is the primary benefit you think will attract customers?

2. Describe "The Four P's" in detail as they apply to your business idea and its marketing plan.

3. How do you intend to practice philanthropy in your community?

Using New Words

logo
marketing
publicity
business card

On a separate sheet of paper, identify the vocabulary term that completes each sentence.

1) _____ is free advertising obtained by getting your business mentioned in the media.

2) Identifying the consumer benefits of your product is the first step toward _____ it.

3) Always carry your _____ to give to customers and contacts.

4) Your _____ is a symbol that represents your business and helps keep your _____ in the mind of the consumer.

Review

Chapter 11 Review

Getting the Facts

On a separate sheet of paper, fill in the blanks using terms from the chapter.

1. Customers aren't actually looking for a product; they are looking for _____.

2. Publicity is _____ promotion received when your product or service is featured in the media.

3. Ray Kroc made McDonald's a huge success by focusing on customer _____, not on making an extraordinary hamburger. He marketed fast, clean _____ and a low _____.

4. When a company makes a public contribution to a charity that gets media attention, it is indirectly buying _____.

Exploration: Preparing a Marketing Plan

Below is a sample marketing strategy for a business selling handmade jewelry. Can you think of other locations, or methods of selling?

MARKETING PLAN LOCATIONS FOR A HANDMADE JEWELRY BUSINESS (WHERE TO SELL)

SELLING METHODS	Door to door	Flea markets	School/ community functions	Street (street vendors)	Through local stores	Your own home	Internet	Other
Business cards	X	X	X	X	X			
Posters		X				X		
Flyers		X						
Phone sales	X			X	X			
Sales calls				X	X			
Brochures		X	X					
Mailings			X					
Website								
Other								

Review

Chapter Summary

I. Selling is bringing the product to the customer; marketing is getting the customer to come to the product.

A. Customers seek benefits.

B. Marketing shows customers the benefits of a product or service.

II. The four essential marketing elements ("The Four P's"):

1. The **product** should fill a consumer need.

2. The **price** should fit the market and create a profit.

3. The **product** should be sold in a place where there is demand.

4. **Promotion** should include advertising and publicity.

III. Always carry your business card as a promotional tool.

IV. Marketing gives your business direction.

A. Decide what product or service benefit to promote.

B. Never stop promoting that benefit to the customer.

C. Choosing the right benefit to promote will generate success.

I found that if you give the consumer a snapshot where he could see himself as he really is and the way he wants to be portrayed, people really respond to it.

— Thomas Burrell,
founder, the Burrell
Communications Group

KEY OBJECTIVES

READING THIS CHAPTER AND DOING THE EXERCISES WILL ENABLE YOU TO:

- Design an ad.
- Choose ways to promote your business — online and in the media.
- Create a logo.
- Develop mailing lists for your business.

ADVERTISING AND PUBLICITY

Promotion

Entrepreneurs use **promotions** to attract customers and increase sales. Promotion is the use of publicity and advertising. As you learned in Chapter 11, *publicity* is free, while *advertising* is purchased. If a newspaper writes an article about your business, that's publicity. If you buy an ad in that newspaper, you've purchased advertising to promote your business. Save all publicity you receive in a portfolio you can show potential customers. Publicity has enormous value because it can attract more publicity and more customers. Be sure to obtain videotapes of any mention your business receives on television — that's another very powerful promotional tool for your business. The goal of promotion is to establish the image of the business in the mind of the consumer.

Visualize the Customer

Before placing an ad, visualize your ideal customer. How old is he or she? What kind of income does he or she earn? What is the benefit your product or service offers that your ideal customer would want? Remember, that your overall marketing vision should drive all your other business decisions.

Once you've done this, you'll be able to make sensible advertising decisions. If you were promoting a rap concert, it would be a waste of money to take an ad out in a magazine for senior citizens. Advertising should not be wasted on customers who don't need your product or service.

The Small-Business Ad

Most ads for small businesses are designed to sell the consumer a specific product or service. Small businesses can't usually afford to engage in **institutional advertising**, as large corporations do. This is non-specific advertising designed to keep a company or industry in the mind of the general public. Most small businesses begin their advertising with a simple print ad in a local newspaper or magazine.

An effective small-business ad concentrates on the aspect of the product or service that is most important to the customer. That aspect is usually one of these three:

1. Price
2. Product/Service
3. Location

The Five Parts of a Print Ad

These are the five basic parts of a printed advertisement:

1. Headline (Title)
2. Deck (Subhead)
3. Copy (Text)
4. Graphics (Photographs or Drawings)
5. Logo/Trademark

As you learned in the previous chapter, a logo is an identifying symbol for a product or business. A **trademark** is a logo that has been registered with the U.S. Patent Office to protect against its use by others.

The logo is printed on the business's stationery, business cards and flyers, and gets the public into the habit of identifying the logo with the product or service.

Promotional Ideas

Here are some great ideas for promoting small businesses. Some of these may be out of your reach financially, at least at first. But many of them can be put in place as part of your marketing plan from the start.

BANNER ADS — These are the advertisements that run on websites.

BILLBOARDS — Billboards are often in highly visible locations and use short, punchy copy that drivers can grasp at a glance.

BROCHURES — Place brochures in "take one" boxes around town.

BUSINESS CARDS — A business card bears the name, address, and phone number of your business, as well as your name and title. If possible, include a short motto or statement about the benefit of doing business with your company. Carry business cards with you wherever you go. You can design business cards on your computer or have them made at a local print shop.

DIRECT MAIL — Whenever you make a sale, get the customer's address, phone and fax numbers, and e-mail address. Once you've developed a mailing list, send out cards or letters regularly to customers informing them of sales and special events. You can even send special discounts for mailing list customers only. You can send e-mail updates to customers. Be sure always to include this statement in the e-mail: "If you wish to be removed from this list, please type Remove in the subject line of your response." It is very important to respect the privacy of your customers. Mailing-list software is easy to use to keep organized and to print labels.

CATALOGS — When you build up a list of 10,000 names, you may be able to afford a four-color catalog. You can afford a two-color catalog with even fewer names.

DISCOUNT COUPONS — Give a discount (price break) to first-time customers or for a limited time. This will encourage consumers to try your product or service.

FLYERS — Flyers are one-page ads you can draw by hand or create on computer. Fax your flyer to customers on your mailing list; photocopy your flyer and distribute it at community functions, sporting events, under windshield wipers, or hand them out on the street. Flyers can also include discount coupons.

FREE GIFTS — "Freebies" draw potential customers the way honey draws flies. But don't disappoint with gifts that look and feel cheap. Go to a wholesaler, where you can get good prices on large quantities of calculators, watches, desk pens, or other desirable items.

PROMOTIONAL CLOTHING — T-shirts or caps bearing the name of your business can turn you and your friends into walking advertisements for your business. You can even put the name of your business on shopping bags.

Sample Flyer

John's Tie Service

Stripes

Polka Dots

Floral

Paisley

Geometrics

Designer

We have a wide variety of ties!

Come see us at The Mott Haven Flea Market on weekends.

Discount Prices! Best Prices Around!

For more information call: (718) 555-7839 or e-mail us at jties@nfte.com

SAMPLES OR DEMONSTRATIONS — Offer samples of your product to potential customers passing by your business. Or take samples to a place where lots of people walk by. If you are selling a service, demonstrate outdoors or in a mall (get permission first!).

SPECIAL EVENTS — Stage contests, throw parties, or organize events to attract attention and customers to your business. Holding contests will gather valuable names for your mailing list, too.

TEAM SPONSORSHIPS — Sponsoring a local sport team is a great way to involve your business in the community and meet potential customers.

800 NUMBERS — Contact your phone company to find out how to set up an 800 number for your business, so your customers can call you for free. Some long-distance providers offer special discounts to small-business owners.

The Media

There are many places to advertise and publicize your business. These are referred to collectively as the **media**. The media is divided into print (magazines, newspapers, etc.), television, and radio. The trick will be to choose the most effective ways to spend your advertising dollars, which for a small business are usually quite limited.

Try to get to know the print, radio, and television journalists in your town so you can get as much publicity as possible. You should call the reporters yourself. Take a whole day to make phone calls pitching your business and explaining why your story is worth writing about. Be totally honest and try to build friendships. Positive reporting often develops because the reporter comes to care about the entrepreneur.

PRINT — Newspapers, magazines, and newsletters are examples of print media. Consider running a coupon in a neighborhood newspaper. A potential customer needs to see an advertisement at least nine times before the marketing message penetrates. In addition, the study found that, for every three times a consumer sees an ad, he or she will ignore it twice. This suggests that a consumer will have to see your ad 27 times before actually visiting your business and buying something.

If you take out a newspaper ad that runs three times a week, therefore, commit to running it for nine weeks at the very least. The most common mistake entrepreneurs make is to give up too soon. If you aren't sure you want to spend the money on an ad in a particular paper or magazine, read it for a few months and see whether your competitors use it regularly. If they do, they are probably seeing a good return on their investment, so you should, too.

As soon as you can afford to place an ad in the *Yellow Pages*, do it, as consumers often look there first when they need a product or service.

TELEVISION — Even though commercial television advertising rates are extremely expensive, an entrepreneur with a new business can sometimes get lower ones, or even receive a free mention (publicity) of his or her business on local cable stations.

RADIO — University and local stations are often willing to mention a new business venture that has an interesting or unusual angle. To get such publicity, you will need to mail a **press release** to the stations. A press release consists of three or four paragraphs of information about your business that you send out to the media. Send out a press release when you open your business, when you get involved with a charity, and when you hold special events. Press releases can generate stories about your business in local newspapers and at local radio stations.

Sample Press Release

FOR IMMEDIATE RELEASE MAY 24, 2001

For More Information Contact:
John Davies — (718) 555-7839

South Bronx High School Student
Opens Tie-Selling Business

Sixteen-year-old John Davies of 34 Fordham Road, the Bronx, announces the creation of "John's Tie Service." A junior at Longfellow High School, John both purchases his ties from the wholesale market and orders them through catalogs. He will be selling his ties on weekends at the Mott Haven Flea Market.

John is starting his own enterprise as a way to learn about business and supplement his income. His short-term goal is to raise enough capital to help pay for college education. John's long-term plan is to own a string of soul-food restaurants in urban communities.

John believes that creating a successful business is a great way to help not only himself but his community.

For interviews with this young entrepreneur,
please call the number above.

Mailing Lists

The best people to market to are those who have already bought or shown interest in your product or service. When a customer makes a purchase or a potential customer asks about your business, ask for his or her address (including e-mail). Use this information to set up a simple *database* on your computer. A database is a collection of information stored and organized for easy retrieval.

Your "customer database" should include the customer's name and address, the date of your last contact, and a note about what he or she bought or was interested in. As your mailing list grows, you can organize it by region or customer interest and send out targeted lists. If you sell gourmet sauces, for example, your notes could tell you whether a customer is interested in hot sauces or dessert sauces. When you add a new hot sauce to your line, you will know whom to target, possibly with a special offer.

Don't send out too much mail (including e-mail), however, or your customers will become annoyed and start ignoring everything you send.

The Internet

The Internet is made up of interconnected computer networks. Governments, universities, and corporations create and manage their own networks. These link with online services to which individuals can subscribe, such as America Online.

The World Wide Web is a set of Internet sites that can deliver graphics and sound as well as text. Websites are not hard to create and can be useful to your business.

Marketing Online

There are millions of people all over the world who are connected to the Internet. Your marketing message might only appeal to a tiny percentage, but even a fraction of the online market represents a lot of people. Better still, the online marketplace is organized into special interest groups, so it's not hard to figure out where to promote your business. There are many ways to market your business online such as:

ONLINE SERVICES — Online services offer classified ads, billboards, and online shopping malls. Talk to a marketing staff person at your online service about setting up your own storefront in such a mall. Online services also have "special interest forums" where you can find people who might be interested in your business.

NEWSGROUPS — A "newsgroup" is an online forum where people leave messages for each other on a selected topic. The messages form an ongoing discussion. Although you can't advertise your business in a newsgroup, you can get to know the other participants and conduct some informal market research.

E-MAIL — Electronic mail is fast and easy to use, but resist the urge to bombard potential customers with it. Most people greatly resent unsolicited e-mail. If you are going to send this type of advertising, it should be informative and entertaining so that customers will be happy to get it. Of course, you can develop a mailing list of customers who want to receive e-mail about your business.

ELECTRONIC STOREFRONT — The major online services offer entrepreneurs the opportunity to buy up a "storefront" in a shopping area. You can also put up a storefront on the internet. Each has advantages. The online service might get more "hits" from curious customers, but then you are limited to that service's subscribers. On the Internet your storefront is accessible to anyone in the world who is online.

Logos and Trademarks

Whether you are advertising your business with flyers at the local laundromat, or through a storefront on the Internet, you will need an easily recognizable logo. When a logo has been registered with the United States Patent Office to protect it from being used by others, it is called a **trademark**. A trademarked product's name is followed by the symbol ^{TM} or ®.*

A company uses a trademark so that people will recognize its product instantly, without having to read the company name, or even having to think about it. The NutraSweet red swirl is an example of a trademark most people would recognize. Rights to a trademark are reserved exclusively for its owner. To infringe on a trademark is illegal.

To file for a trademark, send the Patent and Trademark Office:

1. A written application form.
2. A drawing of the trademark.
3. Three specimens showing the actual use of the mark on or in connection with the company's products or services.
4. A filing fee ($325).

Address: **Patent & Trademark Office**
2900 Crystal Drive
Arlington, VA 22202

Telephone (703) 305-8600

---

* Trademarks will be discussed in more detail in chapter 28.

Logos Help Customers Make Quick Decisions

Customers don't have a lot of time to study different products before deciding where to spend their money. If you can consistently offer a quality product or service and create a logo that successfully represents your company, you are on your way to success. Over time, your logo will become associated with your business. It's up to you to make sure that the customer thinks of quality when he sees your logo. This association can become an advantage over your competition.

McDonald's "golden arches" are a famous logo. When you see them, you expect fast service, inexpensive prices, and a certain kind of food. At this point the arches, just by themselves, embody McDonald's entire marketing vision. Now that's successful promotion!

Chapter 12 Review

NOTE: The exercises printed below can be found in the corresponding chapter of the NFTE MODULE 1 WORKBOOK that came with your textbook. Please write your answers there. If you do not have a workbook, write your answers on a separate sheet of paper.

Critical Thinking about . . . Your Advertising

Label the five parts of this print ad. What is the aspect of the product that the ad focuses on?

There Is No Substitute For Martin Cowboy Boots.

Our cowboy boots are designed by Martin and crafted to Martin's exclusive specifications. They are backed by Martin. Continually refined and enhanced by Martin's extensive research and development program.

Naturally, we believe that there is no substitute for a pair of Martin boots. So we designed Martins to have their own unique look and feel. To be handcrafted to their own high standards of quality and workmanship. To share the Martin tradition of excellence, while being affordable to as many different budgets as possible. Including yours.

Try a pair on at your Martin dealer.   MARTIN
In the Martin tradition.

Using New Words

institutional advertising
media
press release
promotion
trademark

On a separate sheet of paper, write the vocabulary term with the letter of its corresponding definition.

a. announcement sent out to generate publicity

b. general corporate promotion

c. the use of advertising and publicity to attract customers

d. public communication

e. registered company mark or sign

Developing Promotions for Your Business

1. Locate an example of "institutional" advertising in a newspaper or magazine and bring it to class.

2. Create a press release for your business.

3. Develop an ad concept for your own business and use it to create a flyer and a print ad.

4. Sketch possible logos for your business.

5. Create a business card for your business. Include a customer benefit motto or statement on the card.

Review

Chapter 12 Review

Getting the Facts

1. List the five parts of a print ad.

2. What is the difference between a trademark and a logo?

3. What's the most important thing to do before placing or designing an ad?

4. List three ways for a small business to inexpensively advertise its products or services.

5. How many weeks should you commit to running a print ad that runs three times per week?

Exploration: Online Promotion

1. Find an online newsgroup that would be a good source of customers for your business.

2. Contact an Internet service provider to find out how much it costs to set up an electronic store. Write about your findings.

Review

Chapter Summary

I. Visualize your customer before designing an ad.

II. Focus your ad on price, the product or service, or location.

III. Advertising media include: newspapers, magazines, the *Yellow Pages*, television and radio.

IV. The five parts of a print ad are:

1. Headline
2. Deck
3. Copy
4. Graphics
5. Logo/Trademark

A Business for the Young Entrepreneur: John Steele, John's Four Season Care, Minneapolis/St. Paul, Minnesota

John Steele has about 35 customers who depend on him to keep their yards clean. He gets out of bed before dawn to mow lawns in the summer, rake leaves and re-soil in the fall, and shovel snow in the winter.

John started his business at age 14 while participating in the Young Entrepreneurs of Minnesota program. "People give me business because they really like to see kids working hard — not just hanging out doing drugs," John says. "Too many kids want to make money illegally," he adds. "This way you can do it legally and be proud."

John says the most important thing a student entrepreneur can be, is reliable. "People won't ask you back if you show up late or don't do a good job," John says. "They won't recommend you to their neighbors, either." Much of John's business comes from repeat customers and referrals.

Money is the seed of money and the first franc is sometimes more difficult to acquire than the second million.

— Jean-Jacques Rousseau,
French political philosopher
and writer

KEY OBJECTIVES

READING THIS CHAPTER AND DOING THE EXERCISES WILL ENABLE YOU TO:

- Apply cost/benefit analysis to personal and business decisions.

- Determine the opportunity cost of any investment.

COST/BENEFIT ANALYSIS

Cost/Benefit Analysis

When you are trying to decide whether to spend money on an ad or other promotion for your business, you will need a way to figure out if the investment will be worth it. Cost/benefit analysis is a great tool for doing just that. Before making any investment, it is important to look carefully at two factors:

COSTS — money and time you will have to invest

BENEFITS — the rate of return on your money or the advancement of your business or career. If the **benefits** outweigh the costs, the investment will probably be worthwhile. This is **cost/benefit analysis**. It is an important business tool.

You can even apply cost/benefit analysis to your personal life. People often make decisions with their emotions, not their minds. Strong emotions can overwhelm you, however, to the point where you see only the benefits and not the costs of an action (or vice versa). A good example of this is the decision to put a major purchase, such as a stereo, on a credit card. The powerful desire for the stereo can make you lose sight of the costs — a large debt. If you can train yourself always to use cost/benefit analysis, you will be able to make more sensible decisions. Sit down and make a list — in dollars and cents — of all the costs and benefits of a purchase you are thinking of making, before you make it.

Opportunity Cost

Cost/benefit analysis can be inaccurate, however, without a close look at **opportunity cost**. This is the cost of your *next-best investment*.

If you want to go into the army for four years for the experience and travel, and to earn money for college, compare these benefits to the opportunities you will be losing. You will lose the opportunity to go to college immediately, for example. You will lose the opportunity to make money working, or to start a business. If you choose the army, make sure the training and skills will be worth postponing college and/or business experience and income.

People often make decisions without considering opportunity costs, and then wonder why they are not happy with their decisions. Each time you make a decision about what to do with your time, energy or money, think about the cost of the opportunities you are giving up.

A related concept to opportunity cost is **trade-off**. A trade-off is a decision to spend your limited resources on one thing instead of another. Let's say you have a small business selling school supplies to students at your school and you are running low on inventory. Inventory is the amount of product you have available to sell. Now let's say you received $200 for your birthday and you want to spend it on clothes. But you also need **inventory** for your business. Perhaps you will decide to spend only $100 on clothes and $100 on inventory — because you might double the $100 to $200 through sales. Entrepreneurship is the art of choosing the trade-offs that will be the most profitable.

The Value of Your Time

If you were to start a business, what would be your opportunity cost? In other words, what's the next best use of your time? How much money could you make working at a job instead? The answer to this question will give you a rough idea of how to value your time when you start a business and have to figure out how much to pay yourself.

The Desire to Make Money Is Not a Good Reason to Start a Business

Starting a business is an opportunity. Like any opportunity it should be evaluated by taking a careful look at the costs and benefits it offers. You may not reap the financial rewards of owning your own business until after years of hard work. The desire to make money may not be enough to keep you going through the difficult early period of your business.

Most successful companies have been founded by an entrepreneur with a powerful dream — not a powerful desire for money. Henry Ford dreamed of a "horseless carriage" that the average American could afford. The founders of Apple Computer, Stephen Wozniak and Steven Jobs, dreamed of a personal computer in every home. The dream provides the motivation to succeed.

Entrepreneurs say they aren't in business for the money so often that it has almost become a cliché but, like many cliches, it's based on a degree of truth. Successful businesspeople tend to be creative, like Steve Perlman, the founder of WebTV. Perlman developed WebTV when he realized, in the early 1990s, that few Americans were actually "surfing" the World Wide Web but they did watch TV. So he built a box that sits on top of a television and surfs the Web. WebTV provides inexpensive Internet access and e-mail for people who don't own computers.

In 1997, Microsoft made a deal with Perlman and his two partners, Bruce Leak and Phil Goldman, that gave each of them around $70 million. According to Randy Komisar, WebTV's CEO, "The reality is, we didn't do it for the money. We did it for the financing," he said ("Perlmania," by Janice Maloney, *Wired* magazine, July 1999). He added, "Nobody was excited about taking the money, but it was the only opportunity to fund the vision." Real entrepreneurs are much more excited about making their dreams come true than they are about money.

Henry Ford's Dream Built a Great Company

Like Perlman, Henry Ford dreamed of making new technology affordable for the average American family. Many people in the late 1800s realized that a motor car was destined to become a reality in the near future. Only Ford had the vision to imagine them in front of every American home.

Ford needed this strong vision to sustain him through years of business failure. By the time he was almost forty, Ford had been trying to get his vision off the ground for many years. Several of his attempts to produce and sell cars had failed. His neighbors considered him a daydreaming mechanic. He continued to direct all his efforts toward making his vision real, and created the Ford Motor Company. By the time he was fifty, however, Ford was one of the richest and most famous men in the world. Today Ford Motor Company is still a major corporation — all because of one entrepreneur's persistence and belief in his dream.

Understanding the Concept:
Estimating the True Costs of an Action

To make smart decisions, you must be able to estimate the costs. This is hard because it requires thinking into the future. Also, people often make decisions without considering the long-term consequences. Knowing how to create a budget will help you to make better decisions.

Chapter 13 Review

NOTE: The exercises printed below can be found in the corresponding chapter of the NFTE MODULE 1 WORKBOOK that came with your textbook. Please write your answers there. If you do not have a workbook, write your answers on a separate sheet of paper.

Using New Words

benefit
cost/benefit analysis
inventory
opportunity cost
trade-off

On a separate sheet of paper, identify the vocabulary term that completes each sentence.

1. A _____ is a decision to spend your limited resources on one thing instead of another.

2. If the _____ outweigh the costs, the investment will probably be worthwhile.

3. _____ is the amount of product you have available to sell.

4. _____ is the cost of your next-best investment.

5. Before making any business or personal decision, perform a _____.

Getting the Facts

True or False?

1. Businesspeople use cost/benefit analysis to figure out interest rates.

2. You can use cost/benefit analysis in your personal life.

3. "Opportunity cost" is the hidden cost of making an investment.

4. The goal of cost/benefit analysis is to find the best possible return on investment of your time, money, or energy.

Exploration

Assuming you can make $4 an hour after taxes, answer the following questions:

I would need to work ___ hours a week to earn enough to take care of myself.

I would need to work ___ hours a month to earn enough to take care of myself.

I would need to work ___ hours a year to earn enough to take care of myself.

In Your Opinion

For each situation listed below, describe your greatest opportunity cost (that is, your next best investment).

1) You spend $20 on a new shirt.

2) You watch TV for five hours.

3) You invest $10 in your brother's lemonade stand at a guaranteed 100% ROI.

4) You put $10 in your savings account, where it will earn 4% interest.

Chapter Summary

I. Cost/benefit analysis compares benefits and costs of an investment.

A. If benefits outweigh costs, the investment is worthwhile.

B. You can apply cost/benefit analysis to your personal life.

II. Opportunity cost is the cost of what you're giving up when you make an investment (the cost of the next-best investment of your time, energy, or money).

A. Cost/benefit analysis can be inaccurate without considering opportunity costs.

B. People often make bad decisions because they ignore opportunity costs.

A Business for the Young Entrepreneur: Home-baked Goods

Debbi Fields, of Mrs. Fields Cookies, built a multimillion-dollar business from cookies she first started baking when she was thirteen. Do you bake anything really well? Cookies? Banana bread? You can sell home-baked goods at flea markets, garage sales, or school events.

Make your baked goods extra-irresistible by packaging them attractively. Tie a yellow ribbon around the banana bread, or sell cookies in colorful boxes. Make up batches of special items around holidays — green cookies for St. Patrick's Day, or heart-shaped cakes for St. Valentine's Day, for example.

This approach also works for homemade soups, jams and jellies, or any other food item you make that people really like.

Tips

- Don't get too elaborate. Stick to one or two products that you can consistently make really well.

- Figure out your cost of goods sold; that is, the cost of making "one additional unit" (each cookie or cake). Set your price high enough to cover your cost of goods sold and your time and labor.

- Offer a baking service to busy families. Make up a flyer that advertises your service. Perhaps you could supply a hundred cookies a week, for example.

- Buy ingredients in bulk at warehouse or grocery club stores. Bulk purchases are cheaper and lower your costs.

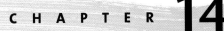

There aren't enough people who care about the future. They are too busy worrying about today and what they can grab now.

— Berry Gordy,
founder of Motown Records

KEY OBJECTIVES

READING THIS CHAPTER AND DOING THE EXERCISES WILL ENABLE YOU TO:

- Conduct a market research survey.
- Use market research to understand your customers' needs.

MARKET RESEARCH

Listen to the Consumer

You can do a lot to control the costs of starting and operating your business by researching your market carefully before you make any decisions. Your cost/benefit analysis of any business decision will be much more accurate if you really understand your market. As you've learned, your market consists of the potential customers for your product or service. *Market research* is the process and technique of finding out *who* these potential customers are and what they want and need.

Through market research, business owners ask consumers questions and listen to their answers.

Types of Market Research

Market research can vary from a simple survey of your classmates that you carry out in one day to detailed studies of a large population. Some types of market research are:

1. **SURVEYS** — People are asked directly, in interviews or through questionnaires, what they would think about a product or service if it were available.

2. **GENERAL RESEARCH** — You can check libraries, city agencies, and other resources for information. If you want to start a sporting-goods shop, you will need to know how many other such stores are already in the area.

3. **STATISTICAL RESEARCH** — **Statistics** are facts collected and presented in a "numerical" fashion — in percentages, for instance. Market-research companies keep records of the typical consumer in a given area. They can then provide statistics based on:

   - Age
   - Annual income
   - Ethnic or religious background
   - Geographic location
   - Interests
   - Occupation
   - Type of dwelling (house or apartment)

Population statistics deal with the characteristics of individuals and groups of people and are called **demographics**.

Marketing Can't Save a Bad Product: the Edsel

Large corporations with nationally distributed products will spend a great deal of time and money on market research in order to get a product "just right." Ford and Chrysler each spent millions on market research before producing, respectively, the Mustang and the mini-van. It was worth millions of dollars to these companies to determine if the public wanted these automobiles, because it was going to cost tens of millions to produce them.

Both the Mustang and the mini-van were successful. One of the most well-known examples of a product that failed despite tremendous marketing efforts, however, was Ford's 1956 Edsel. It was introduced with great fanfare, but was so poorly made and poorly designed that very few were purchased. When the Edsel made its national debut on a live television special, in fact, it wouldn't start! Two years and $450 million later, Ford pulled the plug on the Edsel assembly line. No amount of marketing could convince consumers to purchase a product they didn't want.

Research Your Market before You Open Your Business

When you know your market, you will know how to reach the people in it. This is why it's so important to spend time conducting market research before you open your business. You may be impatient to get started, but don't begin until you've come to know your market intimately.

For example, the Finnish telecommunications company Nokia makes very popular cell phones. But when a reporter from *Wired* magazine asked a Nokia spokesman if anyone was working on making heatproof cell phones for Finns to take into the saunas where they spend a significant amount of time, the spokesman looked very surprised and explained, "In the sauna, we don't even want to hear Bach."* A company that didn't know the Finnish market might have wasted a lot of money making cell phones that Finns could take into their saunas.

Collecting Data on the Market

It is just as important for a beginning businessperson as it is for large corporations to get to know potential customers well. Market research will identify "The Four P's" you have already learned:

- Product
- Price
- Place
- Promotion

Collecting market-research data from your friends, classmates, and relatives can be fun as well as financially rewarding. Here are a few questions you can adapt to your own product or service:

1. Would you buy this product/service?
2. How much would you be willing to pay for it?
3. Where would you buy it?
4. How would you improve on it?
5. Who is my closest competitor?
6. Is my product/service worse or better than my competitors'?

---

* S. Silberman, "Just Say Nokia," *Wired*, September 1999.

Market Research Avoids Costly Mistakes

You can avoid costly mistakes by simply asking your customers what they want. Say you created a design and silkscreened it on five-dozen white T-shirts. After six weeks, you have only sold six. Friends tell you they would have bought shirts if:

- They came in red or blue.
- You had them in different sizes.
- You had them in different styles.
- The shirts had different designs.

With a little market research you could have determined your customers' needs and wishes *before* you made the shirts — and you could have sold many more.

You will learn more specifics about how to conduct market research in Chapter 18. For now, though, you can begin to ask people in your unique market what they think of your business idea.

Chapter 14 Review

NOTE: The exercises printed below can be found in the corresponding chapter of the NFTE MODULE 1 WORKBOOK that came with your textbook. Please write your answers there. If you do not have a workbook, write your answers on a separate sheet of paper.

Critical Thinking about . . . Market Research

Ask three people in your market the following questions about a business you would like to start. For each question, make sure you understand the reasons for each person's answer. Describe your market and explain why you think these three people are representative of it.

1) Do you like the name of my business?

2) Where would you be most likely to buy my product?

3) How much would you pay for my product?

4) How would you improve my business idea?

5) Make up one more question to ask your three potential customers.

Exploration

Would you consider getting a job with one of your competitors? Do you think this would be ethical? Why or why not?

Using New Words

demographics
statistics

On a separate sheet of paper, identify the correct definition for each vocabulary term.

1) Demographics
   a) consumer surveys
   b) market research
   c) population information

2) Statistics
   a) facts presented numerically
   b) records of consumer data
   c) library research

Getting the Facts

1. What are population statistics called?

2. How can market research prevent expensive mistakes?

3. List three types of market research.

4. What four factors should market research include?

Chapter 14 Review

Analyzing the Competition

1. Have you found out who else offers your product/service in your area? Create a chart listing the names and the prices they charge, and the quality of the product or service (this could include complaints customers have or features they really like). Set up a chart like this:

Name of Company	Product/Service	Price	Quality
Super Funk DJs	DJ service	$25/hour	Some customers complain that DJs show up late; some say they would like the DJs to play more hip-hop and less funk.

2. Write an essay explaining why your product/service is going to outperform the competition.

   Example:

   My DJ service is going to outperform the competition because my DJs always arrive 20 minutes before they are supposed to start, in order to have time to get set up. My DJs are also going to have a wider selection of music than the competition, including lots of hip hop, which our customers want to hear.

Chapter Summary

I. Market research uncovers your potential customers and provides information about what they want.

II. Market research can be simple or complex.

A. Surveys

B. General research

C. Statistical research and demographics

III. Market research should identify "The Four P's":

1. Product

2. Price

3. Place

4. Promotion

IV. Conduct market research before you offer your product or service.

BASIC BUSINESS PLAN REVIEW

NOTE: A complete version of the Basic Business Plan can be found after Chapter 14 in the NFTE MODULE 1 WORKBOOK that came with this textbook. Please complete your Plan there. Use the Review Pages below to familiarize yourself with the topics covered in the Basic Business Plan.

A business plan is the road map that gives a business direction.

— Joseph Mancuso, author
How to Write a Winning Business Plan

Why You Need a Business Plan

Every new business–large or small– needs a business plan for two reasons:

1) To serve as a guide for the owner as he or she develops the business.

2) To prove to bankers, venture capitalists, and other potential investors that the business owner has carefully thought through the direction of the business.

Define Your Business Idea

Describe your business idea clearly and concisely. Think about how you got your idea and why it will be a success.

Define One Unit of Sale, Unit Cost and Gross Profit per Unit

Set Goals

Research the Market

Define Your Target Customer

Develop a Marketing Plan

Your Business Idea
(See Chapter 8)

1) Describe your business idea.

2) What is the name of your business?

3) What is the competitive advantage of your business?

4) How did you get your idea?

5) What skills, hobbies, or interests do you have that will help you make your business successful?

Economics of One Unit
(See Chapter 10)

- **Service Business** (Note: A service unit is typically defined as one hour of service or one job.)
  Define your unit.

- **Retail Business**
  Define your unit.

- **Wholesale Business** (Note: A wholesale unit is typically defined as one hour of service or one job.)
  Define your unit.

- **Manufacturing Business**
  Define your unit.

Goal Setting

1) What are your short-term business goals? (less than one year)

2) What are your long-term business goals? (from one to five years)

3) What are your educational and training goals? (from one to five years)

4) What are your personal goals? (for the rest of your life)

5) Why is your product/service going to outperform the competition over time?

6) Have you tried to get a part-time job in your chosen industry?

7) How will your business help you to contribute to your community?

Market Research
(See Chapter 14)

Competition

Ask three people these questions about your business. Ensure that they explain the reasons behind their answers.

1) Do you like the name of my business?

2) Where would you go to buy my product?

3) How much would you pay for my product?

4) Who is my closest competitor(s)?

5) What do you think of my logo?

6) Do you think my product/service has value?

7) How would you improve my business idea?

8) Do you think my product/service is better or worse than that offered by my competitor(s)?

Type of Business You Are In
(See Chapter 8)

- Manufacturer sells to wholesaler

- Wholesaler sells to retailer

- Retailer sells to consumer

- Service retailer sells to consumer

Consumer Description

1) Describe your target consumer

2) Expected age of consumer

3) Expected gender of consumer

4) What need will your product fulfill?

5) Financial status of consumer

Promotion/Advertising
(See Chapter 12)

1) How will you reach this consumer?

2) What is the slogan for your business?

Write a sample press release for your business

Draw a logo for your business

Fill out a marketing plan for your business

Philanthropy

1) Given the needs of your community, how do you intend to practice philanthropy?

2) Are you planning to use cause-related marketing? If so, explain.

Start-up Costs
(See Chapter 10)

These are purchases you need to make to achieve your first dollar of sales. What are your estimated start-up costs? Itemize.

Financing Strategy
(See Chapter 7)

List your sources of financing. Identify whether each source is equity, debt, or a gift. Indicate the amount and type for each source.

2) If you receive equity financing, what percentage of ownership will you give up?

3) If you receive debt financing, what is the maximum interest rate you will pay?

Operating Costs (Fixed & Variable)
(See Chapter 10)

Monthly Fixed Costs

Monthly Operating Costs include USAIIRD: utilities, salaries, advertising, interest, rent and depreciation.

1) Type of Fixed Costs

2) Monthly Fixed Costs

Variable Costs

Estimate those Operating Costs (USAIIRD) that fluctuate with sales and cannot be directly assigned to a unit of sale.

1) Type of Variable Costs

2) Estimated Variable Costs as a percentage of sales

Monthly Budget: Projected Monthly Income Statement
(See Chapter 4)

Complete your Projected 6 Month Income Statement in your NFTE Module 1 Workbook.

Basic Business Plan Review

HOW TO START & OPERATE A SMALL BUSINESS

Basic: *Starting Your Business*
Includes: Chapters 1-14 and the Basic Business Plan

The Basic chapters of NFTE Module 1 will teach you what you need to know to start a simple business. Once you have completed these chapters, you will be able to prepare an income statement, understand marketing basics, perform cost/benefit analysis, and calculate return on investment. You will also learn what it means to be an entrepreneur and how you can use your unique skills and talents to start a small business venture.

After you have finished Chapter 14, you will be ready to apply what you have learned by preparing your Basic Business Plan. A complete version of the Basic Business Plan can be found in your NFTE Module 1 Workbook.

Intermediate: *Running a Business Successfully*
Includes: Chapters 15-28 and the Intermediate Business Plan

The Intermediate Chapters of NFTE Module 1 will teach you how to successfully manage and run your business. Once you have completed these chapters, you will be able to create a cash flow statement, identify your competitive advantage, and keep good records for your business.

After you have finished Chapter 28, you will be ready to apply what you have learned by preparing your Intermediate Business Plan. A complete version of the Intermediate Business Plan can be found in your NFTE Module 1 Workbook.

Advanced: *What You Need to Know to Grow*
Includes: Chapters 29-50 and the Advanced Business Plan

The Advanced Chapters of NFTE Module 2 will teach you how you can grow a small business venture you have already started. Once you have completed these chapters, you will be able to create a balance sheet, do break-even and financial ratio analysis, and select the best financing strategy for your business.

After you have finished Chapter 50, you will be ready to apply what you have learned by preparing your Advanced Business Plan. A complete version of the Advanced Business Plan can be found in your NFTE Module 2 Workbook.

If I had eight hours to chop down a tree, I'd spend six sharpening my ax.

— Abraham Lincoln

KEY OBJECTIVES

READING THIS CHAPTER AND DOING THE EXERCISES WILL ENABLE YOU TO:

- Understand the difference between strategy and tactics.
- Develop a winning strategy.
- Write a mission statement for your business.
- Research the competition.

YOUR COMPETITIVE ADVANTAGE: TACTICS AND STRATEGIES

As you learned in Chapter 8, your competitive advantage is your tool for outperforming the competition. It is something you can do better than the competition that will attract customers to your business. Without a competitive advantage, there's no point to going into business. It's not enough to be excited about your venture and eager to run it — how are you going to outperform the competition and make a profit?

A competitive advantage must be sustainable, meaning that you can keep it going for a long time. If you decide to beat the competition by selling your product at a lower price, your advantage won't last long if you can't afford to continue at that price. Being able to temporarily undercut the competition's price is not a competitive advantage. Being able to *permanently* sell at a lower price, because you have found a cheaper supplier than your competitors use, for example, is a competitive advantage.

Strategy vs. Tactics

Your **strategy** is your plan for how you intend to outperform your current and potential competition. Your business **tactics** are the ways in which you plan to carry out your strategy. If you are planning to open a bookstore, how will you compete with the big chain bookstore in the neighborhood? The big bookstore can probably buy books more cheaply than you can. It buys so many that book wholesalers probably give it discounts. The big bookstore can sell books at a lower price, so you can't compete with their pricing strategy. Your competitive advantage, in this case, is not that you can offer your product at a lower price. How are you going to attract customers away from the big bookstore?

Perhaps you could compete by making your bookstore into a center for the community so people will come to your store instead of your competitor's. That's your strategy. What tactics could you employ to carry out this strategy? You could hold poetry readings and acoustic concerts to promote local poets and musicians. That will draw people in the neighborhood to your store. Offering customers free or very inexpensive tea and coffee might be another tactic. Encouraging them to browse and providing seats for conversations and reading is another tactic that could promote a community feeling so that people begin to prefer your bookstore to the bigger store. You could even set up a binder of personal ads for people who are looking for other people to date.

These are some of the tactics you could use to execute your strategy — which is to make your bookstore a place where people like to gather. If you can attract enough people to make a profit, this is a winning strategy.

Your Competitive Advantage

Your goal as an entrepreneur is to come up with a strategy to outperform the competition and tactics for carrying out that strategy. To discover your business mission, first decide what is the most important benefit the customers in your market will receive from your product or service. After deciding on this benefit, you must then identify how you will deliver it better than any of your competitors can. This will be your company's competitive advantage. Carrying out that competitive advantage in order to satisfy your customers will be your mission as an entrepreneur.

The Mission Statement

Your next step is to express your mission in a clear, simple **mission statement**. A clearly stated mission statement not only tells your customers and employees what your business is all about, it will be a guide for every business decision you make.

The mission statement should express the fundamental goal of a business — its reason for existing. Some people think the mission of a business is to make money, but that is not true. Most great entrepreneurs have discovered that the true mission of a business is to meet a consumer need better than anyone has before. It is by carefully planning and fulfilling this mission that an entrepreneur creates profits and success.

A mission statement does not need to be longer than three sentences. It should express both the business's strategy and its primary tactics. Here's a good example from the Chrysler Corporation:*

"Chrysler's primary goal is to achieve consumer satisfaction. We do it through engineering excellence, innovative products, high quality and superior service. And we do it as a team."

Here Chrysler is saying that it believes its competitive advantage is creating "consumer satisfaction." Chrysler's strategy is to attempt to deliver greater consumer satisfaction than its competition — the other automakers. How does Chrysler intend to carry out its strategy? Through these tactics: "engineering excellence, innovative products, high quality and superior service" and by encouraging its employees to work together as a team.

The Younger Generation's Competitive Advantage

If you are a young entrepreneur, you may have a competitive advantage over entrepreneurs twice your age, because you grew up with the Internet and computers. Twenty years ago, most entrepreneurs kept their financial records in handwritten accounting journals, not on the computer. Almost no one used a cell phone or a fax, and e-mail was just an idea in a computer programmer's brain.

We tend to be most comfortable with the technology we learned to use while we were growing up. Your generation's familiarity with the Internet, laptop computers, beepers, faxes, and cell phones can be a competitive advantage for your business. Let's say there's a video rental store in your neighborhood run by an entrepreneur who does the store's ordering and record keeping by hand. If you open a store that uses scanners and computerized lists, you will probably attract the other store's customers because they won't have to wait in line as long. That's your competitive advantage.

Don't forget, however, that technology doesn't have to be new to be useful to an entrepreneur. Tool-and-die technology, for example, is still very important to an entrepreneur hoping to manufacture a piece of machinery. The phone is still one of a salesperson's most important technological tools.

---

* From *The Ten-Day MBA* by Steven Silbiger, (William Morrow and Co., New York, 1993).

Finding Your Own Competitive Advantage

What if you are having trouble figuring out what your competitive advantage is? The first place to look is at your hobbies and interests. Do you play an instrument? Like to take photographs? We tend to develop our individual talents and skills through our hobbies. These skills can be competitive advantages in the marketplace.

Try looking at your friends, as well. Perhaps you know someone with a special skill who has no business knowledge. With your business knowledge and someone else's skill you could start a partnership that could lead to a successful business.

In defining your competitive advantage, you need to think through your mission, strategy and tactics. Here is an example for a T-shirt business.

MISSION — to create T-shirts and stickers for local bands to sell

STRATEGY — the competing merchandising company in town requires a minimum order of 500 T-shirts; we will outperform them by requiring a minimum order of only 50 at the same per-unit price.

TACTICS — put up flyers at shows and run ads on the college radio station to attract customers; make T-shirts and stickers on weekends, when it's cheaper to rent the manufacturing equipment.

Researching the Competition — Worldwide

Once you choose your competitive advantage and develop a mission statement with your strategy and tactics, it's time to check out the competition. Entrepreneurs keep one eye on their competition at all times. First, you need to research the competition before you start your business. This will help you to figure out whether your competitive advantage will be strong enough to outperform the competition and make a profit. Then, once you're in business, your competition will start reacting to you with new tactics designed to weaken your competitive advantage.

Before the Internet, researching the competition was time-consuming and expensive, but now the entrepreneur has easy, free access to lots of information. In addition, entrepreneurs only had to check out the competition in the neighborhood, or the state, or perhaps nationally, if you were really ambitious. But today's entrepreneurs, even those starting very small businesses, face competition from beyond their neighborhoods because customers can go shopping on the World Wide Web.

Most entrepreneurs are optimistic — optimism is a trait that goes with the territory — so they tend to get very excited about selling to customers all over the world via the Web. What they often don't realize, as Fred Hapgood wrote, in *Inc.* magazine in 1997, is that "the world already is selling to their customers — aggressively and seamlessly."

What can you do? Get online yourself and conduct a thorough search of your industry so you can see your competition's websites.

Is Your Competitive Advantage Strong Enough?

Doing thorough research like this will help you evaluate your competitive advantage and decide upon your strategy and tactics. It will also help you get a clearer picture of your market, and of how well the competition is doing in it. According to entrepreneurship professor Jeffry Timmons, a successful company needs:*

- To sell to a market that is large and growing.

- To sell to a market where the competition is able to make a profit.

- To sell to a market where the competition is succeeding but is not so powerful as to make it impossible for the new entrepreneur to enter the market.

- To sell a product or service that solves problems that customers have with competing products or services (such as poor quality or poor delivery).

- To be able to sell its product or service at a competitive price that will attract customers.

If all of these are in place, and you:

1. really understand the needs of your customers,

2. have a sustainable competitive advantage that no one else has, and,

3. can deliver a product or service that meets your customers' needs at a fair price, you should be able to beat the competition and make a healthy profit.

---

* Timmons, J.A., *New Venture Creation: Entrepreneurship for the 21st Century*, 5th Edition, (Irwin/McGraw Hill, 1999).

Chapter 15 Review

NOTE: The exercises printed below can be found in the corresponding chapter of the NFTE MODULE 1 WORKBOOK that came with your textbook. Please write your answers there. If you do not have a workbook, write your answers on a separate sheet of paper.

Critical Thinking about ...
Your Competitive Advantage

1. What two items should a business's mission statement contain and why?

2. What is the difference between strategy and tactics?

3. Write a mission statement for the neighborhood bookstore discussed in this chapter.

4. Can you think of three competitive advantages for your generation?

Using New Words
mission statement
strategy
tactics

On a separate sheet of paper, identify the vocabulary term that completes each sentence.

Your _____ expresses your competitive advantage and should include both your _____ and the _____ you intend to use to execute it.

Getting the Facts

True or False?

1. A mission statement should be at least five sentences long.

2. A successful company needs to sell a product more cheaply than the competition.

3. A successful company needs to sell a product or service that solves a problem that consumers have with the products or services being sold by the competition.

Exploration

Use the Internet to research the competition for a business you would like to start. List the URLs, e-mail addresses, phone and fax numbers, and addresses for five competitors you located via the Internet.

Analyzing Your Competitive Advantage

1. Write an essay describing your business's competitive advantage. Discuss the strategy and tactics you intend to use.

2. Write a mission statement for your business.

Review

Chapter Summary

I. Your competitive advantage is your strategy for beating the competition.

A. It is something you can do better than the competition that will attract customers to your business.

B. The competitive advantage must be sustainable over a long time.

C. Without a competitive advantage, there's no point to going into business.

II. Your strategy is how you intend to compete. Your business tactics are the ways in which you plan to carry out your strategy.

III. The mission statement should express the fundamental goal of a business — its reason for existing.

A. A mission statement does not need to be longer than three sentences.

B. The mission statement should express both the business's strategy and its primary tactics.

IV. Young entrepreneurs who grew up with the Internet and new technologies may have a competitive advantage over older entrepreneurs who didn't.

V. Research the competition before you start your business.

A. Keep researching the competition once you're in business, because your competition will react to your presence with new tactics designed to undermine your competitive advantage.

B. Use the Internet to research your international competitors — because now they can reach your customers through the World Wide Web.

The second half of a man's life is made up of nothing but the habits he has acquired during the first half.

— Fyodor Dostoyevsky,
Russian novelist

KEY OBJECTIVES

READING THIS CHAPTER AND DOING THE EXERCISES WILL ENABLE YOU TO:

- Develop the valuable habit of keeping good records.
- Use good records to be smart about money.
- Enter expenses and income into a financial record.
- Use receipts and invoices correctly.

KEEPING GOOD RECORDS

A Necessary Habit

There will be nothing more important that you will learn as an entrepreneur than the habit of keeping accurate records. In the 19th century, John D. Rockefeller founded Standard Oil (now Exxon) and built one of the most famous family fortunes ever. It was said that he kept track of every penny he spent from age sixteen until his death in 1937 at the age of 98.

Keeping good records will enable you to be smart about money. The smarter you are about money, the more successful you will be. Business is about the exchange of money, so, as an entrepreneur, you will need to know how it is being spent. You will need to know how much money is coming in and how much is going out — and why.

In this course, you will be asked to keep a record of all your income and expenses. A notation of income is called a **credit** entry and a notation of an expense is called a

debit entry. You will use the record-keeping journal in your workbook to keep track of your income and expenses.

The left-hand page of your journal records cash transactions

In this chapter are sample journal pages. Income is recorded on the left-hand page as "cash received." Expenses are recorded on the right-hand page as "cash disbursed." The six columns of accounting ledger are labeled as follows:

1. Date
2. Explanation
3. Paid to/Received from
4. Cash Received
5. Cash Disbursed
6. Cash Balance

When you sell your product or service to a customer, always give a bill (**invoice**). You will also need to purchase a receipt/invoice book with two-part, carbon-copy receipts/invoices. When you make a sale, give the top copy to the customer as his or her receipt (record of expense). Keep the second copy as your invoice (record of income).

When your customer has paid the bill, the invoice is marked "paid." It represents your customer's receipt. You should keep a record of each invoice, usually in numbered order or organized by customer name. Each invoice that is prepared and sent (or given) to a customer is recorded as a credit entry when the invoice is paid by the customer.

The right-hand page of your journal explains the type of income or expense

You should enter each transaction twice — once on the left page, and once on the right. If you receive cash from making a sale, for example, you enter the amount of the sale under "cash received." You also enter it under "revenue." If you spend money on operating costs, such as making flyers, you enter the amount of the cost under "cash disbursed." You also enter it under "operating cost." The right-hand page is labeled as follows:

1. Start-up Costs/Investment
2. Revenue
3. Cost of Goods Sold
4. Operating Costs

Always get a **receipt** for every purchase you make. A receipt is a slip of paper with the date and amount of your purchase on it. You can use the receipt to fill out your journal.

Using Your Journal

The journal cash **balance** is determined by subtracting total cash disbursements from total cash receipts. The actual physical amount of money you have in your hand after a day of business should match the balance in your ledger.

Keeping good records is really very simple, as long as you do it every day. It's when you start skipping days, or trying to keep numbers in your head, that maintaining a journal becomes difficult. There will be times when you will be too busy to record a transaction in the journal at the moment it occurs. But, if you follow the rules below, you will always have a written record that you can enter in your journal later.

Keeping track of the flow of money in and out of your business will teach you how to adjust your efforts to be successful. The journal shows you how you are spending your money. You can try to improve your balance by cutting expenses or increasing income.

Your income statement tells you if you have made money or lost money. By keeping accurate records in your accounting journal, your income statement will fall into place and you will be able to easily keep track of how your business is doing.

Cash Flow

Start using your journal to keep track of the money your business earns and spends each day. Keep receipts for every purchase you make. This will help you get in the habit of keeping track of your *cash flow*. Cash flow will equal the cash receipts less the cash disbursements for a business over a period of time. One aspect of your cash flow will be the cash balance in your journal.

You can calculate your ongoing cash balance by subtracting cash disbursements from cash receipts. It is very important never to have a negative cash balance or you will not be able to pay your bills.

You could be running a profitable business but still be insolvent (unable to pay your debts) if your cash balance becomes negative. In order to avoid getting caught without enough cash to pay your expenses, follow these three rules:

1. Collect cash as soon as possible. When you make a sale, try to get paid in cash at the time of the sale.

2. Pay your bills as late as possible within the time frame you have agreed upon with your supplier. Most bills come with a due date. The phone bill, for instance, is typically due within thirty days. That means you can take up to thirty days to pay it. Never pay a bill after the due date, however, without getting permission from the supplier first.

3. Always know your cash balance.

Save Receipts for Tax Deductions

Save your receipts until tax time, because they are literally worth money then. The U.S. tax laws allow business owners to deduct many of their expenses from their taxes. These **deductions** can save you money, but you must keep the receipts to prove that you actually paid the expenses. Write the purpose of the expense on the back of the receipt for future reference.

 RULE OF THUMB: Keep your receipts in a box or file. In another box or file, keep your invoices.

Make Record Keeping a Daily Habit

Keeping track of the flow of money in and out of your business will help make it successful. You can try to lower certain expenses or increase income to improve your balance. Record the money you earn and spend each day. Keep receipts for every purchase you make.

Don't expect to keep your financial transactions in your head during the day and then write them down at night. You are bound to forget an item or mix up a number or two and then your record book will not show an accurate **balance**. The balance is determined by subtracting total disbursements from total receipts. The actual physical amount of money you have in your hand after a day of business will match the balance in your journal, if you have been keeping good records.

Keeping Good Records

Jason has a T-shirt silkscreening business. Below are his transactions for the month of July. The transactions are recorded on the journal pages.

1. To start his business, Jason buys a silkscreen frame, ink, a wedge, and other basic supplies on July 1. These cost $250.

2. On July 2 he buys four-dozen T-shirts from a wholesaler for $240.

3. On July 6 Jason registers to sell his T-shirts each weekend in July at a local flea market. Registration costs him $100. He then goes to a print shop and spends $20 on business cards and $10 on flyers.

4. On July 7, Jason goes to the flea market. He sells all his T-shirts at $12 each.

5. On July 10, Jason goes back to the wholesaler and buys five dozen T-shirts for $300.

6. On July 14, he sells four dozen shirts at $12. To get rid of the last dozen, he drops the price to $10 each.

7. On July 16, Jason buys five dozen T-shirts for $300. He spends $50 for designs for his flyers and $10 on printing them.

8. Jason is back at the flea market on July 21, but it rains in the afternoon and he only sells three dozen shirts at $12 each.

9. On July 25 he buys and screens two dozen more shirts for $120. During the final flea market on July 26, Jason sells all his remaining shirts (four dozen) for $12 each.

JASON'S BUSINESS LEDGER					
Date	Explanation	To/From	Cash Received	Cash Disbursed	Cash Bal.
6/30/95					$1000
7/1/95	silkscreen start-up supplies	Ace Arts		$250	$750
7/2/95	4 dozen T-shirts	Joe Wholesale		$240	$510
7/6/95	monthly registration fee	Flea Market		$100	$410
7/6/95	business cards	Print Shop		$20	$390
7/6/95	flyers	Print Shop		$10	$380
7/7/95	sold 4 dozen T-shirts @ $12	Flea Market	$576		$956
7/10/95	5 dozen T-shirts	Joe Wholesale		$300	$656
7/14/95	4 doz. @ $12, 1 doz. @ $10	Flea Sales	$696		$1352
7/16/95	5 dozen T-shirts	Joe Wholesale		$300	$1052
7/16/95	silkscreen ink	Print Shop		$50	$1002
7/16/95	flyers	Print shop		$10	$992
7/21/95	3 doz. @ $12 (rained)	Flea Market	$432		$1424
7/25/95	2 dozen T-shirts	Joe Wholesale		$120	$1304
7/26/95	sold 4 dozen T-shirts @ $12		$576		$1880
Totals			$2,280	$1,400	

Note: For the purpose of simplification, all inventory purchases are expensed immediately as cost of goods sold.

JASON'S BUSINESS LEDGER				
Startup/Invest.	Revenue (1)	C.O.G.S. (2)*	Op. Cost (3)**	
$250				
		$240		**Income Statement:**
			$100	
			$20	Revenue (1): $2,280
			$10	Less C.O.G.S. (2): $960
	$576			Gross Profit: $1,320
		$300		Less Op. Cost (3): $190
	$696			Profit: $1,130
		$300		Taxes: $282.50
			$50	Net Profit: $847.50
			$10	
	$432			
		$120		**Return on Investment:**
	$576			
				Net Profit ÷ Start-up/Inv. x 100
$250	$2,280	$960	$190	$847.50 ÷ $250 = 339%
				Instructions:
				1. Record transactions as they occur.
				2. Keep all receipts and invoices.
				3. Estimate taxes as 25% or
				profit x .25 in this case $1,130 x .25

*Cost of Goods Sold
**Operating Costs

177

Tips on Technology

There are a number of good computer software programs available to help the small business owner keep good records. Software programs that make bookkeeping easier include Microsoft Profit, Peachtree Accounting, and DacEasy Instant Accounting. Other programs, such as Microsoft Money or Quicken can be used to write checks, balance your bank account, and track your income. Intuit also makes QuickInvoice, and QuickBooks.

There are also several new software packages that bundle several programs. *Microsoft Office*, for example, includes *Microsoft Word* for word processing, *Excel* for accounting, and *PowerPoint* for graphics.

 RULE OF THUMB: Collect your cash and pay your bills as late as possible within the time frame you agreed upon with the supplier.

Keeping Personal Records

It is just as important for you to know where your personal income is going as your business income. For this reason, you will be asked to keep a personal record-keeping journal as well as one for your business. You should continue this practice after this course has ended. You will find that having control over your personal finances will give you more control over your life as a whole, because it will give you a better view of where you are going.

The only difference between your business journal and your personal one will be that, on the right-hand page, the headings will be different. For your personal records, they would be, as per the sample ledger below: Business/Work, Allowance/Gift, for Revenue; and for Cost: Food, Clothing, Travel, Entertainment, and Other.

Example:

Left-hand side of page

PERSONAL LEDGER					
Date	Explanation	To/From	Cash Received	Cash Disbursed	Cash Bal.

Right-hand side of page

Revenue		*Cost*				
PERSONAL LEDGER						
Business/Work	Allowance/Gift	Food	Clothing	Travel	Entertainment	Other

Chapter 16 Review

N O T E : The exercises printed below can be found in the corresponding chapter of the NFTE MODULE 1 WORKBOOK that came with your textbook. Please write your answers there. If you do not have a workbook, write your answers on a separate sheet of paper.

Using New Words

balance
credit
debit
deduction
invoice
receipt

On a separate sheet of paper, write the vocabulary term with the letter of its corresponding definition.

a. a recording of income

b. an expense subtracted from income at tax time

c. a bill

d. proof that goods or services were received

e. the difference between credits and debits

f. a recording of an expense

In Your Opinion

Discuss with a partner:

What do you think of the story that John D. Rockefeller kept track of every penny he spent? Do you think that's a wise thing to do? Do you think it's possible? Write a short essay and present your opinions to the class.

Exploration: Preparing Your Own Income Statement

Using the information contained in the record-keeping ledger of your NFTE Module 1 Workbook, prepare an income statement.

Chapter Summary

I. Keeping good records is a necessary habit.

A. A business owner needs to keep track of money.

B. Use a journal, or ledger, to keep track of credits and debits.

1. Credit entries are notations of income.

2. Debit entries are notations of expenses.

II. Keeping records is easy if you make a commitment to do it every day.

III. Always get a receipt for a purchase.

A. Receipts help you keep track of debits or expenses.

B. Receipts are worth money as tax deductions.

IV. Always submit an invoice when you sell a product or service.

A. The invoice is your customer's receipt.

B. Invoices help you keep track of credits or income.

V. Enter each credit or debit twice in your journal.

A. Record each credit or debit in the Cash Received or Disbursed column and then in the appropriate category column.

B. Keep all credit information on the Cash Receipts page.

C. Write all debit information on the Cash Disbursements page.

You don't get what you deserve, you get what you negotiate.

— Chester L. Karrass,
pioneer of negotiation theory

KEY OBJECTIVES

READING THIS CHAPTER AND DOING THE EXERCISES WILL ENABLE YOU TO:

- Handle a negotiation well.
- Practice the art of compromise.
- Seek a Yes or No answer instead of a Maybe.

NEGOTIATION

Negotiation Is about Compromise

Negotiation is the process of achieving one's goals through give-and-take. An example of negotiation is a buyer and seller discussing the price of an item until an agreement is reached.

As a small business owner, you will have to negotiate frequently — with suppliers, with customers, and with employees. How well you negotiate will greatly affect the success of your business.

Negotiation is about **compromise**, not about winning. Compromise is sacrificing something you want so that an agreement can be reached that is acceptable to both you and the person with whom you are negotiating.

When negotiating, keep in mind that the other person is not your enemy. The best negotiations are those in which both parties are satisfied — a "win/win" agreement.

Conduct your negotiations as if you would be dealing with that person again very soon. You never know when you might need his or her help.

The best negotiators are tough and resourceful. They are also honest and careful to make sure the other person is as pleased with the end result as they are.

Before the Negotiation

1. **Set your goals and organize your thoughts.** What do you want to achieve in the negotiation? Write down your goals and thoughts on note cards to keep with you during the discussion.

2. **Decide what your boundaries are.** Think about what the best deal for you would be. Then think about the worst. What is the minimum you would be willing to accept? What is the maximum you are seeking? Knowing this ahead of time will prevent you from getting carried away and giving up too much of one thing in order to get something else. You don't want to win the battle and find you've lost the war.

3. **Put yourself in the other person's shoes.** What does he or she want from the negotiation? What is his or her minimum? maximum? Things that aren't very important to you could be very important to the other person. You could give up something during the negotiation that doesn't mean much to you, but means so much to the other person that he or she might give in on something you want.

4. **Don't talk dollars until you have to.** When buying or selling, don't begin by mentioning an actual dollar amount. Talk to the seller or buyer first. Try to get an idea of what his or her position is. The more information you can gather beforehand, the better.

During Negotiations

1. **Let the other person name a price first.** When discussing a price, try to let the other person make the first offer. This will reveal his or her position.

2. **Try extremes.** If the person won't reveal a position, try throwing out an extreme figure — very high or very low (depending on what your own position is). This will force the other person to come forward with some type of response that will help guide you.

3. **Show willingness to bargain.** As negotiations proceed, respond to each counter-offer by giving up something you decided in advance that you could afford to give up.

4. **Listen.** The greatest negotiators are also the best listeners. Through listening, you will gain the information you will need to arrive at a win/win situation.

5. **Silence can be an important tool.** After you have initially stated your case, don't say anything for a few moments. This can prompt the other person to say something that you can turn to your advantage.

6. **Always ask for more than has been offered.** When the other person wants you to pay back a loan in ten days, for instance, ask for fifteen. You may have to settle for twelve, but that's better than the original demand.

Don't Let "Maybe" Waste Your Time*

When you need an answer, the most frustrating negotiations are not those that end in a firm No, but those that end with a Maybe.

If you find that many of your negotiations are ending in Maybe's, you could be seeking the wrong answer. You could be trying too hard to seek a Yes from someone who is not really willing to give you one. You are letting that person string you along with a Maybe. Maybe's can feel encouraging, but actually waste your time and keep you from pursuing other options.

When someone can't seem to give you an answer, say something like, "I understand you can't say Yes right away, but I think it's fair for me to ask you to give me a definite No by the end of the week."

If he or she says No at the end of the week, fine. Now you can move on to a new situation and explore new possibilities. But first, don't forget to ask the person who says No: "If you can't do it, can you recommend someone who might?"

---

* With thanks to Joseph Mancuso, founder of the Center for Entrepreneurial Management.

Chapter 17 Review

N O T E : The exercises printed below can be found in the corresponding chapter of the NFTE MODULE 1 WORKBOOK that came with your textbook. Please write your answers there. If you do not have a workbook, write your answers on a separate sheet of paper.

Critical Thinking about . . . Negotiation

1. Play the Negotiating Game with your teacher's guidance. Write an essay about how you did and how you might improve the next time you play the game.

2. Use negotiation strategies to negotiate for something you want, such as a later curfew, a favor from a friend, time off from work, etc. Write a paragraph describing your negotiation experience.

Using New Words

compromise
negotiation

On a separate sheet of paper, identify the correct definition for each vocabulary term.

1) negotiation

   a) achieving mutual goals through give-and-take

   b) achieving all your own goals at the other person's expense

2) compromise

   a) an agreement in which both parties have given up something

   b) failure to come to an agreement

Getting the Facts

1. What is the difference between negotiating and playing a game?

2. Why is it smart to seek a win/win conclusion to a negotiation?

3. What's a good way to get organized before a negotiation?

4. What should you always determine before entering a negotiation?

5. Name three tactics you can use to try to get the other person to reveal his or her position.

In Your Opinion

Do you agree that negotiation is about compromise, not winning? Write a short essay about your opinion and share it with classmates.

Review

Chapter Summary

I. Negotiation is about compromise, not about winning.

    A. The best negotiators are honest and fair.

    B. The best negotiations are those in which both parties win.

        1. Both parties are then more likely to stick to the agreement.

        2. Both parties are more likely to help each other out in the future.

II. Prepare yourself before a negotiation.

    A. Organize your thoughts and determine your limits.

    B. Imagine the other person's goals and limits.

III. During negotiation, try different tactics to get the other person to reveal his or her position.

    A. Let the other person name a price first.

    B. Try extremes.

    C. Show your willingness to bargain.

    D. Listen.

    E. Try silence.

    F. Always ask.

IV. A No is better than a Maybe because it lets you move on to new prospects.

KEY OBJECTIVES

READING THIS CHAPTER AND DOING THE EXERCISES WILL ENABLE YOU TO:

- Learn the four steps of developing a marketing plan.

- Learn how to develop a successful marketing mix for your business venture.

- Learn the basic principles of pricing strategy.

CONSUMER ANALYSIS AND DEVELOPING YOUR MARKETING MIX

The art of listening applies not only to negotiation but also to all your decisions about how to run your business. As we discussed in Chapter 14, listening to what your potential customers have to say is very important. Conducting market research will help you determine what benefits the customers in your market are looking for in your product or service. That is your *"marketing strategy."* It should direct all your future business decisions — from where to locate your business to how to price your product or service. Successful entrepreneurs are market driven. Every decision they make is designed to strengthen the consumer perception that their product or service is the best provider of the benefit that the customer is seeking.

Price: What It Says about Your Product

Pricing is a critical marketing decision. To choose the lowest possible price does not necessarily communicate the best marketing message to customers. However new entrepreneurs usually assume they should simply sell their product at the lowest price they can afford.

According to *Guerrilla Marketing Attack,* by Jay Levinson,* a study of consumers in the furniture industry found that price came ninth, when consumers were asked to list factors affecting their decision to make a purchase. *Quality* turned out to be the number two influence on buying patterns. *Confidence* in the product was number one. *Service* was third.

Simply selling at a lower price than the competition will not necessarily win you the largest market share. Sometimes consumers even think that a low price means the product is of poor quality. If you are selling BMWs, and you lower the price, you could damage the "image" of the car as a luxury item.

You need to know how the customers in your market think before you can make good business decisions. You need to develop a carefully researched marketing plan.

The Four Steps of Developing a Marketing Plan

The marketing plan introduces your product to your market. Developing a plan is a four-step process. These steps are:

1. Consumer analysis

2. Market analysis

3. Development of a **marketing mix**

4. Break-even analysis (We'll discuss break-even analysis in Chapter 31.)

Step One: Consumer Analysis

Before you can develop a marketing vision for your business, you will need to know who your customers are and what they want. The Home Depot chain of hardware stores markets itself as a company that teaches people how to use tools to improve their homes. Home Depot doesn't just sell tools; it sells what people really need — the skills to use the tools. Home Depot's marketing vision focuses on what customers need their products to do.

---

* Levinson, J.C. *Guerrilla Marketing Attack,* (Houghton Mifflin Co., 1989).

Successful businesses are not built on single sales but on repeat business. The owners of Home Depot have calculated that a satisfied customer is worth more than $25,000 in sales over the customer's lifetime. Bernie Marcus, one of the company's founders, has said, "All of our people [employees] understand what the Holy Grail is. It's not the bottom line. It's an almost blind, passionate commitment to taking care of customers."*

Market Segments

If the best marketing strategies are focused on the customer, an entrepreneur clearly has to choose which customers to target. After all, you can't please all of the people all of the time! Chances are, not every single consumer in the market will need your product. As you make decisions about your target customer, consider each level of the production/distribution chain (to be discussed in Chapter 20): manufacturer, wholesaler, retailer, and consumer. You should decide which level(s) of this chain you will need to reach in order to make your marketing strategy successful.

The customers you decide to target will be your **market segment**. A market segment is composed of consumers who have a similar response to a certain type of marketing. In the cosmetics industry, for instance, one segment really likes luxurious, expensive products. Another segment is looking for products that claim to reduce signs of aging. Another's primary concern is price. A company that recognizes these segments and chooses one or two as its target market will do well, because of its focus on its target consumer.

Successful Segmenting:
The Body Shop

The Body Shop is a good example of successful targeting of a market segment. Anita Roddick was fed up with paying for expensive packaging and perfumes when she bought cosmetics. Price had become part of the image for many cosmetics. One perfume was marketed as the most expensive in the world!

Roddick saw an opportunity here to create a different line of cosmetics. She decided to use natural products that would be packaged inexpensively. Her products appealed to women

---

* Marcus, B. and Blank, A. *Built from Scratch: How a Couple of Regular Guys Grew the Home Depot from Nothing to $30 Billion*, (Randon House, 1989).

who didn't like all the hype in the cosmetics industry. Her success has proven that selling an honest product straightforwardly can be the best marketing strategy of all.

Step Two: Market Analysis

But what if Roddick had found out that there were very few women interested in natural cosmetics? Her business would not have survived because, even though the cosmetics market is very large, her segment would have been too small to support a business.

This leads us to Step Two of the marketing process: Market Analysis. As we have seen, a market is a group of people with the potential interest in buying a given product or service. You'll need to figure out how large your market is. Then you'll need to figure out how large the segment interested in your product or service might be.

Marketers have developed four basic ways to analyze a market:

BY LOCATION — Segmenting consumers by where they live. You could decide that the market for your home-cooked baked goods will be everyone within five miles of where you live, for example.

BY POPULATION — Segmenting consumers based on age, sex, income, or education. You could decide to only market your all-natural cosmetics to women between the ages of 15 to 35.

BY PERSONALITY — Segmenting consumers by personality (conservative vs. liberal, for instance), or lifestyles. You could decide to market your services as a hiking guide to people who go camping.

BY BEHAVIOR — Segmenting consumers by *purchasing* behaviors that have been observed, such as brand loyalty or responsiveness to price. If you are making hacky-sacks, you could decide to focus on people who already play Frisbee, because they show up as consumers interested in outdoor skill games.

Analyzing the Market Segment

Let's say you want to make and sell hacky-sacks at your high school, where there are about 2,000 students. How do you determine which segment of that market to target? You could use any of the above segmentation methods. For example:

BY LOCATION — You could decide that your market is everyone who lives within two miles of the school.

BY POPULATION — You could decide to limit your marketing efforts to juniors and seniors.

BY PERSONALITY — You could decide to market to students who play soccer, because using a hacky-sack will help them improve their soccer skills.

BY BEHAVIOR – You could decide to market to people who buy Frisbees, because they are likely also to buy hacky-sacks.

You could research the market by taking a survey of 50 students. Show them the product and ask questions like:

Do you play soccer? How often?

Would you be interested in purchasing this hacky-sack, if it were available?

If 50 of the 200 students surveyed seem interested in your hacky-sack, you could expect that roughly 500 of the 2,000 would represent your market. Now you can focus your marketing efforts on those students.

Step Three: The Marketing Mix

Now that you know who your target consumer is, you are ready for Step 3: development of a "marketing mix." This is the combination of four factors — *product, price, place, and promotion* — that together communicate your marketing vision to your consumer.

"The Four P's" are the essential elements of your marketing plan. Together, they communicate your total vision. If you change one "P" you must also pay attention to how it affects the other three. If you raise your price, for example, are you still selling the product in the right place? Or do you need to move to a location that will better attract consumers willing to pay (and will even be attracted by) the new price?

PRODUCT – The product or service should meet or create a consumer need.

PRICE — The product or service must be priced low enough for the public to buy it and high enough for the business to make a profit.

PLACE — The product or service should be sold where there will be a demand for it. Don't try to sell ski hats in Hawaii!

PROMOTION — Create an advertising and publicity strategy for your product or service.

Place: Location, Location, Location!

For a retail business, *location* is the key to attracting customers. Ideally, you'll want your store or business to be where your market is.

For other types of business, though, the key to location might be cost or convenience. More and more people are operating service businesses from their homes. Wholesale businesses, on the other hand, require a great deal of storage space and are best located in out-of-the-way areas where rent or property costs are low.

Pricing

By now you understand that just offering the lowest price may not be the best strategy. An increasingly popular alternative is **value pricing**. Value pricing is not just price-cutting. It means finding the balance between quality and price that gives your target customers the value they seek. Remember, "value" is not the same as "cheap." Most consumers are driven by a strong desire to get value for their money. They want to feel okay about spending it. If the quality of a product is very good, a consumer will be willing to pay a higher price than for a poor-quality product.

In general, entrepreneurs who focus on providing value to customers will do well. Giving free gifts or spending a lot of money on advertisements are marketing strategies that might bring customers to your business for the first time, but only consistently offering good value will keep them coming back.

Retailers' Rule of Thumb: Keystoning

Retailers who buy goods wholesale and resell them sometimes use "keystoning", or doubling the wholesale price, as a rule of thumb for estimating what price to charge. If you buy cell phones for $22 each from a wholesaler, for example, selling them for $44 in your store will probably cover your costs and provide you with an acceptable profit.

In general, keystoning is a good way to estimate a price. If you are selling hacky-sack balls that cost $4, sell them for $8. When pricing, however, the entrepreneur must always be sensitive to the market and to what competitors are charging.

Other Pricing Strategies

Some other pricing methods include:

COST PLUS: A simple method of taking your cost and adding a desired profit margin. This method, however, fails to take your marketing vision into consideration.

PENETRATION STRATEGY: This method can work well during the early stages of the product life cycle, as it is based on using a low price to gain market share. Japanese companies used this method to dominate the VCR market.

SKIMMING STRATEGY: The opposite of Penetration Strategy, this method seeks to charge a high price during the introductory stage of the product life cycle, when a product is novel and has few competitors. RCA used this strategy when it first introduced color TVs.

MEET OR BEAT THE COMPETITION: This is a common strategy in commodities and service businesses — airlines tend to compete heavily via pricing, for example.

So how do you pick a pricing strategy? It's simple, just pick a price that reflects and supports your marketing vision. All your business decisions should be market driven.

Chapter 18 Review

NOTE: The exercises printed below can be found in the corresponding chapter of the NFTE MODULE 1 WORKBOOK that came with your textbook. Please write your answers there. If you do not have a workbook, write your answers on a separate sheet of paper.

Critical Thinking about . . . Pricing

1. Why is it important for an entrepreneur to be market driven? What does "market driven" mean?

2. Give an example of a business in which having the lowest price has been a successful strategy. Give an example of a business that uses a different pricing strategy.

3. What do you think is the market segment for your business? How do you intend to learn more about your target market?

Using New Words

market segment
marketing mix
value pricing

On a separate sheet of paper, identify the correct definition for each vocabulary term.

1. Value pricing is
   a. pricing the product or service at the lowest possible price.
   b. pricing the product or service at a price that gives target customers the balance between quality and price that they seek.
   c. price-cutting.

2. Your market segment is
   a. all the people who make up your market.
   b. the people in your market interested in your product or service.
   c. people with the money to buy your product or service.

3. Which is not part of the marketing mix?
   a. place
   b. price
   c. product
   d. plan

Review

Chapter 18 Review

Getting the Facts

In your NFTE Module I Workbook, use terms from the chapter to complete the sentences.

1. All your business decisions should be _____ .

2. "Keystoning" is a common _____ strategy.

3. Retail businesses need to be located where the _____ is.

4. The four components of the marketing mix are: _____, _____, _____, and _____ .

5. The four steps of developing a marketing plan are: _____, _____, _____, and _____.

Exploration

Visit three different fast food restaurants, then answer the following questions.

1. Did you observe any differences in how the employees handled customers' orders? Describe them.

2. Describe what you believe to be the marketing vision of each restaurant, based on what you observed.

3. Describe what you think the pricing strategy of each restaurant is.

Review

Chapter Summary

I. Successful entrepreneurs are market driven.

    A. Every decision they make proves to the customers that their product or service is the best choice.

    B. Price is an example of a decision that should be market driven.

    C. Simply selling at the lowest price may not be the best decision.

    D. Research the market to determine the right pricing strategy for your business.

II. There are four steps to a marketing plan.

    A. Consumer analysis: who are your consumers? What do they want?

    B. Market analysis: what is your market segment? How large is it?

    C. Marketing mix: how can you combine its four factors to communicate your marketing vision to your customers?

        1. product

        2. price

        3. place

        4. promotion

    D. Break-even analysis (discussed in chapter 31)

III. Market-driven pricing strategies

    A. Value pricing — finding a balance between price and quality that makes consumers feel that they are getting value for their money.

    B. Keystoning — retail rule of thumb: doubling the wholesale cost.

The secret of success in life is for a man to be ready for his opportunity when it comes.

— Benjamin Disraeli
English novelist and politician

KEY OBJECTIVES

READING THIS CHAPTER AND DOING THE EXERCISES WILL ENABLE YOU TO:

■ Define personal liability.

■ Explore the pros and cons of sole proprietorships.

■ Discuss the advantages and disadvantages of partnerships.

■ Learn how to register a sole proprietorship.

SOLE PROPRIETORSHIPS AND PARTNERSHIPS

Sole Proprietorships

The **sole proprietorship** is owned by one person, who may also be the only employee. The owner receives all the business's profits, but also suffers all the losses. Most student businesses are sole proprietorships.

The sole proprietor is personally **liable**, or responsible, for any lawsuits that arise from accidents, faulty merchandise, unpaid bills or other business problems. This means the winner of a lawsuit against a sole proprietor can collect money not only from the business, but from a court forcing the owner to sell private possessions — such as a house or a car. A young person should start a business where the risk of the product or service physically hurting someone is very low.

When deciding which business to go into, stick to simple and safe products, such as neckties, watches, or headbands. Businesses that market products that might harm someone (skateboards are a good example) should consider incorporating and purchasing liability insurance. Incorporation offers the business owner *limited liability*. This protects personal assets, because a lawsuit against a corporation can only seek payment from the assets of the corporation.

Advantages of a Sole Proprietorship

- It is relatively *easy to start*. Registration does not require much paperwork and is less expensive than for a partnership or corporation.
- The business owner pays *personal income tax* on the business's earnings.
- There are *fewer government regulations* than for the other forms of business.
- Sole proprietors can make *quick decisions* and act without interference from others.
- A sole proprietor keeps *all the profits* from the business.

Disadvantages of a Sole Proprietorship

- It can be *difficult to raise enough money* by oneself to start or expand the business.
- A sole proprietor must often put in *long hours*, often working six or even seven days a week.
- There is unlimited personal **legal liability** from lawsuits related to the business.
- There is often *no one to offer encouragement* or feedback.
- The odds of *failure* are high, usually because of a lack of financing or business expertise.

Partnerships

A **partnership** consists of two or more owners who make the decisions for the business together and share the profits and losses. As in a sole proprietorship, the owners face unlimited liability in any lawsuits. The exception is the **limited partnership**. The "limited partners" have no say in the daily operation of the business and have, as a result, limited liability. Even so, there must still be at least one "general partner," who is liable for all partnership debts.

Partners bring different strengths and skills to a business. This can help the business grow and succeed. In addition, partners can support and advise each other. On the other hand, partnership disagreements can become quite unpleasant and destroy the partnership, the friendship — and the business.

Despite the advantages of partnerships, we suggest being very cautious about entering into one, even with a good friend or relative. A lawyer should be consulted and a Partnership Agreement drawn up that carefully defines the responsibilities of each partner.

Advantages of a Partnership

- Financing can be easier to secure because partners can combine assets.

- The business risks, long hours and **legal liabilities** are shared.

- Different skills and contacts are brought into the business.

Disadvantages of a Partnership

- The profits must be shared.

- Although shared, legal liability still includes personal property.

- Disagreements among the partners can destroy the business.

- Partnerships can be difficult and unpleasant to dissolve.

Registration of a Sole Proprietorship

It is easy and inexpensive to register a sole proprietorship. When you do, you will have a real business!

Rules and regulations vary greatly from area to area, however. Contact the county courthouse or your local chamber of commerce to find out which licenses and permits are necessary in your locality. If you do *not* register your business, you may be fined or prosecuted by the IRS or other government agencies. You can't use the court system or bring a lawsuit. Your business will not be able to really grow. Being "legal" will allow you to concentrate on your business.

Registration usually takes the following steps:

1. Choosing a name for your business.

2. Filling out a "Doing Business As" (D.B.A.) form with the name of the business and your name, so the state will know the name of the person who owns the business.

3. An official may then conduct a name search to make sure the name you have chosen is not already being used. You may even be asked to help research the records yourself.

4. After the name of your business is established, you will fill out a registration form and pay the registration fee.

5. You may be asked to take the form to a notary, have it *notarized* and bring it back to the registration office. As discussed earlier, a notary is a person who has been given the authority by the state to witness the signing of documents. You will have to show the notary identification so he or she knows who is signing the registration form. A notary usually charges a fee of around one dollar.

State and Local Law

Once registered, the name of the business officially belongs to you. Now you'll need to research local regulations at your local chamber of commerce.

Zoning regulations, for instance, prohibit certain businesses from operating in certain areas. There are also licensing regulations, such as restrictions on obtaining a liquor license for a bar or restaurant. These can vary not only from state to state but from town to town.

Federal Regulations

If you hire employees to work for you, there are federal, state and city regulations that come into effect as well. If you are the owner and only employee, however, those regulations will not affect you (with the important exception of paying federal income tax on your profits).

Sales-Tax Identification Number

In many areas, every business, regardless of its size, must obtain a Sales Tax Identification Number and collect the appropriate taxes on all retail sales.

Collecting sales taxes from businesses is one way government pays for paved roads, street lights, police and fire departments — all of which make it easier for businesses to operate.

To find out which sales taxes are required in your locality, consult your phone book for your state's sales-tax office or other relevant government office.

It is extremely important to follow all federal, state and local regulations, and to pay all applicable personal and business taxes. As your business expands, your records and dealings must be completely aboveboard and legal.

Sample Tax Identification Number Application

CIS-1
(6-90)

STATE OF NEW JERSEY
DIVISION OF TAXATION
APPLICATION FOR REGISTRATION
Read instructions before completing this form
ALL SECTIONS MUST BE FULLY COMPLETED ON BOTH SIDES OF THIS APPLICATION

MAIL TO:
CN 252
TRENTON, N.J. 08646-0252

REGISTRATION DETAIL

A. Please indicate the reason for your filing this application.
(Check only <u>one</u> block)
☐ Original application for a new business.
☐ Application for a new location of an existing business
☐ Amended application for an existing business.
☐ Moved previously registered business to new location (UTF-C can be used in lieu of CIS-1)
Give name and NJ Registration Number of existing business.

☐ Other · please explain

B. FID # ☐☐ - ☐☐☐☐☐☐☐   OR   Soc. Sec. # of Owner ☐☐☐ - ☐☐ - ☐☐☐☐
☐ Check Box if applied for

C. Name
(IF INCORPORATED - give Corp. Name; IF NOT- give Last Name, First Name, MI of Owner, Partners)

D. Trade Name

E. Business Location:
(Do not use P.O. Box for Location Address)

Street

City _____ State ☐☐

Zip Code ☐☐☐☐☐ - ☐☐☐☐
(Give 9-digit Zip)

(See instructions for providing alternate addresses)

F. Mailing Name and Address · (if different from business address)

Name

Street

City _____ State ☐☐

Zip Code ☐☐☐☐☐ - ☐☐☐☐
(Give 9-digit Zip)

G. Beginning Date For This Business In New Jersey _____ / _____ / _____ (see instructions)
month   day   year

H. Type of Ownership (check one):
☐ NJ Corporation   ☐ Sole Proprietor   ☐ Partnership   ☐ Out-of-State Corporation
☐ Limited Partnership   ☐ Other - explain _____

O/C _____
NCT ☐

Sample Business Certificate

Business Certificate

I HEREBY CERTIFY *that I am conducting or transacting business under the name or designation*

of

at

City or Town of   *County of*   *State of New York*

My name is*

and I reside at

     I FURTHER CERTIFY *that I am the successor in interest to*

the person or persons heretofore using such name or names to carry on or conduct or transact business.

IN WITNESS HEREOF, *I have this*   *day of*   *20*   *, made*
and signed this certificate

_____

* Print or type name.
* If under 21 years of age, state "I am   years of age."

STATE OF NEW YORK
COUNTY OF

     On this   *day of*   *20*   *, before me personally*
appeared

to me known and known to me to be the individual described in and who executed the foregoing
certificate, and he (she) thereupon duly acknowledged to me that he (she) executed the same.

_____

Chapter 19 Review

N O T E : The exercises printed below can be found in the corresponding chapter of the NFTE MODULE 1 WORKBOOK that came with your textbook. Please write your answers there. If you do not have a workbook, write your answers on a separate sheet of paper.

Critical Thinking about . . . Sole Proprietorship or Partnership?

1. What can happen to a business owner who is personally liable?

2. How should partners protect themselves from disagreements?

3. Why should you choose a product or service that is unlikely to injure anyone when starting your own business?

Analyzing

List the advantages and disadvantages of partnerships and sole proprietorships.

Sole Proprietorship or Partnership?

Pretend you are a lawyer asked by a client to explain the differences between a sole proprietorship and a partnership. Use the lists of advantages and disadvantages you made to help you write a business letter to this client.

Using New Words

liable
legal liability
limited partnership
partnership
sole proprietorship

On a separate sheet of paper, identify the vocabulary term that completes each sentence.

1) In a sole proprietorship, the business owner is completely _____ for any debts or legal judgments incurred by his or her business.

2) _____ is shared equally by business owners involved in a general partnership, unless otherwise provided for in the partnership agreement.

3) The _____ is an attractive form of business ownership because it offers the owner complete control.

4) Partners in a _____ have no say in the daily operation of the business.

5) One disadvantage of a _____ is the potential for disagreements between the owners of a business.

Getting the Facts

1. What kind of personal tax does a sole proprietor pay?

2. What government identification number must you have before you can sell a product or service?

3. Name two types of local regulations you need to research before opening for business.

4. As a sole proprietor, what form must you file with your state?

5. What is the purpose of having a form notarized?

Review

Chapter Summary

I. The sole proprietorship is a business owned by one person.

A. That person receives all profits and suffers all losses.

B. That person is personally liable for any business lawsuits.

II. A partnership consists of two or more business owners.

A. The partners share profits and losses.

B. The partners share personal liability.

III. The registration of a sole proprietorship has several steps.

A. Filling out the D.B.A. form.

B. Going to the county courthouse or other designated office.

C. Paying a registration fee.

A Business for the Young Entrepreneur:
Home and Office Plant Care

Do your friends say you have a green thumb? People like to have plants in their homes and offices but don't always have time to care for them. Home and office plant care is a business that is inexpensive to start and doesn't require a lot of time. Most plants only need attention once or twice a week, so plant care is a great small business for a busy student.

Make a flyer and ask if you can put it up in the lobbies of office buildings near your home or school. To learn how to care for different types of plants, visit your local plant nursery or shop. Ask the owner to recommend some books you can read.

Supplies

watering can

plant food

rags for dusting plant leaves

notebook for instructions on how to care for plants

calendar to keep track of visits

Where to find them

hardware store or nursery

nursery or flower shop

make from old shirts

stationery store

stationery store

Tips

- Ask customers for details on how to care for each plant. Write them down!

- Offer customers a discount on your services if they refer you to another customer.

You give birth to that on which you fix your mind.

— Antoine de Saint-Exupéry
French author

KEY OBJECTIVES

READING THIS CHAPTER AND DOING THE EXERCISES WILL ENABLE YOU TO:

- Understand the manufacturer-to-consumer chain.
- Calculate markup percentages.
- Calculate gross profit margin.
- Calculate net profit margin.

THE PRODUCTION/ DISTRIBUTION CHAIN*

The consumer is the final link in the chain that extends from the manufacturer through the wholesaler and retailer. When a consumer buys a pair of athletic shoes in a sporting-goods store, the chain would be:

1. Manufacturer produces a great quantity of a particular shoe.

2. Wholesaler buys a large number of these shoes from the manufacturer.

3. Retailer buys a smaller number to stock his/her store.

4. Consumer walks into retailer's store and buys one pair of shoes.

---

* With special thanks to Diana Kidd of Koch Industries for the ideas she contributed to this chapter.

Manufacturer → Wholesaler → Retailer → Consumer

This manufacturer-to-consumer chain is called the **production/distribution structure**, or the distribution channel.

There can be other links in this chain besides the four above. A manufacturer may have to buy raw materials or other manufactured goods to make the product. There may be other *middlemen* — agents or brokers or other wholesalers — between manufacturer and wholesaler or between wholesaler and retailer. On the other hand, sometimes there is no middleman in the chain, if the retailer is purchasing directly from the manufacturer.

Delivery

Inexperienced entrepreneurs sometimes don't realize how important the distribution channel is to the success of a business. You need to know how long it will take to get each item you want to sell from your supplier. If your product moves too slowly through the distribution channel, you can lose customers who don't want to wait for it. A clothing store owner can lose business if she is not able to get the latest fashions into her store while they are in fashion. Customers looking for new trends will buy from her competition, instead.

If you are running a business that requires quick delivery of your product, try to find suppliers in your area to cut down on delivery time.

Markups

At every link in the chain, the price of the product is increased to cover expenses and to generate a profit for that link. These increases in price are called **markups**. At each step along the chain the price of a product is "marked up," usually anywhere from 25% to 100%.

When consumers purchase a product from a retail store, they are paying the retailer's **gross profit margin** — the markup from the price the retailer paid the wholesaler to the price the retailer is charging the consumer. This markup, related to *gross profit* *per unit*, is used to cover operating costs as well as, hopefully, to provide a profit to the entrepreneur.

The old expression "I can get it for you wholesale" means the person making the offer can get the product at the wholesaler's price, that is, without the retailer's markup. The tradition of bargaining in certain cultures is carried on with the knowledge that the seller has marked up the cost. The bargainers are really negotiating the seller's profit margin.

If you are able to purchase a product at a relatively low wholesale price, and customers are willing to pay a retail price that includes a relatively high markup, you will have a very profitable business.

Retail Markup Percentage

Because most entrepreneurs sell many items at different prices and different wholesale costs, it would be time-consuming to try to figure an acceptable markup for each item. Instead, retailers use percentage markups. Every item in a gift shop, for example, might be marked up 50 percent.

Wholesale Cost x Markup % = Markup

If you know the markup and wholesale cost of an item, you can figure the markup percentage using this formula:

$$\text{Markup \%} = \frac{\text{Markup}}{\text{Wholesale Cost}} \text{ x } 100$$

Let's say the gift shop buys cards for $2.00 each from the wholesaler and sells them for $3.00 each.

Markup = $3.00 – $2.00 = $1.00

$$\text{Markup \%} = \frac{\$1.00}{\$2.00} \text{ x } 100 = 50\%$$

If the gift shop owner finds, while doing her monthly income statements, that she is not generating enough profit, she can raise her markup percentage slightly to try to increase revenue. Or she can try to find a cheaper wholesale supplier to lower her wholesale costs.

The Relationship Between Price, Gross Profit, and Cost

As we have learned, if a shoe store buys a pair of sneakers from the wholesaler for $20 and sells it for $45, the retailer's markup is $25. This $25 markup is also called the *gross profit per unit*.

$$\textbf{Gross Profit = Retail Price – Wholesale Cost}$$
$$\$25 \quad = \quad \$45 \quad – \quad \$20$$

Gross Profit Margin per Unit

A business that can't cover its operating costs (USAIIRD) won't stay in business very long, so business owners like to know what percentage of each dollar of revenue is covering their operating costs. To calculate this gross profit margin per unit, divide the retail price of an item into its gross profit.

$$\textbf{Gross Profit Margin per Unit} = \frac{\textbf{Gross Profit per Unit}}{\textbf{Retail Price}} \times \textbf{100}$$

In the case of the gift shop owner:

$$\text{Gross Profit Margin per Unit} = \frac{\$1.00}{\$3.00} \times 100 = 33\%$$

For every dollar the gift shop owner receives from selling an item, therefore, 33 cents of that dollar will be used to pay operating costs, and hopefully provide a profit.

Profit Margin

Finally, for the business as a whole, the **profit margin** is calculated by dividing profit by sales and multiplying by 100. This shows how much of each dollar of sales is profit.

$$\textbf{Profit Margin} = \frac{\textbf{Profit}}{\textbf{Sales}} \times \textbf{100}$$

Chapter 20 Review

NOTE: The exercises printed below can be found in the corresponding chapter of the NFTE MODULE 1 WORKBOOK that came with your textbook. Please write your answers there. If you do not have a workbook, write your answers on a separate sheet of paper.

Getting the Facts

1. What does the expression, "I can get it for you wholesale" mean?

2. What happens to the price of a product at every link in the manufacturer-to-consumer chain?

3. Name a key business principle of buying and selling.

4. List two reasons why a wholesaler increases the price of a product before selling it to a retailer.

Using New Words

markup
gross profit margin
production/
distribution structure

On a separate sheet of paper, identify the correct definition for each vocabulary term.

1) markup
   a) the difference between the price and the cost per unit
   b) the retailer's cost
   c) the wholesale price

2) production/distribution structure
   a) the four types of business
   b) the manufacturer-to-consumer chain along which a product travels
   c) the method by which consumers communicate to entrepreneurs

3) profit margin
   a) retail price
   b) markup
   c) profit divided by sales

Review

Chapter 20 Review

Analyzing ... Markup Percentage

Formulas:

Retail Price – Wholesale Cost = Markup

$$\text{Markup percentage} = \frac{\text{Markup}}{\text{Wholesale Cost}}$$

Example: Item	A Retail Price	B Wholesale Cost	C Markup	D Markup Percentage
Watch	$20.00	$12.00	$8.00	66%

Analyzing ... Retail Gross Profit Margin per Unit

Formulas:

Retail Price – Wholesale Cost = Gross Profit per Unit (also called Markup)

$$\text{Gross Profit Margin per Unit} = \frac{\text{Gross Profit per Unit}}{\text{Retail Price}} \times 100$$

Example: Item	A Retail Price	B Wholesale Cost	C Gross Profit	D Gross Profit Margin per Unit
Watch	$15.00	$12.00	$3.00	20%

Chapter Summary

I. The manufacturer-to-consumer chain has four links:
   Manufacturer ➤ Wholesaler ➤ Retailer ➤ Consumer

   A. This chain is also called "the production/distribution structure."

   B. There may be additional wholesalers or middlemen in the chain.

II. At every link, the product price is raised.

   A. These increases in price are called markups.

   B. Markup is equal to gross profit per unit.

III. Most retailers use percentage markups.

   A. Applying one percentage markup to every item in a store is easier than figuring a dollar markup for each item.

   B. Markup % = $\dfrac{\text{Markup}}{\text{Wholesale Cost}} \times 100$

IV. Retailers like to know their retail gross profit margin and their profit margin.

   A. Retail gross profit tells the retailer how much of each dollar of revenue goes to cover operating costs.

   B. Retail Gross Profit Margin = $\dfrac{\text{Gross Profit per Unit}}{\text{Retail Price}} \times 100$

   C. Profit Margin equals = $\dfrac{\text{Profit}}{\text{Sales}} \times 100$

Man is still the most extraordinary computer of all.

—John F. Kennedy,
35th President of the
United States

KEY OBJECTIVES

READING THIS CHAPTER AND DOING THE EXERCISES WILL ENABLE YOU TO:

■ Explore ways that entrepreneurs use computers.

■ Expand your business on the Internet.

TECHNOLOGY*

The Information Age

Smart entrepreneurs take advantage of the latest breakthroughs in business technology. Technology is science that has been applied to industry or commerce. You are probably aware of the rapid improvements in computer technology. This phenomenon has been called the Information Revolution, because it has made it so much easier for data to be communicated around the world by telephone or over the Internet.

Computers

The computer is a very helpful tool for the entrepreneur. Even the least expensive model can help you:

---

* Thanks to Mike Caslin, Duane Moyer, Nick Gleason for assistance with material in this chapter.

- Create stationery and business cards.

- Type professional-looking letters and correct your spelling before you print them out.

- Keep financial records.

- Make flyers and posters.

- Keep a mailing list of customers and print labels for mailing.

If you can't access a computer in your home or neighborhood, ask a teacher or counselor if it's possible to use one at school. The local library may be a place to gain access to a computer. In addition, some communities have nonprofit technology centers that are available to the public.

Protect Your Computer Data

Collections of information are called **data**. Important business data on your computer might include mailing lists, invoices, letters, and financial records. If anything happens to your computer, you could lose valuable data. You'll need to protect your computer from:

1. Power surges or outages. A "power surge" can send too much electricity through your computer and "fry" the circuits. Plug all your computer equipment into a power strip that has a surge protector. Another safety feature, Uninterruptible Power Supply (UPS), may be purchased in computer stores. This is a type of battery backup that enables you, should the electricity fail, to shut down your computer safely without loss of data.

2. Computer viruses. A virus is a computer program that can attach itself to your software files and hard drive and destroy them. Safeguard your computer input with virus-protection software, such as programs from Norton or McAfee.

3. Disk failure. Hard drives can "crash," destroying valuable data. To prevent this, save everything you do by transferring it to backup disks.

Computer Software Programs

There are software programs for just about every business need you might have. But where's the best place to buy them? Office supply and computer stores will carry most of the software you want, but sometimes the best prices can be found elsewhere.

Mail-order companies offer some of the best deals on computer software. Some popular ones are:

- MacWarehouse/MicroWarehouse: (800) 397-8508 to order a catalog.

- The PC Zone: (800) 258-2088.

A lot of software is available for free or at a low cost on the Internet. Many software companies offer their programs directly to customers as **shareware**. Although free of charge, shareware usually does not include upgrades or technical support, so that if a problems develops, it may be difficult to solve.

Most good anti-virus programs will "monitor" the installation of any software including shareware. However, if you install software without an anti-virus program being present, make sure to run a virus check as soon as possible.

Several software packages designed to help you write a business plan are on the market. Some are:

- Biz Builder

- Tim Berry's Business Plan Toolkit: for Macintosh users

- B-Tools for Windows

- Success, Inc.

Keep in mind that you do not really own the software you use. It is "intellectual property" in the same way that books and music belong to those that create them. That's why when you install software you will be asked to agree not to copy it for anyone else.

The Internet

The **Internet** began in the 1960s as a network of computers created by the Department of Defense so that military leaders could communicate with each other. It became available to the public in the 1970s and presently operates in more than 60 countries and is accessed by millions of people worldwide. It is used daily for sending and receiving *electronic mail* (**e-mail**), obtaining information, and maintaining databases, among many other applications.

Going Online

To go "online," your computer must be equipped with a **modem**. The modem lets your computer send and receive data. You will also need an **ISP**, or Internet Service Provider. Smaller ISP's will simply provide you with the software for direct connection to the Internet. Larger servers, such as America Online or Microsoft Network, give access to the Internet plus a wide range of "extras," such as shopping malls, magazines and newspapers, reference works, chat rooms (where subscribers can "talk" directly with each other), health and fitness advice, classified ads, and other features. Another advantage of the larger ISP's is that they are well packaged and easy to use.

The existence of the Internet has raised a variety of issues regarding privacy and censorship. At present, there is no single governing authority for the Internet, but service providers voluntarily maintain a set of standards.

The World Wide Web

The World Wide Web is a subset of the Internet, made up of documents that include graphics, not just text. To "surf the Web" you need a *web browser*. Most ISP's provide a web browser when you subscribe.

Websites

Web pages are the material you look at while surfing the Web. "Home Pages" are personalized **websites** on the World Wide Web.

Web pages are *hypertext* documents. This means that they combine text with graphics. Web pages are also marked with **hyperlinks**. These are areas on the page that, when clicked on, lead somewhere else — another website, for example, or other pages, graphics, sounds or videos within the website being visited. Web pages have addresses called URLs (Uniform Resource Locators). If a Web page URL starts with "http:" you'll know to expect a hypertext document to appear. Many entrepreneurs design websites for their businesses. That way they can reach customers around the world. To create your own website, you may have to learn HTML (Hypertext Markup Language), although some ISP's offer pre-programmed home pages that are very easy to build even if you don't know HTML. A good resource for learning HTML is the book *HTML for Dummies*.*

The Computer as Equalizing Tool

The Internet, or "Information Superhighway" can be a great equalizing force. It makes vast amounts of information available to anyone with access to the Internet (for which only a modem is necessary), and can help the new entrepreneur compete with established businesses. The "Information Age" is still just beginning. More and more, people will have immediate access to the same information resources. Information is crucial to business. The right information at the right time can mean the difference between success and failure.

---

* Tittel, E., et al. *HTML for Dummies*, 3rd Edition (Hungry Minds, 1997).

Instant Financial News

Like many other publications, *The Wall Street Journal* is available online, as are other business publications such as, *Inc.* magazine, *Entrepreneur, Business Week,* and *Barron's.*

If you are interested in *investing* (buying stocks and bonds), you will love the Internet because you can get instant information about your investments. America Online provides financial information updated continuously during market hours. Charles Schwab and E*TRADE^SM are two electronic services through which you can buy and sell stocks and other investments online. A popular website dedicated to educating small investors is The Motley Fool. It is informative and well-written and demystifies investing. It also has some special services for young people. The Microsoft Investor website offers a free stock-tracking device with graphs.

The Internet as Business Opportunity

There are three types of businesses that can be operated over the Internet:

1. Selling goods, services, and information,

2. Selling advertising space (particularly if you're getting many "hits," that is, visits to your website), on a daily basis, and

3. Charging a subscription fee to those wanting to visit your site.

You can also use the Internet to find the best deals. Many Internet businesses offer products at low prices by cutting out the wholesaler and selling direct. This could really improve your product/distribution chain.

The Internet allows you to reach far beyond your immediate geographical area for potential customers. Selling collectibles (such as baseball cards and stamps) is a good Internet business because the collectors of these items are usually spread all across the country. "Information businesses" are another possibility. If you have access to a facility such as the New York Public Library, you could do valuable research for those who are too far away to make use of this resource. Whatever you choose, make sure you understand government regulations and tax laws relating to the Internet.

E-mail

As discussed earlier, e-mail is electronic mail. These are messages sent between computers via the Internet. If you join a large ISP, like America Online or Microsoft Network, you will get an e-mail account. If your ISP does not provide e-mail, you can get it free from Yahoo (http://www.yahoo.com) or at www.hotmail.com. Set up an e-mail address for your business from the beginning. It's a great way for customers to reach you with questions or orders. You can also use e-mail to stay in touch with your suppliers. Just be careful not to annoy anyone with e-mail promoting your business. Annoying advertising on the Net is called "spam." Sending spam can result in your e-mail inbox being jammed with "flames," which are angry e-mails.

Newsgroups

Newsgroups are public message boards that usually focus on a particular topic. Sending e-mail or posting messages on newsgroups can be used to contact sales prospects and keep in touch with customers you already have, but you must use these methods carefully. In the "real world," you can search for sales prospects by distributing flyers or cold-calling people on a list. Most newsgroups do not appreciate spam, and members may respond angrily.

Becoming involved in a newsgroup can lead to increased business, if it is handled properly. Let's say you sell photographic supplies and you hear about an interesting newsgroup for photographers. Don't blitz it with ads for your business! Instead, before posting any messages, observe for awhile. Just read messages for a week and get a feel for the discussions taking place. Once you feel comfortable, try posting a message such as the following:

> *The discussion this week on the advantages of the new Nikon mini-camera was very interesting. I'm in the photography supply business and I'm looking for new items to add to my website. I have already posted articles from* Advanced Photography *magazine and gotten tips from some of my clients. Does anyone have any ideas for other useful information I could post?*
>
> *Thanks!*
>
> *Sandra Bowling*
>
> *PhotoSupply Online*
> *http://www.photosupply.com*
> *e-mail: photosupply@aol.com*
> *The Photographer's Source for Supplies and Advice*

Because this is not a sales pitch, no one in the newsgroup should take offense, and it could certainly attract some potential customers to your website.

Whether you use e-mail or newsgroups, it is important that you never give out personal information such as a home phone number or address. Providing an e-mail address and business phone number, separate from your home phone number, will enable customers to get in touch with you.

The Electronic Storefront

No matter what type of business you have, opening a website called an **electronic storefront** could introduce your business to customers all over the world. Through this "store" you can display your catalog, price lists, and other information.

You'll need to decide whether you want to create a store yourself or use an online service storefront. An online service storefront offers many advantages — online services typically build your storefronts for you, and promotion and advertisements are part of the deal to help make subscribers aware of your business. On the other hand, if you put a store up on the Internet yourself, you will have more control over what it looks like and where it is located, and your potential customers won't be limited to the subscribers of the online service.

One of the smartest ways to set up an electronic storefront on the Internet is to hire a website designer to do it. Otherwise, you could spend a lot of time and money figuring out how to do the necessary programming.

At the present time, electronic storefronts are almost always created as websites. However, two "servers" that have been used in the past, and which you should be familiar with, are:

- FTP (File Transfer Protocol) server. This allows you to store text and graphic files that customers can retrieve. The problem with an FTP is that customers have to download your files to look at them at all. Since this takes time, it can discourage people with only a mild interest in your business. Also, FTP sites are very expensive to set up, and are a good option only if you are selling to a community with built-in interest in your business.

- Gopher server. A gopher site stores text-only information that customers can view while surfing the Web. They don't have to download it. More people have had access to Gopher technology than to FTP. On the other hand, pictures of your product cannot be shown on a Gopher site.

Books about the Internet

Some helpful resource books include: *The Internet for Dummies*, by J.R. Levine (Hungry Minds, Inc., 2000); *Dern's Internet Guide for New Users*, by D.P. Dern (Computing McGraw-Hill, 1997); *The Internet Companion: a Beginner's Guide to Global Networking*, by Tracy LaQuey (Addison-Wesley, 1994), and *Whole Internet: User's Guide and Catalog-Academic Edition*, by Ed Krol (Wadsworth, 1995). Since the technology is constantly evolving, however, entrepreneurs should keep their eyes open for the latest books and magazines about information technology. Visit your local library or bookstore regularly.

Bill Gates: Opening the Windows on Software

The most successful entrepreneurs love risk, adventure, and possess great vision and drive. Bill Gates has these qualities in abundance. He has used them, along with his formidable brainpower, to build Microsoft Corporation into one of the most powerful players in the computer industry and made himself one of the richest people in the world in the process.

Steven Jobs and Stephen Wozniak, the founders of Apple Computer, were the kings of personal computer hardware. In the 1970s, software, the programs that make computers do things, were not considered so important. Software was not considered "interesting."

Gates's great insight was to commercialize software. He and his company of computer programmers designed software that made computers do things ordinary people wanted them to do: calculate budgets, edit manuscripts, be able to design graphics, and make graphs and charts. Gates made software fun and user-friendly. And the consumer responded enthusiastically.

Sleepless Nights

While still a student at Harvard, Gates worked on improving a software program called BASIC, with his friend Paul Allen. BASIC was a program that a lot of computer programmers were trying to improve, so that it could be used by non-experts. Gates and Allen approached a company called MITS, which had developed a computer called the Altair that was looking for a software program for its "people's computer."

The two partners spent eight sleepless weeks until they developed a BASIC program that would run the Altair computer. When MITS tested their program, it worked, and Gates and Allen began an association with the company. Gates dropped out of Harvard and in 1975 he and Allen founded Microsoft.

By the following year, Microsoft had hired other talented programmers and landed two big customers who needed software to go with their hardware: National Cash Register (NCR) and General Electric. Later, Microsoft landed a contract with IBM. That Gates was able to keep the copyright to the software that IBM was using was an important key to Microsoft's future growth.

By 1983 Microsoft's revenues had reached $34 million and it was employing more than 200 people. The age of the personal computer had arrived and people needed software to operate their new computers. Microsoft had developed a reputation for hiring the best and the brightest and getting them to put forth their best efforts. The environment in the company was both casual and a little offbeat. The youthful employees dressed in jeans and sneakers and engaged in plastic sword fights in the halls. Gates himself developed a reputation for being somewhat eccentric.

Throughout, Gates did not lose sight of his goals. His vision led to the development of Windows, a comprehensive program that was easy to understand. Virtually any-one who could read and type could follow the simple on-screen instructions. Gates unveiled Microsoft Windows 3.0 in May 1990, before reporters, business analysts, and industry watchers. He was just 34 and already a billionaire. Microsoft was now also directly taking on IBM, which was developing its own competing operating system, called OS/2.

Gates was taking a big risk but it paid off. In just two years, Microsoft's equity value was worth $22 billion, making Gates's personal worth more than $7 billion. Microsoft programmers have continued to work on bringing improved programs to the public.

Microsoft grew significantly in the 1990s, posting revenues of $22.9 billion in 2000 and employing 39,000 people. Gates himself has stated that when he reaches retirement age he will donate most of his personal fortune to worthwhile charities.

Chapter 21 Review

N O T E : The exercises printed below can be found in the corresponding chapter of the NFTE MODULE 1 WORKBOOK that came with your textbook. Please write your answers there. If you do not have a workbook, write your answers on a separate sheet of paper.

Critical Thinking about ... Technology for the Entrepreneur

1. Do you have access to a computer? If so, list five ways you could use it for your business. If you don't have a computer, write a plan for how you intend to get access to one.

2. What kind of newsgroups do you think would be valuable for the type of business you are starting? If you have access to the Internet, go online and find three newsgroups that would be good resources for your business.

3. Do you think it would be a good idea to create a website for your business? Why or why not?

4. List three dangers that can threaten computer data. How would you protect your data from being damaged?

Getting the Facts

1. What's the main difference between an FTP server and a Gopher server?

2. What is a hyperlink?

3. What are "flames"?

4. List three types of businesses entrepreneurs could start over the Internet.

5. What three items does your computer need to communicate on the Internet?

Chapter 21 Review

Using New Words

data
electronic storefront
e-mail
hyperlink
Internet
ISP
modem
newsgroup
shareware
website

On a separate sheet of paper, identify the vocabulary term that completes each sentence.

1. Entrepreneurs can store _____ like customer addresses and supplier information on their computers.

2. To access the Internet with your computer you need to have a _____ so you can connect over a phone line with your _____.

3. If you join an online _____, be careful not to post any _____ that seems like an advertisment for your business, as members will find that annoying.

4. The _____ is a network made up of computers from all over the world communicating with each other.

5. If you set up a _____ for your business, you will be able to reach customers all over the world. An _____ will let you buy and sell over the Web as if you owned a regular store.

6. A _____ is a word or phrase on a Web page that is underlined, indicating that if you click on it you will be linked to a new page.

Exploration

1. Go online and visit some software suppliers, such as Staples or Mac Warehouse. Find five software packages you think would be useful for your business.

2. Using your imagination, write a paragraph describing what you think will be possible with the Internet in 20 years.

3. Do you have any favorite electronic storefronts on the Internet? If not, do some exploring until you find three you like. Would you order a product from the Internet? Why or why not? What would your concerns be?

Review

Chapter Summary

I. There are exciting new technological advances in the computer industry that are affecting this country and the entire world.

II. Entrepreneurs can take advantage of this "information superhighway."

    A. Computers can be important to the young entrepreneur and can be an important "equalizer" when competing with larger businesses.

    B. With a computer and modem, one can access the Internet with an Internet service provider (ISP).

        1. Internet "newsgroups" can supply a wide variety of useful information.

        2. The World Wide Web, combining sound and image, can be used for marketing your business.

III. These technological breakthroughs give beginning entrepreneurs the means to get information formerly available only to larger, established companies, and reach customers around the world very cheaply.

A Business for the Young Entrepreneur: Baby-sitting Service

Parents of young children are always searching for responsible baby-sitters. You probably have friends who baby-sit. Why not start a baby-sitting service?

Each week, have the baby-sitters who work for your service call to tell you when they can work. In return for matching baby-sitters with jobs, you will earn a commission. A commission is a percentage of each sale. You could charge ten percent, for example.

Let's say the Smith family needs a baby-sitter on Friday night for four hours. You look on your list and see that Sara can work Friday night and lives near the Smiths. Mrs. Smith agrees to pay Sara five dollars per hour. That means Sara will earn:

$5 per hour x 4 hours = $20

Sara pays you ten percent of that twenty dollars because you got her the job. Here's how you figure your commission:

1. "Percentage" means "out of a hundred." Ten percent (10%), means ten out of a hundred. Divide one hundred into ten.

$$\frac{10}{100} = 10\%$$

2. Another way to express any percentage as a number is simply to move the decimal point two places to the left (this is the same as dividing the percentage by 100).

    20% percent becomes .20

    45% becomes .45

    10.5% becomes .105

3. To figure your commission, multiply the percentage, expressed as a number, by the total sale.

    Commission on Sara's job = $20 x .10 = $2.00

    Your commission is two dollars.

Remember that time is money.

— Benjamin Franklin, American
statesman, inventor and writer

KEY OBJECTIVES

**READING THIS CHAPTER AND DOING
THE EXERCISES WILL ENABLE YOU TO:**

- Write a business memo.
- Write a business letter.
- Use "cc:" to send copies of
  memos or letters.
- Remember to proofread
  business correspondence
  carefully.

BUSINESS COMMUNICATION

Time Is Money

Entrepreneurs need to move fast — and communicate even faster. If your business is
making furniture and the lumber stores in your community decide to compete with
each other by cutting prices, you will need to know about it so you can stock up on
wood. Are you on the e-mail and fax lists for your suppliers so you get up-to-the-
minute information from them?

Business Cards

Business cards display your name and that of your business. They should also show
your mailing address, phone and fax numbers, website URL and e-mail address. A
business card can also include a short catchy phrase that describes your business, such
as "For Sound Advice" if you are running a stereo-repair business.

Businesspeople exchange business cards when they meet. This is called networking. You can hand out your card to suppliers and others you do business with so they will know how to reach you. You can also give your card to potential customers you meet outside your business. Keep a stack of your cards at your business for customers to take with them when they leave.

Collect the business cards you receive in a rolodex, where you can keep them in alphabetical order for easy reference.

The Business Memo

Have you heard the expression "Time is money"? It's especially true for the entrepreneur. You don't have time to read, or write, long letters when you need to make a point. One of the best ways to save time is through the use of the business **memo**.

The word "memo" is short for *memorandum*, from the Latin word meaning "to be remembered." A memo is usually a brief, clearly written note from one businessperson to another. It is usually written or typed on plain paper. The purpose of the memo is to inform or remind the reader of an idea, suggestion, observation, or request from the writer.

A memo is most often sent **interoffice**, that is, from one person to another within the same company. Memos are sent to business associates, not customers. On occasion, memos are sent from a person in one company to someone in another. Today, it is common practice to send such memos by *facsimile* (**fax**). Ideally, a memo should be written, sent, and received on the same day.

You may be wondering, why not just telephone the person, instead of going to the trouble of writing a memo? The answer is that a memo provides you with proof of the communication.

If you call up to share important information, they, or you, can forget you called. Also, *nobody* can remember *exactly* what was said in a conversation.

Have you ever had someone deny that you told them something when you were sure you did? This can be very annoying in one's personal life, but in business such a misunderstanding could cost you money, your job, or your reputation. With a memo in front of both of you, no one will "forget" who said what and when.

Whenever you write a memo, make a copy for your files. Sometimes a copy is sent to others who may be concerned with the subject discussed.

How to Write a Business Memo

A business memo is usually composed of the following parts:

1. A heading at the top of the page:

    To: (Name of addressee)

    From: (Name of sender)

    Date: (Date memo is written)

    Re: (Briefly what memo is about)

    Many businesses have preprinted memo stationery with the above heading.

2. An introduction, in which the subject of the memo is introduced.

3. The body of the memo, where the main points are discussed as concisely as possible.

4. The *conclusion*, where the sender closes the memo with a polite restatement of the main point.

5. *Signature or initials*. A memo differs from a business letter in that a full, formal signature, including your title, is not necessary. If you know the person to whom you are sending the memo fairly well, you might just sign your first name or put initials next to it in the heading.

    For more formal memos, write in your full name.

6. A *"cc:"* (pronounced "cee-cee") stands for "carbon copy," though now usually a photocopy. This is used only when copies of the memo will be sent to other people. For example, if you've written a memo to George Louis, but you want your partner, Bill Jones, to see it too, you would type (in the lower left-hand corner of the page):

cc: Bill Jones or
cc: B. Jones *(if Mr. Louis knows who Bill Jones is).*

This lets Mr. Louis know that you keep your partner informed of business details. After you sign the original memo, photocopy it. Keep one for your files and give one to Bill Jones.

Here is an example of a memo.

(Notice how the first letter of each line begins at the left-hand margin.)

To: C.J. Meenan
From: Darnell Jones *D.J.*
Date: April 1, 2001
RE: Request for business financing

I am hereby requesting a venture loan of $200 to start my business, "Darnell's Candy." I would use the money in the following way:

1. Business cards: $22
2. Advertising (posters and flyers): $20
3. Registering business at County Clerk's Office: $30
4. Telephone-answering machine: $50
5. Candy inventory: $78
Total: $200

I look forward to hearing from you.

cc: S. Mariotti

Memos effectively convey a sense of urgency. Perhaps that is why Prime Minister Winston Churchill sent this memo to the head of the British Navy in 1940 during World War II.

To: The First Lord of the Admiralty

From: Winston Churchill
Date: April 1940
Re: The Preparedness of the Royal Navy

Please send me today, on no more than one sheet of paper, your evaluation of the strengths and weaknesses of the Royal Navy and how the weaknesses may be remedied.

This seemingly simple request was made at a time when England was in danger of being invaded by Hitler's Germany. It was not a simple request at all, and Churchill knew it. He wanted his admirals to look accurately and honestly at their resources because the country was in a life-or-death situation.

As Churchill's famous memo did, good business memos cut through the "baloney."

The Business Letter

Like the business memo, the business letter should be concise and clear. Its tone is usually more formal and its form is somewhat different.

A business letter should be typed on stationery, ideally on **letterhead** (stationery with printed name, address, phone number(s) and business logo). Business letters are used for first contact or when a serious matter needs to be discussed. Always keep a copy of every business letter you send.

There are two basic business letter formats:

- Your name and address, the date, and your signature flush right. Place the address of the person to whom you are writing flush left. A variation on this format is to center your name and address at the top of the page as if on letterhead.

- All addresses, the date and your signature flush left (lined up against the left margin).

Notice how the business letter, unlike the memo, provides full address and title information for both the sender and the receiver. Also, the salutation or greeting is followed by a colon (:) not a comma (,). A comma follows a greeting only in a personal, non-business letter. A personal letter would begin "Dear Chris," for example. The note "Encl." in the lower-left-hand corner indicates that the reader of the letter should look for an enclosure in the envelope; in this case, Darnell's check to Mr. Meenan.

Here is a letter from the young entrepreneur using the traditional format.

Darnell's Candy
235 East 13th Street
New York, NY 10009
(212) 555-3210

April 7, 2001

Mr. C.J. Meenan, Vice President
Meenan and Associates, Inc.
116 East 59th Street, Suite 3
New York, NY 10021

Dear Mr. Meenan:

I am writing to thank you for approving the venture loan of $200. I have used the money, as we discussed when we met, to start Darnell's Candy.

Business is going very well. I am enclosing my first payment to you of $50 and expect to be able to continue paying you $50 for the next three weeks, which will be payment in full.

Thank you again for giving me the chance to start my own business.

Sincerely,

Darnell Jones

Darnell Jones,
President

encl: $50 check
cc: Steve Mariotti

Here is the same letter using the flush-left format.

Darnell's Candy
235 East 13th Street
New York, NY 10009
(212) 555-3210

Mr. C.J. Meenan, Vice President
Meenan and Associates, Inc.
116 East 59th Street, Suite 3
New York, NY 10021

April 7, 2001

Dear Mr. Meenan:

I am writing to thank you for approving the venture loan of $200. I have used the money, as we discussed when we met, to start Darnell's Candy.

Business is going very well. I am enclosing my first payment to you of $50 and expect to be able to continue paying you $50 for the next three weeks, which will be payment in full.

Thank you again for giving me the chance to start my own business.

Sincerely,

Darnell Jones

Darnell Jones,
President

Encl: $50 check
cc: Steve Mariotti

Proofread Carefully

In both memos and business letters, making grammatical errors and spelling mistakes can lower the respect the reader of your memo or letter has for you. Proofread all your business communications carefully before you send them. It's a good idea to have someone else proofread them, too.

Electronic Communication

The skills you develop from writing business memos and letters will serve you in good stead no matter what kind of business you are in.

Today there are an increasing variety of ways to communicate, including:

- Voice mail — a phone system that allows the leaving and receiving of messages through phones not on the users' premises.

- Fax — machines that send printed material over phone lines.

- E-mail — messages sent over phone lines between computers.

Whether you're leaving a message on an answering machine or a voice-mail system, sending a fax or using electronic computer mail, you'll still need to use good grammar and spelling. People are more willing to do business with an entrepreneur who can express him or herself briefly and correctly.

Memos are a great way to save time and prevent confusion.

Chapter 22 Review

NOTE: The exercises printed below can be found in the corresponding chapter of the NFTE MODULE 1 WORKBOOK that came with your textbook. Please write your answers there. If you do not have a workbook, write your answers on a separate sheet of paper.

Critical Thinking about ... Business Communication

1. Write a memo for each subject below.

   Memo 1) You received A's on all your exams, but your teacher gave you a B+ for the class because you were late four times. Write a memo to the teacher about your grade.

   Memo 2) Your school is hosting a picnic and you would like to supply the soda because you can buy cans for fifty cents and sell them at the picnic for a dollar. Write a memo to an adult relative or mentor requesting a loan of $100.

   Memo 3) You have a part-time job but would like to take off a day to attend a track meet. Write a memo to your boss asking permission to miss one day of work.

2. Proofread the memos you have written, then have a friend proofread them too. Did your friend find any errors you had missed?

3. What information would you put on your business card? Do you have a motto or slogan?

Getting the Facts

1. How soon after it is written should a memo be received?

2. What advantage does communicating by memo have over the telephone?

3. What is the difference between the signature for a memo and a business letter?

4. What does "cc:" stand for?

5. What's one thing that should be done with both memos and business letters?

Exploration

The Rumor Game:

Play this game with the whole class to test the efficiency of verbal communication: Have one person make up a sentence, write it down, and then whisper it into the ear of the person sitting next to him/her. Then have that person pass it on until the message has gone through the whole class. Have the last person who hears the sentence say it aloud. Is it the same as the original sentence?

Review

Chapter 22 Review

Using New Words

fax
interoffice
letterhead
memo

On a separate sheet of paper, identify the vocabulary term that completes each sentence.

First, Darnell Jones sent a _____ to Mr. Meenan asking for a loan.

He could have sent the memo by mail or by _____. On April 7, Darnell wrote a formal business letter on _____ to Mr. Meenan and enclosed his first payment. Since he and Mr. Meenan do not work in the same office, Darnell did not use _____ mail.

Chapter Summary

I. Entrepreneurs need to stay in constant, fast communication with suppliers, customers and other business connections.

    A. Always carry business cards to hand out to other businesspeople and customers.

    B. Keep a stack of business cards near the entrance to your business or next to the cash register.

    C. Make sure all your business contacts have your business card and know how to reach you quickly.

II. Business memos save time and increase productivity.

    A. A memo is a note between businesspeople.

    B. A memo provides proof of a communication.

III. A business memo has six parts:

    1. heading
    2. introduction
    3. body
    4. conclusion
    5. signature or initials
    6. "cc:" (if appropriate)

IV. The business letter is more formal and looks different from a memo.

    A. It is written on letterhead stationery.

    B. It always includes a formal signature and title.

V. All business communications should be carefully proofread.

    A. All business communication should be concise and clear.

    B. Use correct grammar and spelling to make the best impression.

We started off with a very idealistic perspective — that doing something with the highest quality, doing it right the first time, would really be cheaper than having to go back and do it again.

— Stephen Wozniak, co-founder of Apple Computer

KEY OBJECTIVES

READING THIS CHAPTER AND DOING THE EXERCISES WILL ENABLE YOU TO:

■ Explain why quality leads to profit.

■ Discuss W. Edwards Deming's ideas about the relationship between quality and profit.

■ List ten ways to improve quality in your business.

■ Apply the Japanese concept of kaizen to your life.

QUALITY

Profit Comes From Quality

The **quality** of a product is its degree of excellence. The consumer is usually willing to pay more for quality because:

- A quality product will last longer.
- A quality service will be more satisfying.

"Quality" is the buzzword of American business in the new millennium. "Total quality control" is the subject of many business-magazine articles.

Quality was not always considered such an important concept by American corporations. For many years, American business focused on short-term profits. Less attention was given to the quality of the product.

In the early 1950s, though, an American named W. Edwards Deming argued that the quality of the product was the very essence of business. His position was that in the long run it was cheaper to produce quality goods. Deming insisted that profits came from quality.

This simple notion was actually quite profound: If profits come from quality, then a business that focuses on improving quality should find profits increasing as a result. Deming's theory suggested that *a business's goal should be quality, not short-term profits.*

Deming Goes to Japan

Deming's revolutionary concept was ignored by the American business community, so he went to Japan. Japan was rebuilding its economy after the destruction of World War II.

In those days Japan was notorious for the poor quality of its manufactured products. The phrase "Made in Japan" was found on cheap toys and gift items. People sometimes used it to refer to anything poorly made.

Deming gave lectures to business leaders in Japan that totally changed the Japanese philosophy of manufacturing. The Japanese took Deming's advice to heart and focused on making high-quality products, not short-term profits.

Today, Japanese products are known for their *excellent* quality. Deming's thesis that *profits follow quality* has been proven correct. The quality of Japanese cars broke the American automakers' control of the market. Today, millions of Americans buy Japanese cars.

The Japanese government presents annual Deming Prizes to Japanese companies that have demonstrated the very highest standards of quality control. To win one of these awards is one of the greatest honors a Japanese company can achieve.

Many American businesspeople have traveled to Japan to study why Japanese companies have become so successful. They have brought Deming's ideas back home, where they are finally being adopted by American businesses.

Why Quality Is Actually Cheaper

A high-quality product is actually cheaper than one made by cutting corners, for the following reasons:

1. *You don't have to fix it.*

2. You get the most valuable advertising possible — your satisfied customers tell others how good the product is, bringing new customers to your business.

3. You earn *customer loyalty*. Quality builds a base of repeat customers. Repeat customers generate profits.

This vision of quality is expressed as **continuous improvement**. The idea is that continually seeking to improve quality will steadily increase profits. This concept is expressed in Japanese as ***kaizen*** (pronounced "KYE-zen"). Many American companies now teach continuous improvement to their employees.

Start with Quality

Build the foundation of your business on quality from the very beginning. When you are estimating your start-up costs, for example, you might be tempted to cut them by getting the cheapest possible items. If you are running a delivery business and you buy an old van cheaply, however, it might cost you a lot in repairs in the long run. Start with the best possible quality you can afford.

Ethics

Ethics are rules that govern how we treat each other. Another aspect of *kaizen* is that both the suppliers and employees must be treated ethically.

- Suppliers will not be loyal to a company that deals with them unfairly.

- Employees won't focus on continuous improvement unless they feel good about their company.

The Japanese try to make employees feel that their interests and the interests of the company are one and the same. American companies are realizing that this is a good idea and are using this approach to improve relations between workers and management.

Ten Ways to Improve Quality:*

1. *Adopt a philosophy of continual improvement.* Create, write, and implement a motto to inspire your continual commitment to improvement.

2. *Be consistent.* Don't attempt one big effort, but constantly look for small improvements.

3. *Do it right the first time.* This is cheaper than having to fix a job later and possibly irritate and lose a customer.

4. *Develop long-term relationships with suppliers based on loyalty and trust*, even if it means not getting the lowest price every time. Some sacrifice of profit now can be repaid many times over when you need help or credit, and the supplier helps you because he or she has become your friend.

5. *Focus on quality* in production and customer service.

6. Have a *training program* for yourself and your employees.

7. *Get rid of fear.* Your employees and customers should not be afraid to point out ways to improve your business.

8. *Don't ask for perfect performance* from your employees (or yourself). Instead, work a little smarter and better every day.

9. Focus on the quality of what your business does, *not the quantity*.

10. Quality is everybody's job. *Ask for comments and help* from employees, customers and suppliers, and provide incentives for continued improvement in quality.

Debbi Fields: "Good Enough Never Is."

Debbi Fields was only nineteen years old when she opened her first cookie store. Fields knew nothing about running a company, but she'd been baking cookies since she was thirteen. She believed that if her cookies were made from quality ingredients and were served with a smile, people would buy them. Fields' commitment to quality and customer service was an excellent business strategy. By age thirty, she owned more than five hundred Mrs. Fields Cookies stores in twenty-five states and five foreign countries.

---

* These ten suggestions have been adapted by the National Foundation for Teaching Entrepreneurship from the works of W. Edwards Deming and others.

Fields always put quality before profit. She refused to substitute margarine-butter blends for pure butter, for example, even though the substitution would have saved the company money.

One day Fields walked into her third store and noticed that the cookies looked flat and overcooked. When she asked the store clerk what he thought of the cookies, he said, "Aw, they're good enough." Fields silently slid each tray of cookies into the garbage — losing about five hundred dollars worth of cookies. She told the clerk, "Good enough never is." That's been the motto of Mrs. Fields Cookies ever since.

In 1984, Fields began to expand internationally by opening stores in Japan, Hong Kong, and Australia. Instead of hiring expensive consultants to tell her what type of cookies would sell best in different countries, Fields conducted hands-on market research. She simply traveled to each country, opened a store, and began giving away cookies. She would ask customers what they preferred. Fields learned that, in some countries people preferred dark-chocolate to milk-chocolate chips, or liked macadamia nuts better than pecans. Her new stores were successful because Fields used quality ingredients to make the cookies people told her they would buy.

Chapter 23 Review

Critical Thinking about ... Quality

1. Write a motto for the business you want to start.

2. What are two reasons why a customer might be willing to pay more for quality?

3. What was W. Edwards Deming's thesis (argument)?

4. What are your own personal ethics? State each one in a sentence.

Getting the Facts

1. What is the name of the quality prize given out in Japan?

2. What happened in Japan to convince American entrepreneurs to pay more attention to quality?

3. What does the Japanese word *kaizen* mean?

4. What are three reasons why the entrepreneur should focus on quality?

Using New Words

continuous improvement
ethics
kaizen
quality

Write a paragraph describing how you intend to apply the principles of ethics and quality to your business. Use all the vocabulary words.

Exploration

Count how many commercials use the word "quality" during one hour of television. Count how many use the word "price." Report your findings to the class. Explain what they reveal about Americans' attitudes about quality.

In Your Opinion

Discuss with a group:

When you buy something, are you willing to pay more for better quality?

Do you care more about quality or price when making a purchase?

Review

Chapter Summary

I. Profits stem from quality.

A. Traditionally, American business focused on profit.

B. Deming's focus on quality was initially ignored in the United States.

II. In Japan, Deming's theory that quality leads to profits helped rebuild a war-torn economy.

A. Japan's auto industry used Deming's principles to compete with U.S. automakers.

B. Japan's success proved Deming's theory.

III. *Kaizen* is the commitment to continuous improvement.

A. Continuous improvement means trying, every day, to improve the quality of a product or service.

B. *Kaizen* includes striving for excellence in relationships with employees, suppliers, and customers.

A Business for the Young Entrepreneur: Clothing Boutique

Did you know that you can buy fashionable clothes for half the price you would pay at the mall if you buy from a wholesaler? Of course, to buy from a wholesale merchant you have to have a business. Why not start a clothing boutique?

You know what kind of clothes your friends love. The best place to find these clothes wholesale is in a wholesaling district of a large city. You can buy the latest fashions wholesale and sell them from your home at a lower price than the stores at the mall charge.

The key to making this a successful business is market research. Ask your friends the following questions:

- What size do you wear?
- What kind of clothing would you be interested in buying?

The secret to getting ahead is getting started.

— Sally Berger

KEY OBJECTIVES

READING THIS CHAPTER AND DOING THE EXERCISES WILL ENABLE YOU TO:

■ Prepare a monthly cash flow statement.

■ Guard against losing your business because you have run out of cash.

■ Manage your cash flow.

CASH FLOW

Entrepreneurs Use Three Basic Financial Statements to Track Their Businesses:

1. Income statement

2. Cash flow statement

3. Balance sheet

Chapter 4 explained how you can create a financial statement that will give a clear picture of your business. But an entrepreneur can't just use an income statement. Once you start running a business you'll notice that, sometimes, even when the income statement says you are making a profit, you have no money! This can happen because there is often a time lag between making a sale and actually getting paid. If you sell something and the customer promises to pay you in one week, the sale goes onto the income statement — but you don't actually have the cash yet.

Cash is the lifeblood of your business. Run out of cash and your business will soon be finished. Without cash on hand, you can find yourself unable to pay important bills, even while the income statement says you are earning a profit. That lag can be a dangerous period for your business. If you can't pay the phone company and your phone gets cut off, it doesn't matter that the income statement says you are profitable!

You cannot guide your business's daily operation using the income statement alone. You also will need to use a monthly cash flow statement to track the cash going in and out of the business. *Cash flow is the difference between the money you take in and the money you spend.*

Cash Flow

In Chapter 16 you learned to use an accounting journal to keep track of the money your business earns and spends each day. This will help you keep track of your **cash flow**. One measure of your cash flow is the cash balance in your journal.

In order to avoid getting caught without enough cash to pay your bills, follow these three rules:

1. Collect cash as soon as possible. When you make a sale, try to get paid on the spot.

2. Pay your bills on time, but as late as possible within the time frame you agreed upon with your supplier. Most bills come with a due date but you don't have to pay it the day it arrives in your mailbox. Never pay a bill after the due date, however, without getting permission from the supplier first.

3. Check on your cash balance every day. Always know how much cash you have on hand.

The Cyclical Nature of Cash Flow

The cash flow statement records inflows and outflows of cash when they occur. If a sale is made in June, but the customer doesn't pay until August, the income statement will show the sale in June. If you only looked at the income statement, you might think that you had more cash to spend than you really did. The cash flow statement won't show the sale until August, when the cash "flows" into the business.

In addition, cash flow is **cyclical** for many businesses. The amount of cash flowing in may depend on the time of year. A flower store will have a lot of cash coming in around Mother's Day and Valentine's Day, but may have very little coming in during the fall. A college campus bookstore will have to spend a lot of cash before September to buy books for resale to students for the new semester. At that time the business will have very little spare cash. In contrast, it will have a lot of cash coming in during the following month or two as students buy books for their courses.

The phone company or the bank will not care whether you will have a lot of cash coming in over the next three months; they will want their regular monthly payments. When you write your business plan, include a "seasonality scenario" describing your expectations for seasonal changes in your cash flow.

Reading a Cash Flow Statement

Below is a simple cash flow statement for Jason's T-Shirts, the business from Chapter 16. The first section of the statement records all sources of income. These are cash *inflows*, or *receipts*. (Here the word receipt does not mean the same thing as the slip of paper you get when you buy something — those receipts are proof of purchase.)

The next section reports cash *outflows* or *disbursements* that must be made that month — the phone bill, cost of goods sold, salaries, etc.

The last section shows the net change in cash flow. This tells the entrepreneur whether the business had a positive or negative cash flow that month. You can have a lot of sales and still go out of business if you don't have enough cash coming in to cover your monthly cash outflows. The cash flow statement is essentially the business's analysis of cash position.

Cash Flow Statement for Jason's T-Shirts, July 2001

Cash Inflow:

Sales	$ 2,280.00	
Total Cash Inflows	2,280.00	

Cash Outflows:

Cost of Goods Sold	960.00	
Operating Costs*	190.00	
Total Cash Outflow	1,150.00	
Net Cash Flow Before Taxes	1,130.00	($2,280.00–$1,150.00)
Taxes	282.50	
Net Cash Flow	$ 847.50	($1,130.00–$282.50)

The Cash Flow Equation: Cash Flow = Receipts — Disbursements

---

* Remember to add back depreciation, as it is a non-cash expense.

Forecasting Cash Flow

As you get your business off the ground, you'll need to prepare monthly cash flow **projections** to make sure there is enough cash coming in to pay your bills. A projection is an educated guess or forecast about the future.

There are two steps to forecasting cash-flow receipts:

Project your receipts from all possible sources. *Remember* — orders are not cash receipts because you cannot guarantee that every order will become cash. Some orders may be cancelled and some customers may not pay. Cash receipts are checks that you know will clear, or credit card orders that have been phoned in, or cash itself.

Subtract expenses you expect to have from these projected cash receipts. Cash expenses are *only* those expenses you will actually have to pay during the projected time period.

How can you be sure that these projections will be accurate? You can't be completely sure, but create them anyway. Review and update them daily.

Risking Your Cash on Inventory

The entrepreneur takes a risk every time he or she spends cash. If you buy inventory, you are taking the risk that no one will buy it at a price that gives you a profit. When Jason bought T-shirts to sell at the flea market, he was taking a risk by tying up his cash in inventory.

There are two other risks with inventory: storage costs and **pilferage**. If you have to pay rent to store your inventory somewhere, you will have to make sure you can sell it at a price that will include storage costs. Pilferage is the stealing of inventory by employees or customers. Barney's, the famous New York clothing store, had a 7% pilferage rate. This was one of the reasons the store went bankrupt.

Finally, if you aren't keeping track of your cash flow statement, you can get caught in a squeeze between your suppliers and your customers. If the suppliers want you to pay for inventory you've purchased and you are short on cash because your customers haven't paid you yet, you could get into trouble with your suppliers. They might not want to give you credit in the future. If you get into a position where you can't pay your suppliers back at all, you could be forced to sell your business to pay them.

The "Burn Rate"

Your **burn rate** is your negative cash flow per month. It is normal to have a negative cash flow for the first few months of your cash flow projections when you start your business. You are likely to spend more than you earn in the beginning stages. That's why you'll want to have a good business plan that attracts investors who are willing to give you money to pay the bills for the first few months!

This negative cash flow is serious and cannot continue for long. Of course, just because you are "burning" cash in the beginning doesn't mean you should forget about cash flow. Use this ratio to figure out how many months of negative cash flow you can cover before you'll go through the cash you currently have available.

$$\frac{\text{Cash on Hand}}{\text{Negative Cash Outflow Per Month}} = \textbf{Number of Months before Cash Runs Out}$$

Chapter 24 Review

NOTE: The exercises printed below can be found in the corresponding chapter of the NFTE MODULE 1 WORKBOOK that came with your textbook. Please write your answers there. If you do not have a workbook, write your answers on a separate sheet of paper.

Critical Thinking about . . . Cash Flow

1. Describe the difference between the income statement and the cash flow statement.

2. Write a "seasonality" scenario for one year for a business you would like to start. Describe how you think the cash flow would be affected during the course of the year.

3. What are three rules for managing your cash?

4. Give an example of a situation where a cash flow crunch could develop and force an entrepreneur to declare bankruptcy.

Getting the Facts

1. What is a "burn rate"? What is the formula for calculating the number of months before you run out of cash?

2. What are the three risks an entrepreneur takes when he or she buys inventory?

3. What are the two steps to projecting cash flow?

Using New Words

burn rate
cash flow
cyclical
pilferage
projection

On a separate sheet of paper, identify the vocabulary term that completes each sentence.

1. The Christmas tree business is _____ because the amount of cash depends on the time of year.

2. A cash flow _____ is an estimate of how cash flow is going to look in the future.

3. _____ is the stealing of inventory by employees or customers.

4. A business that has to spend a lot of money to get started will probably have a high _____.

5. _____ is the difference between the money a business takes in and the money it spends.

Chapter Summary

I. Cash flow is the difference between the money you take in and the money you spend.

    A. Unlike the income statement, the cash flow statement keeps track of the actual cash flowing in and out of the business.

    B. Cash is the lifeblood of your business. Use the cash flow statement to make sure you don't run out of cash and become unable to pay your bills.

II. Your cash flow is the cash balance in your accounting journal.

    A. Collect cash as soon as possible. When you make a sale, try to get paid on the spot.

    B. Pay your bills as late as possible within the time frame you agreed to with your supplier.

    C. Check on your cash balance every day. Always know how much cash you have on hand.

III. Cash flow is cyclical for many businesses.

    A. The amount of cash flowing into a business may depend on the time of year.

    B. When you write your business plan, include a "seasonality scenario" describing your expectations for seasonal changes in your cash flow.

IV. Prepare monthly cash flow projections to make sure there is enough cash coming in to pay your bills.

    A. A projection is a guess or educated forecast about the future.

    B. Project your cash receipts from all possible sources.

    C. Subtract expenses you expect to have from these projected cash receipts.

V. When you spend cash on inventory, you are taking risks.

    A. The risk that no one will buy it at a price that gives you a profit.

    B. Risks of storage and pilferage (employee stealing).

VI. It is normal to have a negative cash flow for the first few months of your cash flow projections when you start your business.

    A. This negative cash flow is called the "burn rate."

    B. To calculate the number of months before cash is out, divide cash on hand by negative cash outflow per month.

Courage is doing what you're afraid to do. There can be no courage unless you're scared.

— Eddie Rickenbacker, pilot and airline executive

KEY OBJECTIVES

READING THIS CHAPTER AND DOING THE EXERCISES WILL ENABLE YOU TO:

- Locate wholesalers in your area.
- Find trade fairs (flea markets) in your area.
- Sell your merchandise at a trade fair.
- Practice selling and negotiating.

FROM THE WHOLESALER'S TO THE TRADE FAIR*

This chapter outlines how to buy products at a wholesaler's and resell them for a profit at a trade fair (flea market). This is a very simple way to begin a business. Hopefully, you will do this on a field trip with your class to a wholesale district or online. This experience will allow you to put into practice many concepts you have studied so far, including sales, and negotiation. Next, you'll sell your inventory at a trade fair or flea market. In the next chapter we'll discuss preparing an income statement and cash flow statement with the records from your trip.

---

* Remember, only go to a trade fair to sell merchandise if you have approval from a parent or guardian.

Finding a Wholesaler

Most businesses are retail businesses that sell directly to the consumer. Wholesalers buy in large quantities from the manufacturer and sell in smaller quantities to retailers.

If you live in a city, there will be wholesale stores you can visit in person. Find them by looking through your local phone company's *Business to Business Guide*. Libraries usually carry these directories.

If you live in a small town or rural area without wholesale suppliers, pick the largest city nearest you and look in its *Business to Business Guide*. You can call wholesalers whose products interest you and order goods through the mail.

You can also look up wholesalers by industry or location in the *American Wholesalers and Distributors Directory*. Your library should have a copy.

Another way to locate wholesalers is to contact the Manufacturers' Agents National Association:

> **Manufacturers' Agents National Association**
> **23016 Millcreek Road**
> **P.O. Box 3467**
> **Laguna Hills, CA 92654**
> **1-877-626-2776**

In addition, most major product lines (sporting goods, candy manufacturers, etc.) have *trade associations* — many of which are located in Washington, D.C. These associations will be happy to tell you about wholesalers in your area.

Selling at a Trade Fair

A trade fair or flea market is an open-air market made up of entrepreneurs who rent space by the day or by the season. Sometimes the space is free, on a first-come, first-served basis.

Traditionally, prices at such events are low. Consumers shopping here are looking for bargains. You can get a list of such markets in any community by calling the local chamber of commerce. It is a great way to gain basic business experience.

Making Change

Before your trade fair field trip, you should practice making change. Try this exercise:

You find the following amount of change in your wallet. What is your total? Calculate your answers on a separate sheet of paper.

4 quarters:

6 dimes:

11 pennies:

5 dollars:

TOTAL:

RULE OF THUMB FOR SELLING AT TRADE FAIRS:
1. Arrive early to get a spot where the most people will see your merchandise.
2. Have plenty of business cards and flyers to give away, even to people who don't buy anything.
3. Display posters or other eye-catching advertisements.
4. Bring plenty of change.
5. Keep track of your merchandise on inventory/record sheets.
6. Write a sales receipt for every sale.
7. Put on your "sales personality" — be outgoing and friendly.

Chapter 25 Review

NOTE: The exercises printed below can be found in the corresponding chapter of the NFTE MODULE 1 WORKBOOK that came with your textbook. Please write your answers there. If you do not have a workbook, write your answers on a separate sheet of paper.

Critical Thinking about . . . Selling at a Trade Fair or Flea Market

1. Call your local chamber of commerce and make a list of trade fairs and open markets in your area.

2. Use a *Business to Business Guide* or *The American Wholesalers and Distributors Directory* to locate wholesalers you could visit or from whom you could order products for resale.

Exploration

Trip to the wholesaler:

After you have purchased inventory at a wholesaler's for your trade fair field trip, write a short essay analyzing your experience. What did you buy? How much did you pay? How well do you think you negotiated?

Use a *Business-to-Business* telephone directory to call two vendors of a product you would like to sell.

Chapter Summary

I. There are several ways to find a wholesaler:

A. Business-to-Business phone books

B. *American Wholesalers and Distributors Directory* (http://www.manaonline.org)

C. Manufacturers' Agents National Association

D. Trade associations

II. A trade fair (flea market) is an open-air market composed of small businesses.

A. It can be an opportunity to promote your own new business venture.

B. There are seven rules of thumb for selling at trade fairs:

1. Arrive early.

2. Give away business cards and flyers.

3. Display posters or other eye-catching advertisements.

4. Bring plenty of change.

5. Keep accurate records during the day.

6. Write a receipt for every sale.

7. Be outgoing and friendly.

The world turns aside to let any man pass who knows whither he is going.

— David S. Jordan,
educator and naturalist

KEY OBJECTIVES

READING THIS CHAPTER AND DOING THE EXERCISES WILL ENABLE YOU TO:

- Prepare an income statement from the trade fair field trip.
- Use an inventory sheet.
- Calculate net profit for the field trip.

TRADE FAIR FINANCIALS

Now that you've made a trip to a wholesaler and sold your goods (products) at a trade fair, you can prepare an income statement.

To prepare your income statement you should have:

- The money from your sales
- Your sales receipts
- Your leftover merchandise

1. **Cash Sales:** First, count your cash. Separate your "personal" money from your "business" money. Subtract the amount of business money you had at the beginning of your day at the trade fair from the amount you have now. This will give you your Total Cash Sales.

   (End of Day Cash) – (Beginning of Day Cash) = (Total Cash Sales)

2. **Sales Receipts:** Next, add up your sales receipts. Your total cash sales should match exactly the total of your sales receipts. If it does not, you made a mistake in your transactions during the day, or you simply lost some money. Ultimately, the amount of total cash sales you have on hand is your revenue from the day.

3. **Total Cost of Goods Sold:** Now you must figure your Total Cost of Goods Sold. This is the cost of the items you bought for resale. These items are your inventory (the list of what you have on hand to be sold). To do this:

   - Take the cost of your beginning inventory.

   - Subtract the cost of the inventory you have left.

   - The result is your Total Cost of Goods Sold.

(Beginning Inventory) – (Ending Inventory) = (Total Cost of Goods Sold)

Example: Let's say you purchased ten watches for $5 apiece at the wholesaler. Your beginning inventory is: 10 x $5 = $50.

Say you sold five of the watches for $12 apiece.

Your sales: $12 x 5 = $60.

You still have five watches left, so your ending inventory is: 5 x $5 = $25.

Total cost of goods sold:	Beginning inventory	$50
	Less ending inventory	– 25
	Total Cost of Goods Sold	$25

4. Now you have enough information to calculate your Gross Profit. Gross profit is what you have left from sales after you have covered your total cost of goods sold. Therefore:

(Total Sales) – (Total Cost of Goods Sold) = (Gross Profit)

For the watches example:

Total Sales	$60
Less Cost of Goods Sold	– 25
Gross Profit	$35

5. You still have to subtract any additional costs, such as:

   - Travel
   - Advertising
   - Permits
   - Rentals (chairs, tables, etc.)

These are your operating costs. Let's consider these to be fixed costs. To calculate your Net Profit, subtract Operating Costs from the Gross Profit.

(Gross Profit) – (Operating Costs) = (Net Profit)

Using the example above, let's say it cost you $2.00 to take the bus to and from the trade fair with your watches; you spent $1.00 photocopying some flyers; and the trade fair provided you with a table for a rental fee of $10. Your fixed costs would be:

Bus	$ 2.00
Photocopying	1.00
Table rental	+ 10.00
Total Fixed Costs	$13.00

Your Variable Costs are zero.

Figure Net Profit:

Gross Profit	$35
Less Operating Costs	– 13
Net Profit	$22

How do I make sense of all this?

Now you have figured out everything you'll need to prepare an income statement. The watch-selling experience would be documented as follows:

INCOME STATEMENT		
Income Statement		**Financial Analysis of Income Statement**[*]
Revenue:	$60.00	100%
Less Total Cost of Goods Sold:	25.00	42%
Gross Profit:	35.00	58%
Less Operating Costs:		22%
Fixed Costs:	$13.00	
Variable Costs:	0.00	
	13.00	
Net Profit:	$22.00[**]	36%

[*] Review from Chapter 13: How to express line items as percentages of revenue: $\frac{\text{line item}}{\text{revenue}} \times 100$

[**] Note: You still have $25 of inventory left.

Now you can prepare a cash flow statement that shows the effect of your inventory investment and trade fair trip on your cash position.

CASH FLOW STATEMENT	
Cash Inflow:	
Sales:	$ 60.00
Other:	0.00
Total cash inflow:	60.00
Cash Outflow:	
Cost of Goods Sold:	25.00
Operating Costs:	13.00
Investment in Inventory:	25.00
Total cash outflow:	63.00
Net Cash Flow:	($ 3.00)

Developing a cash flow statement shows that you have a negative cash flow of $3.00, despite the fact that you made a profit. You must therefore plan how you will finance this negative cash flow.

An efficient way to keep track of your goods and sales is through the use of an *inventory sheet*. The inventory sheet allows the businessperson to keep track of goods that are sold and their prices. It also shows at a glance how much profit is being made on each sale. This will make preparation of income statements easier later on.

Inventory sheets also keep track of the markups on each item by expressing the profit both in dollars and as a retail markup percentage

INVENTORY SHEETS								
Product	Wholesale Cost Per Unit	Selling Price	Gross Profit Per Unit	Markup* Percentage	Quantity	Total Cost of Goods Sold	Total Sales	Total Gross Profit
Comb	$2.00	$4.00	$2.00	100%	100	$200	$400	$200
Brush	3.50	8.75	5.25	150%	40	140	350	210
Socks	1.00	3.00	2.00	200%	50	50	150	100

$$* \text{Markup \%} = \frac{\text{Gross profit per unit}}{\text{Wholesale cost per unit}} \times 100$$

TRADE FAIR INVENTORY SHEET (SAMPLE)

Product	A x Units Sold (make mark for each sale)	B = Wholesale Cost Per Unit	C Total Cost of Goods Sold	D Selling Price Per Unit	(A x D) Total Sales
Hat	IIIII (5)	$9.00	$45.00	$15.00	$75.00
Lipstick	IIIIII (6)	$0.50	$3.00	$2.00	$12.00
			$48.00		$87.00

My Income Statement

My Total Sales are: $87.00

My Total Cost of Goods Sold is: 48.00

My Gross Profit is: 39.00   ($87.00 – $48.00)

My Operating Costs are:
     My Fixed Costs are: $4.00
     My Variable Costs are: 0

My Total Operating Costs are: $4.00

My Net Profit/(Loss) is: $35.00   ($39.00 – $4.00)

Cash Flow Statement

My Cash Inflow is:
     Sales: $87.00

My Cash Outflow is:
     COGS: $48.00
     Operating Costs $4.00

My Total Cash Outflow is: $52.00

My Net Cash Flow is: $35.00

Chapter 26 Review

N O T E : The exercises printed below can be found in the corresponding chapter of the NFTE MODULE 1 WORKBOOK that came with your textbook. Please write your answers there. If you do not have a workbook, write your answers on a separate sheet of paper.

Critical Thinking about . . . Selling at a Trade Fair

Use your inventory sheet to create an income statement and cash flow statement after your trade fair or flea market selling experience.

Analyzing Your Trade Fair Financials

1. Is your net cash flow different from your net profit/(loss)? If so, what do you think happened? Write an essay describing what you learned from your selling experience and what you would do differently next time.

2. What are non-cash expenses and non-cash revenues? Will your business sell on credit or buy on credit?

3. In looking back, how might you have increased your profits?

Chapter Summary

I. Before preparing your income and cash flow statements, collect:

    A. The money from your sales

    B. Sales receipts

    C. Leftover inventory

II. Use the following formulas when preparing your income and cash flow statements:

    A. Beginning cash – Ending cash = Total cash sales

    B. Beginning inventory – Ending inventory = Cost of goods sold

    C. Total sales – Total cost of goods sold = Gross profit

    D. Gross profit – Operating costs = Net profit before taxes

    E. Cash inflow – Cash outflow = Net cash flow

III. Use inventory sheets to keep track of goods and sales.

> *A minute's success pays the failure of years.*
>
> — Robert Browning
> English poet

KEY OBJECTIVES

READING THIS CHAPTER AND DOING THE EXERCISES WILL ENABLE YOU TO:

- Turn product features into customer benefits.
- Turn customer objections into sales advantages.
- Apply the principles of selling.

PRINCIPLES OF SUCCESSFUL PERSONAL SELLING

Business Is Based on Selling

All business is based on selling products or services for money. A successful sale matches a product or service with a consumer need.

Salespeople often become successful entrepreneurs because they hear what the consumer needs and wants on a daily basis. If the customer is dissatisfied, it is the salesperson who hears the complaint. Successful salespeople work hard at getting to know their customers.

From Salesperson to Entrepreneur

Many of America's great entrepreneurs started out in sales:

Ray Kroc, founder of McDonald's, was selling milkshake machines when he was inspired to turn the McDonald brothers' hamburger restaurant into a national operation.

Aristotle Onassis was a wholesale tobacco salesman before becoming a multimillionaire in the shipping business.

King C. Gillette was a traveling salesman when he invented the safety razor.

W. Clement Stone started out selling newspapers at the age of six before going on to build a great fortune in the insurance industry.

William C. (Billy) Durant, the founder of General Motors, began his career as a buggy salesman. He liked to say, "The secret of success is to have a self-seller, and if you don't have one, get one."

Methods of Selling

There is more than one way for products or services to be sold. Here are some of them:

- By appointment (personal sales call)
- Trade fairs or flea markets
- Direct mail (sending out product or service offers through mailing lists)
- Door to door
- Through school
- Through community or Boy Scout/Girl Scout functions
- "Cold calling" (without appointments)
- By telephone
- Through listings in a catalog
- From home
- From your own store
- Through other stores
- Through outside salespeople on commission
- Through your own sales team
- Through newspaper, radio, or television advertising

Not all of these methods of selling, of course, are within reach of the beginning entrepreneur. Consider each of them carefully. Many of them may be useful to you.

Sales Presentations

However you choose to sell your product or service, every businessperson has to be able to make an effective personal sales presentation, or personal sales call (see next chapter). The following principles of selling apply to any product or service:

1. **Make a good personal impression** when selling your product or service. Prepare yourself. Be neat, clean, and dress appropriately.

2. **View selling as teaching.** This is your chance to "teach" the customer about your product or service. Explain the benefits to your customer.

3. **Believe in your product or service.** Good salespeople believe in what they are selling.

4. **Know your product or service.** Understand how its features can benefit the consumer.

5. **Know your field.** Read the trade literature. Learn about your competitors.

6. **Listen to your customers.** Gain their trust and understand their needs. How does your product or service address them?

7. **Prepare.** Practice your sales presentation. Know ahead of time how you want to present your product or service.

8. **Think positively**, so you can deal with the many rejections you will probably experience before you successfully sell your product or service.

9. **Keep good records.** Set up your record-keeping system, including invoices and receipts, before you go on your first sales call.

10. **Make an appointment.** People are more likely to listen when they have set aside time to hear your sales pitch. They will be less patient if you interrupt their day unannounced.

11. **Stay in touch** with your customers and potential customers. Cultivate your customers for repeat sales. Build relationships.

Features Become Benefits

The essence of selling is showing *how* and *why* the outstanding features of your product or service will benefit customers (fulfill their needs).

Let's say you are selling hats that fold, don't wrinkle, and come in a wide range of colors. These features create the product's benefits: a *durable* hat will not have to be replaced soon; an *easy-to-clean* hat will save money; a hat that *fits into a pocket or bag* will be used often. The *benefits* sell the hat, not the features.

The features of a product are facts about the product. The creative art of selling is teaching the customer how the features will be of benefit to him/her.

PRODUCT: HAT	
Feature	**Customer Benefit**
Durable	Will not have to be replaced soon.
Washable	Will look neat. Customers will save on cleaning costs.
Folds	Can be kept in pocket or bag.
Many colors available	Can match hat to coat.

Focus

Many entrepreneurs stress that the more you are able to concentrate your time, energy, and resources on one or two products, the better your chances of success. An overly diversified business can become unorganized and inefficient. A good rule for the young entrepreneur is to find one product or service and focus on it until the business is successful. Also, remember that each product should have its own name. If a name comes to represent too many products, you run the risk of losing loyalty because the customer becomes unsure as to what the name represents.

Shawn Blakely, Cheep Bird Feeders, Wichita, Kansas

Shawn Blakely designs and builds decorative wooden bird feeders. He sells them wholesale to pet stores. A national chain of pet stores has contracted with him to sell his entire line.

Shawn began his business as a 17-year-old student in an entrepreneurship course run by Young Entrepreneurs of Kansas. The demand for his feeders took off so fast that he started manufacturing them in his uncle's garage, a few blocks from his home.

Moving into his uncle's garage brought Shawn into violation of local zoning laws, though. The laws prohibited manufacturing operations in residential areas. Because zoning laws change from town to town, however, Shawn was able to move his business to his grandfather's tool shed in rural Butler County, where it was not illegal to build his bird feeders.

After placing his product line with the national chain, Shawn had to hire five other people to help him fill orders. He has used some of his money to buy and maintain 17 snack-vending machines. These generate even more profits for this enterprising young man.

Chapter 27 Review

Critical Thinking about . . . Features and Benefits

Develop a list of features and customer benefits for the following products.

1) Diet soda

2) Earrings

3) Necktie

4) Delivery service

5) T-shirt

Getting the Facts

1. Why do salespeople tend to make good entrepreneurs?

2. List three famous American entrepreneurs who began their careers in sales.

3. To sell effectively, turn your product's features into customer _____.

4. The essence of selling is _____.

Chapter Summary

I. All business is based on selling.

    A. Many great entrepreneurs started as salespeople.

    B. Salespeople hear directly about what the customer wants and needs.

II. Principles of selling include: believing in the product, knowing the customer and product well, and being prepared.

III. The essence of selling is teaching.

    A. Teach the customer about the product.

    B. Sell the benefits of your product, not its features.

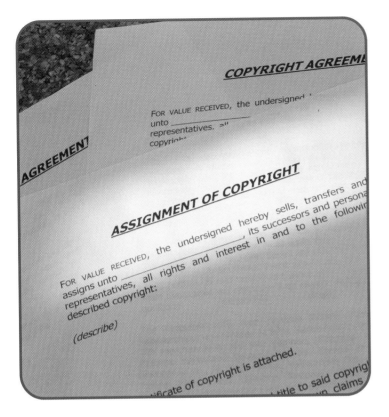

> *Don't ask whether something can be done; find a way to do it.*
>
> — An Wang, founder, Wang Laboratories

KEY OBJECTIVES

READING THIS CHAPTER AND DOING THE EXERCISES WILL ENABLE YOU TO:

- Know how to secure a patent.
- File for trademarks and copyrights.

PROTECTING YOUR INTELLECTUAL PROPERTY*

Intellectual Property

Your thoughts have value. They can influence how you feel about yourself — positively or negatively. They can also be the foundation of a very successful business. Every great business started as a thought, after all.

Your thoughts are your **intellectual property**. If you create a work of art or invent a product, you can use it to build a business. But to do so, you must protect it so that other entrepreneurs can't use it themselves.

If you have developed a good invention, you can either go into business for yourself or sell the idea to a manufacturer. Before taking either step, however, you must protect your rights as inventor by patenting the invention.

---

* Some of this material is repeated from chapter 6.

A **patent** grants to the inventor the exclusive privilege of making, using, selling, and authorizing others to make, use, and sell his/her invention. A patent can be obtained for any original and useful device or process and is valid for twenty years. After that time, anyone may sell the invention without paying the inventor.

When Filing a Patent Is Necessary

As discussed in Chapter 6, a patent cannot be obtained on a mere idea or suggestion. Your invention must be fully developed and actually work before you can seek patent protection. You may have to prepare detailed drawings showing exactly how it works.

You don't need to obtain a patent unless you:

- Have invented a product that you intend to market yourself or sell to a manufacturer and

- Believe that someone else could successfully sell the product by copying your invention.

The average patent takes over two years to obtain. A patent search has to be undertaken, to make certain that the idea is a new idea. Obtaining a patent is a complex legal process. Before starting it, see a registered patent agent or an attorney.

A patent application must include the following:

1. An in-depth description of the invention.
2. A drawing of the invention (when appropriate).
3. A completed "Declaration for Patent Application."
4. A notarized statement from the inventor to the effect that he or she is the original inventor of the subject of the application.
5. The filing fee (typically ranges between $345 and $690).

Public Domain

If an invention is put into use by the inventor for more than one year without obtaining a patent, the invention is considered **public domain** and a patent will no longer be granted.

Remember, however, that you don't need to go to the trouble and expense of obtaining a patent unless your invention is unique and you intend to sell it.

Trademarks

Another valuable type of intellectual property for the entrepreneur is the trademark. The symbol for trademark is ™. **Trademarks** are "any word, name, symbol, or device, or any combination thereof adopted and used by a manufacturer or merchant to identify his goods and distinguish them from those manufactured or sold by others," according to the United States Patent Office.

A company uses a trademark so that people will recognize its product instantly, without having to read the company name, or even having to think about it. The Nike "swoosh" is an example of a trademark most people recognize. A trademark is potentially worth millions of dollars, so if you develop one for your business, you must protect it by registering it with the government. Rights to a trademark are reserved exclusively for its owner. To **infringe** on a trademark is illegal.

To file for a registered trademark, send the United States Patent and Trademark Office:

1. A written application form.
2. A drawing of the trademark.
3. Three specimens showing the actual use of the mark on or in connection with the goods or services.
4. A filing fee ($325).

You can also apply online at: www.uspto.gov

Copyrights

Art is another form of intellectual property. If you are a songwriter, author, or painter, you may create works that you could sell. But if you don't protect your work, someone else can sell it. A *copyright* is the form of legal protection offered to literary, musical, and artistic works. The owner of a copyright has the sole right to print, reprint, sell and distribute, revise, record and perform the work under copyright. The copyright protects a work for the life of the author/artist plus seventy years thereafter.

To file for a copyright, request forms from the Copyright Office. The forms are easy to fill out. To secure a copyright, send a completed form and two examples of the work with a registration fee of $30.

Addresses and Phone Numbers for the United States Patent & Trademark and Copyright Offices:

1. **Patent & Trademark Office**
    2900 Crystal Drive
    Arlington, VA 22202
    (703) 305-8600

2. **Copyright Office**
    Information and Publications Section, LM-455
    Library of Congress
    101 Independence Ave. S.E.
    Washington, DC 20231
    (202) 707-9100

Technology Tip: Copyrights Online

Like so many organizations today, the U.S. Copyright Office is also online and all copyright application forms are now available on the Internet. However, you must have Adobe Acrobat® Reader software installed on your computer to download the forms. A free version can be downloaded through links at the home page for the Copyright Office. The address is: http://www.loc.gov/copyright. Also, circulars and announcements (but not application forms) are also available via fax. Call (202)707-2600 for more information.

Electronic Rights

Now that writing and art and music can be posted on the Web, entrepreneurs have to be careful about protecting their intellectual property online, as well. The rights to reproduce someone's work online are called **electronic rights**.

In 2000, the National Writers Union sued *The New York Times* — and won — because the *Times* was publishing articles from the newspaper on its website without paying writers any additional fees. Many websites have done this — published art or writing or music without paying the creators of that intellectual property for the right to use it.

How can you protect your electronic rights? First, watch out for contracts that say:

- "Work-made-for-hire" — this means you are giving up the copyright of your work to the buyer. Now the buyer can use it anywhere without paying you anything beyond the original fee you negotiated.

- "All rights" — this means you are handing over all rights to your work to the buyer.

Here are some strategies for negotiating to protect the electronic rights to your intellectual property*:

1. Get the buyer to define exactly what is meant by "electronic rights" — online publication? CD-ROMs? Anything else?

2. Put a limit on how long the buyer can have electronic rights — one year, for example.

3. Ask for an additional fee for each additional set of rights. A good rule of thumb would be to ask for 15% of the original fee every time your work is used somewhere else electronically. If you sell a drawing to a newspaper for $100, you could ask for $15 if the paper wants to use the drawing on its website.

---

* Adapted from the National Writers Union Guide to Negotiating Electronic Rights. For more information see http://www.nwu.org.

Chapter 28 Review

NOTE: The exercises printed below can be found in the corresponding chapter of the NFTE MODULE 1 WORKBOOK that came with your textbook. Please write your answers there. If you do not have a workbook, write your answers on a separate sheet of paper.

Critical Thinking about ... Intellectual Property

1. Define intellectual property.

2. What are three methods of protecting intellectual property?

3. When is it a good idea to apply for a patent?

Using New Words

electronic rights
infringe
intellectual property
patent
public domain
trademark

On a separate sheet of paper, identify the vocabulary term that completes each sentence.

1. If a piece of art is _____, it is okay to put it on your website without paying the artist.

2. To protect your _____ online, you will have to negotiate your _____.

3. A _____ is a symbol that is valuable because it represents your business in the customer's mind.

4. If you protect your invention with a _____, another entrepreneur will not be able to _____ upon it.

Getting the Facts

1. What is the difference between a copyright and a patent?

2. For how many years does a copyright protect a work?

3. What's a good rule of thumb when you are negotiating a fee for electronic rights?

Exploration

1. Write a business letter to the United States Copyright Office requesting information on how to file for a patent, trademark, or copyright. Or, if you have access to a computer, visit their website at http://www.loc.gov/copyright and print out this information.

2. Copyright-infringement lawsuits have been brought against some rap artists who "sample" other people's music. Write a letter to the United States Copyright Office asking what the current policy is on "music sampling."

Review

Chapter Summary

I. A patent grants the inventor exclusive rights to the invention for twenty years.

A. A patent takes about two years to obtain.

B. An invention that has been in use for more than a year cannot be patented.

II. Trademarks are exclusive words, names, symbols, or devices that identify a company.

III. Copyrights protect literary, musical, and artistic works.

IV. With the development of the Internet, entrepreneurs now have to protect their intellectual property on the Web, also.

A. Make sure all contracts include electronic rights.

B. If possible, do not sign "work for hire" contracts, which give your copyright to the buyer.

A Business for the Young Entrepreneur: Handmade Crafts

Do you like to sew? Or work with wood? If making things comes easy to you, consider making a simple product to sell. People enjoy buying handmade products. Some products you could make include:

- decorative pillows
- stuffed animals
- puppets
- bird cages
- jewelry
- candles

Think of something you will enjoy making that people in your market will want to buy!

A great place to sell handmade crafts is at a local trade fair (flea market). You can obtain a list of these retail selling opportunities from the Chamber of Commerce in your area. Find out how to rent a booth or table.

Bring:

- colorful flyers
- business cards to give to customers and potential customers
- a receipt book; give each customer a receipt
- lots of change

INTERMEDIATE BUSINESS PLAN REVIEW

NOTE: A complete version of the Intermediate Business Plan can be found after Chapter 28 in your NFTE MODULE 1 WORKBOOK. Please work on your Plan there. The review pages below will help to familiarize you with the topics covered in the Intermediate Business Plan.

Intermediate Business Plan

Now you are ready to write a more detailed plan for your intended business. If you are satisfied with your Basic Business Plan, use those worksheets to help you fill out your Intermediate Business Plan. This is an opportunity, however, to improve your Plan or even change it entirely. Maybe you have decided to start a different business, for example, or perhaps you have done more research on your costs and can write a more accurate plan now. In addition, the Intermediate Plan will include more detailed marketing planning, a cash flow statement and a projected income statement for your first year of business.

Your Business Idea
(See Chapter 8)

1) Describe your business idea.

2) What is the name of your business?

3) What is the competitive advantage of your business?

4) How did you get your idea?

5) What skills, hobbies, or interests do you have that will help you make your business successful?

Legal Structure
(See Chapter 19)

1) Is your business a sole proprietorship or a partnership?

2) If it is a partnership: What skills, hobbies, interests, or equipment does your partner(s) have that will help make the business successful?

3) How have you and your partner(s) agreed to divide ownership in the business?

Economics of One Unit
(See Chapter 10)

- **Service Business** (Note: A service unit is typically defined as one hour of service or one job.)
  Define your unit.

- **Retail Business**
  Define your unit.

- **Wholesale Business**
  Define your unit.

- **Manufacturing Business**
  Define your unit.

Goal Setting

1) What are your short-term business goals? (less than one year)

2) What are your long-term business goals? (from one to five years)

3) What are your educational and training goals? (from one to five years)

4) What are your personal goals? (for the rest of your life)

5) Why is your product/service going to outperform the competition over time?

6) Have you tried to get a part-time job in your chosen industry?

Philanthropy

1) How do you intend to practice philanthropy? How will your philanthropy benefit your company in terms of marketing?

2) How will your business help you to contribute to your community?

Type of Business You Are In
(See Chapters 8 and 20)

- Manufacturer sells to wholesaler

- Wholesaler sells to retailer

- Retailer sells to consumer

- Service retailer sells to consumer

Consumer Description
(See Chapter 18)

1) Describe your target consumer.

2) Expected age of typical customer.

3) What consumer need will your product fulfill?

4) Expected financial status of consumer.

Market Analysis
(See Chapter 18)

1) How have you analyzed your market?

   a) by location

   b) by population

   c) by personality

   d) by behavior

2) Using the categories above, describe the characteristics of your market, and explain how your marketing plan targets that group.

Market Research
(See Chapter 14)

Competition

Ask three people these questions about your business. Ensure that they explain the reasons behind their answers.

1) Do you like the name of my business?

2) Where would you want to go to buy my product?

3) How much would you pay for my product?

4) Who is my closest competitor(s)?

5) What do you think of my logo?

6) Do you think my product/service has value?

7) How would you improve my business idea?

8) Do you think my product/service is better or worse than that offered by my competitor(s)?

The Marketing Mix
(See Chapter 18)

Product

How is your product or service going to meet the needs of the consumers in your market segment?

Price

Explain your pricing strategy.

Place

Where will you sell your product or service? What is your location strategy?

Promotion/Advertising
(See Chapter 12)

1) What is your business slogan?

2) Where do you intend to advertise?

3) How do you plan to get publicity for your business?

4) Fill out the marketing plan for your business in your NFTE Module 1 Workbook. Redo your marketing plan based on your new marketing mix.

5) Are you planning to use cause-related marketing?

Write a sample press release for your business.

Draw a logo for your business.

Wholesalers/Suppliers

Using a Business-to-Business Directory, list key wholesalers or suppliers that you will need to get your business started.

The Production/Distribution Chain
(See Chapter 20)

1) Describe the distribution channel, including all markups. If you sell more than one product, pick one as an example.

2) What is the estimated delivery time between when you place an order with your supplier and when you will have the product available for your customers?

Intellectual Property Protection
(See Chapter 28)

1) Have you contacted the United States Copyright and Trademark Office to determine whether someone else has registered your business name or logo? As a result, what action will you take?

2) Is your business based on an invention? If Yes, have you applied for a patent?

Your Record-Keeping System
(See Chapter 16)

1) What are your plans for keeping good financial records?

2) Describe your filing system.

Technology
(See Chapter 21)

Identify which technology tools you plan to use for your business and why.

Costs and Financing
(See Chapter 10)

These are the purchases you need to make to earn your first dollar of sales. What are your estimated start-up costs? Itemize.

Financing Strategy
(See Chapter 7)

1) List your sources of financing. Identify whether each source is equity, debt, or a gift. Indicate the amount and type for each source.

2) If you receive equity financing, what percentage of ownership will you give up?

3) If you receive debt financing, what is the maximum interest rate you will pay?

Operating Costs (Fixed)
(See Chapter 10)

Monthly Operating Costs include USAIIRD: Utilities, Salaries, Advertising, Interest, Insurance, Rent and Depreciation.

1) Type of Fixed Costs

2) Monthly Fixed Costs

Operating Costs (Variable)
(See Chapter 10)

Estimate those Operating Costs (USAIIRD) that fluctuate with Sales, and cannot be directly assigned to a Unit of Sale.

1) Type of Variable Costs

2) Estimated Variable Costs as a percentage of Sales

Yearly Budget: Projected Yearly Income Statement
(See Chapter 4)

Complete your Budgeted Yearly Projected Income Statement in your NFTE Module 1 Workbook.

Cash Flow Statement
(See Chapter 24)

Complete your Cash Flow Statement in your NFTE Module 1 Workbook.

Intermediate Business Plan Review

HOW TO START & OPERATE A SMALL BUSINESS

Basic: Starting Your Business
Includes: Chapters 1-14 and the Basic Business Plan

The Basic chapters of NFTE Module 1 will teach you what you need to know to start a simple business. Once you have completed these chapters, you will be able to prepare an income statement, understand marketing basics, perform cost/benefit analysis, and calculate return on investment. You will also learn what it means to be an entrepreneur and how you can use your unique skills and talents to start a small business venture.

After you have finished Chapter 14, you will be ready to apply what you have learned by preparing your Basic Business Plan. A complete version of the Basic Business Plan can be found in your NFTE Module 1 Workbook.

Intermediate: Running a Business Successfully
Includes: Chapters 15-28 and the Intermediate Business Plan

The Intermediate Chapters of NFTE Module 1 will teach you how to successfully manage and run your business. Once you have completed these chapters, you will be able to create a cash flow statement, identify your competitive advantage, and keep good records for your business.

After you have finished Chapter 28, you will be ready to apply what you have learned by preparing your Intermediate Business Plan. A complete version of the Intermediate Business Plan can be found in your NFTE Module 1 Workbook.

Advanced: What You Need to Know to Grow
Includes: Chapters 29-50 and the Advanced Business Plan

The Advanced Chapters of NFTE Module 2 will teach you how you can grow a small business venture you have already started. Once you have completed these chapters, you will be able to create a balance sheet, do break-even and financial ratio analysis, and select the best financing strategy for your business.

After you have finished Chapter 50, you will be ready to apply what you have learned by preparing your Advanced Business Plan. A complete version of the Advanced Business Plan can be found in your NFTE Module 2 Workbook.

This land was made for you and me.

— Woody Guthrie,
American folksinger

KEY OBJECTIVES

**READING THIS CHAPTER AND DOING
THE EXERCISES WILL ENABLE YOU TO:**

■ Understand the economic
definition of efficiency.

■ Define GNP and GDP.

■ Understand how
government regulations
impact small businesses.

■ Analyze global business
opportunities.

SMALL BUSINESS AND GOVERNMENT

The Economic Questions*

Since time began, people have had to answer the same basic questions:

- What should be produced?
- How will we produce it?
- Who gets to have what we produce?

Families, individuals, entrepreneurs, charities, corporations and nations all have had to answer these questions. The study of how these different groups make decisions and answer these questions is called economics. The system a group of people creates by making these decisions is an economy.

---

* See *Master Curriculum Guide, Economics: What and When,* edited by June Gillird. et al., Joint Council on Economic Education (1989), for an excellent discussion of economics.

To answer these questions, people must decide what to do with resources. Resources are things, such as land, labor and capital, which are used to produce products (goods) and services. Land includes all natural resources, such as minerals, trees and water. Labor is work that helps produce products or services. Capital refers to equipment, factories and tools needed to make a product.

The entrepreneur's role is to use these resources to produce products and services that meet consumer needs.

Scarcity

Economic decisions are made in response to scarcity. Scarcity means that there is a limited supply of resources. Many successful entrepreneurs add value to scarce resources and make a profit. For example, in a neighborhood with few clothing stores, one could say that fashionable clothing is scarce. An entrepreneur who brings in fashionable clothes from another neighborhood has added value by making shopping more convenient for residents. She has made a scarce resource available, and is likely to make a profit. The profit demonstrates that she was able to make use of a scarce resource in a way that appeals to consumers.

Changes in Prices Communicate Information to Entrepreneurs

An economic system is considered **efficient** when consumer needs are met with very little waste of resources (both labor and capital). An entrepreneur who makes economically efficient decisions is likely to make a profit, both by meeting consumer needs and by paying close attention to the price consumers will pay to have their needs met.

In a free market system, changes in price send signals to entrepreneurs. If the price of a pair of sneakers rises from $45 to $55, and other factors, such as the cost of materials, remain the same, more entrepreneurs will decide to sell sneakers. These entrepreneurs, taking advantage of the growing difference between the sneakers' cost and retail price, expect to make a profit in the sneaker business.* A rise in prices attracts producers and leads to growth in production, as well as increased competition.

If the price of sneakers falls from $45 to $35, and other factors remain the same, some entrepreneurs will stop selling sneakers. They will look for something more profitable to do with their labor and resources. A fall in prices can lead to a decrease in production.

---

* It is important always to start a business that interests you and matches your talents and hobbies. A business that is highly profitable this year may be less so next year; therefore, choose a business you would like to run, rather than one that will make the most money right away.

Small Business and the Economy

Small businesses are an important part of the national economy. As an entrepreneur, the value you create contributes to the **Gross National Product (GNP)** of your country. The GNP is the annual market value of all products and services produced by a country's resources. The United States GNP includes value created by American companies, whether their operations are in the U.S. or abroad. As an entrepreneur, every sale you make in your business, no matter how small, contributes to the GNP. Each year, the GNP increases or decreases (usually by a very small percentage).

A decrease in the GNP means businesses are selling fewer goods and services. They have less money to hire people, and some even have to close. This causes unemployment. Since fewer people have jobs, there is less money spent on goods and services. This can create a **recession**, or economic downturn.

The Gross Domestic Product (GDP) is a major component of GNP. GDP is the annual estimated value of all products and services produced within a country (excluding exports). An increase in GDP means businesses are making profits and entrepreneurs are making wise decisions and using resources efficiently.

Government and Business

The United States has a free-market economy, meaning that anyone can start a business. The government itself does not own or control private businesses, but it does make laws about business practices. For example, it enforces minimum age requirements in the workplace and prosecutes employers who discriminate for reasons of gender, race or sexual orientation. The government also provides a court system that enforces contracts between businesses and consumers. For example, an entrepreneur who has paid a Web designer for a homepage may take the designer to court if he fails to complete the task. The court acts as a neutral judge of the situation and provides a solution. In this case, the designer might be asked to pay back the entrepreneur, or to complete the homepage.

In the United States, city, state and federal government regulations govern many elements of business. Therefore, as an entrepreneur, you should always call your local chamber of commerce and ask about regulations that apply to your business. Examples of government regulations, discussed in later chapters, include taxation, insurance and legal incorporation. These will have a direct impact on your business. Therefore, it is very important always to be fully informed of and to follow all government laws and regulations.

The Money Supply

In addition to regulating business, government plays an important role in a country's political and economic stability. It is difficult to run a business during wartime, as factors that bring people together to buy and sell are disrupted; governments' decisions about war and peace therefore directly impact both small entrepreneurs and large corporations.

It is also critical that consumers and businesspeople be able to value goods and services using a stable currency. When currency values change rapidly, consumers and businesses are harmed because they are unable to make long-term decisions. Instead these groups must make choices in a situation where they are uncertain about the future value of their money.

When the value of currency goes down, so do consumers' and businesses' ability to buy products and services. An entrepreneur who plans to buy a computer next month might choose to buy it today for fear that it will be two times as expensive if she buys it then. In making this purchase, she has given up cash which could otherwise be used to grow other elements of her business.

Keeping the Value of Money Stable

In the United States, the government tries to keep the value of money constant in order to prevent these problems; if an entrepreneur knows that the buying power of a dollar will be worth the same today as it will next week, she will make decisions based on her business needs, not on other factors.

As the central source of printed money, the government maintains a stable currency value. In carefully monitoring the quantity of money it prints, the government can influence consumer and business behavior to keep the value of money constant.

When the government prints large amounts of money, interest rates fall. Because money is more easily available, banks charge less interest on loans. Low interest rates encourage entrepreneurs and corporations to take out loans and expand their businesses. This can be good for awhile, but if it goes on too long, entrepreneurs may borrow too much money and their businesses will fail because they have too much debt. In contrast, when the government cuts back on the money supply, interest rates rise.

As an entrepreneur, you are directly affected by government decisions about the money supply, and should pay close attention to changes in interest rates and the resulting changes in your suppliers' and competitors' business behavior.

Globalization

In deciding to start a business, you have entered not only a national economy, but also play a key role in a broader global economic system. Because of improvements in technology, communication between businesspeople has become much faster, allowing them to work effectively at different locations around the world. Airplanes enable rapid travel across vast distances, while the Internet allows customers to place orders reliably and quickly for products manufactured abroad. Good management and careful planning allow successful businesses to operate in many countries at once.

As an entrepreneur, you should consider international opportunities. These may include imports, which help you to bring in new or improved products from abroad, or exports, through which you can reach markets in other countries. Whichever one you choose, you will be contributing to your country's **trade balance**, which is the difference between its overall imports and exports. A trade balance is positive when a country's businesses export more than they import. The trade balance sometimes affects the ease with which businesses may do business in other countries, as the government usually prefers to maintain a positive trade balance. If you decide to import goods from abroad, carefully research whether there are special taxes, called **tariffs**, which could make your imports more expensive.

Business and Culture*

If you decide to take advantage of opportunities abroad, it is very important to remember that business practices in other countries may be different from those in your own. What is polite or acceptable in one culture may be viewed differently in others; always take the time to find out about differences in social behavior before you approach a new market. For example, in Western cultures, businesspeople often like to get down to business right away. However some cultures may find this approach rude or offensive. In Mali, West Africa, meetings often begin with long greetings and pleasantries. Sometimes people talk and drink tea for hours before the matter at hand is discussed. Knowing and following cultural preferences, like this one, can greatly add to your success. This will help you to create strong relationships with your new customers or suppliers.

Most importantly, never consider your market or business opportunities to be limited to a single country, state or city; there are valuable lessons to be learned from businesses in other countries with different cultures and business practices. Even if your business maintains a local focus, research on companies in other countries may help you to better understand new directions you can take in your own market.

---

* Many thanks to Kerri Kennedy for the ideas she contributed.

Chapter 29 Review

NOTE: The exercises printed below can be found in the corresponding chapter of the NFTE MODULE 2 WORKBOOK that came with your textbook. Please write your answers there. If you do not have a workbook, write your answers on a separate sheet of paper.

Critical Thinking about . . . Business Formation

With your teacher's guidance, calculate the following statistics for your class.

1) Class GNP for one day.

2) Class GNP for one week.

3) Part-time employees.

Getting the Facts

1. Why is price important to entre-preneurs?

2. How is GDP different from GNP?

3. Explain why entrepreneurs should understand government regulations.

4. Why should an entrepreneur research the culture where he or she plans to conduct business?

Using New Words

efficient
Gross Domestic Product
Gross National Product
recession
tariff
trade balance

Identify the correct definition for each vocabulary term below:

1) Gross National Product
    a) the annual estimated value of all products and services produced by a country
    b) the annual estimate of successful businesses in a country
    c) the annual estimate of a country's balance of trade

2) Gross Domestic Product
    a) Gross National Product minus imports
    b) Gross National Product minus exports
    c) Gross National Product minus production abroad

Review

Chapter 29 Review

3) recession

   a) economic downturn

   b) economic upturn

   c) unemployment

4) tariff

   a) the free-trade price of goods

   b) a tax levied on an import to make it less attractive

   c) a restriction on the number of goods that can be imported

5) trade balance

   a) the difference between a country's exports and imports

   b) the difference between a country's domestic sales and international sales

   c) the balance between trade and manufacturing

Exploring the Internet

Why do you think some Americans are worried about globalization? Search the Internet for two news articles about anti-globalization protests. Write a short essay giving your opinion about how you think globalization will affect entrepreneurs.

Review

Chapter Summary

I. **Economics is the study of how groups and individuals make decisions about the use of resources.**

A. Economic decisions are made in response to scarcity.

B. Entrepreneurs can make a profit by adding value to scarce resources.

II. **An economic system is considered efficient when consumer needs are met with very little waste of resources.**

A. Entrepreneurs should always be alert to changes in price.

B. A rise in prices attracts producers and leads to growth in production and increased competition.

C. A fall in prices can lead to a decrease in production.

III. **Gross National Product (GNP) is the annual market value of all products and services produced by a country's resources.**

IV. **Gross Domestic Product (GDP) is a component of GNP. It is defined as the market value of all products and services produced within a country (excluding exports).**

V. **City, state and federal government regulations govern many elements of business.**

A. The government regulates the money supply.

B. The court system evaluates contract disputes and enforces government business regulations.

VI. **Entrepreneurs should be alert to international opportunities to do business.**

A. They can import or export goods abroad.

B. It is important that an entrepreneur familiarize herself or himself with the culture in which he or she plans to do business.

A Business for the Young Entrepreneur: House Cleaning

It's hard for working mothers and fathers to keep up with housework. This can be a great money-making opportunity for you.

You probably have already had some "on-the-job training" doing chores at home. Make flyers to advertise your services. A flyer is a one-page advertisement for your business that you hand out to potential customers and post on bulletin boards. You can draw a flyer by hand or design it on a computer. It can be simple or fancy, but should be eye-catching and include your name, the name of your business, and your phone number. Include the following jobs on your flyer:

- Sweeping
- Mopping
- Dusting
- Emptying garbage
- Doing dishes
- Cleaning bathrooms
- Doing laundry

Put up your flyers in grocery stores, laundromats, and community bulletin boards. You could offer your customers the option either to have you use the cleaning supplies at their houses, or bring your own.

Tips

- Do a great job so you can build a base of repeat customers.
- Offer a discount to any customer who refers you to someone else.
- Try to expand into office cleaning.

There's no such thing as a free lunch.

— Milton Friedman,
American economist

KEY OBJECTIVES

READING THIS CHAPTER AND DOING THE EXERCISES WILL ENABLE YOU TO:

- Explain the relationship between supply, demand, and price.
- Analyze how competition keeps prices down and quality high.
- Discuss monopoly's effect on price and quality.
- Use a supply-and-demand graph.

SUPPLY AND DEMAND

In a free–market economy, what is produced, the price, and the quantity bought and sold are determined by **supply** and **demand**.

Supply is a schedule of the quantities that a business would make available to consumers at various prices. If you are making and selling dresses, you will probably be more motivated to supply them if you can sell them for $50 than if you can sell them for $5.

Demand is a schedule of the quantities that consumers would be willing to buy at various prices. Customers will probably want to buy a lot more of your dresses if you sold them for $5 than if you sold them for $50.

Price relays information between the consumer and the entrepreneur. The entrepreneur knows quickly when the price of a product is too high, because most consumers refuse to buy it. The entrepreneur knows when the price is too low when the product sells out quickly and consumers want more. The price of a product is determined by the laws of supply and demand.

Law of Demand*

According to the *law of demand*, as price goes up, the quantity demanded by consumers goes down.

Let's say you get permission to sell soda at a Little League game. During the first half of the game, you charge $2 per can of soda and sell two-dozen cans. During the second half of the game, you try lowering your price to $1 per can. You sell five-dozen cans. The people attending the game have "obeyed" the law of demand: If everything else remains the same, people will demand more of something at a *lower* price than they will at a *higher* price.

Law of Supply

On the other side of every market is a *supplier*. The supplier also reacts to price changes. If your business is baking and selling cookies, how many would you be willing to make if you thought they would sell for $.25 each? What if people were willing to pay $1.00? You would probably work harder and try to bake and sell more cookies at the higher price.

The entrepreneur who acts in this way is obeying the *law of supply*: If everything else remains the same, businesses will supply more of a product or service at a *higher* price than they will at a *lower* price.

Using the Laws of Supply and Demand to Predict Market Behavior

Understanding the laws of supply and demand will help you predict market behavior. For example, what would you expect to happen to the demand for air conditioners in the summer? What would likely happen, therefore, to the *price* of air conditioners in the summer?

The demand for air conditioners will rise in the summer because more people will want one. Suppliers of air conditioners will be able to raise their prices in late spring because more people will be "demanding" this product then. As summer draws to a close, and most people who wanted air conditioners have already bought them, the price should come down.

Competition affects the price of a product (or service) by increasing the supply. Typically, what happens is that an entrepreneur starts a business to fill a consumer

---

* See *Master Curriculum Guide in Economics, Part II, Strategies for Teaching Economics,* edited by Ronald A. Banaszak and Elmer U. Clawson, the Joint Council on Economic Education (1981), for an excellent discussion of supply and demand.

demand. If the entrepreneur is making a profit meeting that demand, other entrepreneurs notice and also move into that business. The supply increases, therefore, driving the price down as the businesses strive to compete with each other. If you suspect that the supply of the product you sell is going to rise, it would make sense to get out of that business and start selling something else.

Together, demand and supply determine how much will be bought and sold and what the price will be in any given market. Remember, a market is a group of people buying and selling a product or service. Businesses would like to charge high prices for their products and services. Consumers seek low prices. The **market clearing price** occurs when what the buyer wants to pay coincides with what the entrepreneur wants to charge.

Supply and Demand Schedules

George goes to the grocery store to buy apples. What he will do at the store depends on the price of the apples. If apples cost 90 cents each, George might only be willing to buy one. If the price is ten cents each, he might be willing to buy nine.

The owner of the grocery store might be willing to sell (supply) ten apples, if he could sell them for $1.00 each. At ten cents each he only wants to supply one.

A list of how many units of a product consumers are willing to buy at different prices is called a *demand schedule*. Here is a demand schedule for George.

You can see from the demand schedule that, as the price of apples declines, George is willing to buy more.

Price of one apple	Number of apples George is willing to buy at the price
$1.00	0
$ .90	1
$ .80	2
$ .70	3
$ .60	4
$ .50	5
$ .40	6
$ .30	7
$ .20	8
$ .10	9

A list of how much of a product producers are willing to supply at different prices is called a *supply schedule*. Here is a supply schedule for the grocer.

You can see from the supply schedule that, as the price of apples rises, the grocer is willing to supply more.

Price of one apple	Number of apples grocer is willing to supply at the price
$ .10	1
$ .20	2
$ .30	3
$ .40	4
$ .50	5
$ .60	6
$ .70	7
$ .80	8
$ .90	9
$ 1.00	10

The Market Clearing Price

The supply and demand schedules have been plotted on the following page. The point at which the supply and demand lines cross is the market clearing price. This is the price at which the number of apples George is willing to buy and the grocer is willing to supply are the same. The trade will take place at this point.

According to the graph, the market clearing price is fifty cents. At this price George will buy five apples and the grocer will sell five.

Supply, demand, and price information are communicated quickly and clearly between consumers and entrepreneurs in the free-market system. Learning to forecast supply and demand in your market will be a key to your success.

1. What is the market clearing price of apples?

2. How many apples is the grocer willing to sell at $0.20?

3. How many apples is George willing to buy at $0.20?

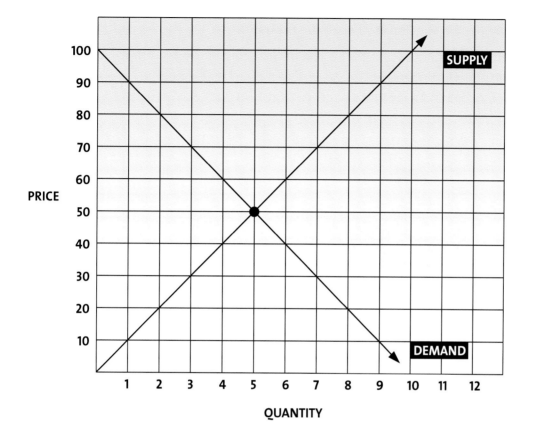

Competition Keeps Prices Down and Quality High

The laws of supply and demand work best in competitive markets. When businesses are competing with each other, they try to attract consumers by lowering prices, improving quality, and developing new products and services. If a business has no competition, it is called a **monopoly**. A monopoly can charge consumers whatever prices it wants to charge for its products.

Anything that keeps entrepreneurs from entering a market, will make it less competitive and encourage monopolies. Less competition leads to higher prices, poorer quality, and fewer new products and services.

Many things can put pressure on a price. Several years ago a flood in Louisiana made it difficult to get milk into the state. The supply of milk was cut off. Distributors of milk had to bid against each other for supplies from out of state. They had to pay high prices and so they charged Louisiana consumers high prices, as well. Because the price of milk rose so high, however, it attracted other suppliers who rushed more milk to the state. As the supply of milk increased, the price began to come down. Gradually, the price of milk returned to what it was before the flood.

Use Supply and Demand as Guides

Entrepreneurship is a discovery process full of risk and uncertainty. But, each time you make a choice regarding your business, you will quickly get feedback from your market. The demand for your product or service will rise or fall. If the demand falls, the market may be telling you to change your product or service. If the supply of your product or service rises, the price will start to fall. You might find that you can't sell enough to make a profit. If you are in the marketplace competing, there's nothing to be ashamed of if the market pushes you to move on to something new.

Chapter 30 Review

NOTE: The exercises printed below can be found in the corresponding chapter of the NFTE MODULE 2 WORKBOOK that came with your textbook. Please write your answers there. If you do not have a workbook, write your answers on a separate sheet of paper.

Critical Thinking about . . . Supply and Demand

1) What is likely to happen to the price of air conditioners in December? Why?

2) What would you expect to happen to the demand for gasoline if everyone began using electric cars? How would you expect this to affect the availability of gasoline and its price?

3) Explain why a monopoly can charge any price for the products it sells. Can monopolies develop in a free-market system? Why or why not?

Using New Words

demand
supply
market clearing price
monopoly

On a separate sheet of paper, identify the vocabulary term that completes each sentence.

1) Consumers communicate to business owners through their _____ for a product or service.

2) Business owners have to study the market to determine how much to _____.

3) The price at which quantity supplied equals quantity demanded is the _____.

4) A company that has a _____ in a market can control supply and, therefore, price.

Review

Chapter 30 Review

Exploring Supply and Demand

1. You may have noticed prices being affected by supply and demand. Is there a product that you stop buying when its price goes up, even a little? Is there another product that you would keep buying even if its price rose considerably? Write a short essay discussing the difference in your demand for these products.

2. Create a demand schedule for each product above, showing the quantity you would buy at different prices.

3. If other suppliers move into the market for the product (or service) your business sells, what are ways you could compete other than lowering your price?

Review

Chapter Summary

I. Market price and quantity are determined by supply and demand.

A. Price relays information between customer and producer.

1. If the price is too high, consumers won't buy the product.

2. If the price is too low, the product sells out too quickly.

B. Businesspeople must forecast supply and demand in their markets.

II. Competition keeps prices down and quality high.

A. A monopoly tends to keep prices high and quality down.

B. Competition encourages entrepreneurs to be creative and develop new businesses.

III. Making a profit tells the entrepreneur that he/she is successfully responding to competition, scarcity, and consumer demand.

A. Scarcity means limited supply.

B. The entrepreneur may change businesses many times in response to changes in competition, scarcity, and consumer demand.

If you do your job well, the last thing you have to worry about is money, just as if you live right, you'll be happy.

— Edwin Land,
founder of Polaroid Corporation

KEY OBJECTIVES

READING THIS CHAPTER AND DOING THE EXERCISES WILL ENABLE YOU TO:

- Identify the "break-even" point.

- Define one unit of sale.

- Figure how many units a business has to sell to break even.

BREAK-EVEN ANALYSIS

The Break-Even Point

Remember the first three steps of the marketing process? They are: consumer analysis, market analysis, and development of a "marketing mix." As you work through these procedures you will figure out how supply and demand affect your market. Once you've done your market research and have created a marketing plan, you will have to answer one more important question: Can you *afford* your marketing plan? Luckily, there's a tool to help you answer that question. It's the fourth and final step of the marketing process: break-even analysis.

Break-even analysis helps you find the point at which your business will be selling enough units to cover its costs. This will help you figure out how many units you need to sell to be able to afford your marketing plan. If you estimate your market to be 2,000 sales a month, but your analysis shows that you have to sell 5,000 units to cover the cost of advertising, you will have to rethink your strategy.

Break-even analysis is based on the *income statement*. The income statement shows whether a business has earned a profit or suffered a loss. When sales and costs are equal, there is no net profit or net loss. The total at the bottom of the income statement is zero.

This condition is called the break-even point. Many new businesses lose money or just break even for a while before they begin making a profit. Eventually, as the business owner gains experience, he/she may begin to make more than enough sales to cover costs.

On the other hand, the business owner may find that not enough sales revenue is coming in to cover costs. The business is not "breaking even." Businesses that are not breaking even are eventually forced into closing, or bankruptcy. A bankrupt business is declared legally unable to pay its bills. It's wise, therefore, to always save a part of your profit, when you are making one, to cover periods when you are not.

To survive in the short run, therefore, a business must break even. To survive over the long run, a business must make a profit so the owner has enough money to pay his/her own living expenses.

It is important for the entrepreneur to know how much will be necessary to sell during a month so the business will break even. Break-even analysis shows how many units of the product or service will need to be sold in a month to do this.

Unit of Sale

First, though, the business owner must define the **unit of sale**. If you are selling ties, one unit of sale can be defined as one tie. If you are selling a baby-sitting service, you can define one unit of sale as one hour of baby-sitting.

Once you've defined the unit of sale, you can figure **gross profit per unit**. This is the first step toward determining how many units you will have to sell to break even. Gross profit per unit is the selling price of the unit minus the cost of producing it (the cost of goods sold).

Selling Price per Unit – Cost of Goods Sold per Unit = Gross Profit per Unit

Let's look at David's income statement from Chapter 4 again.

David bought 25 ties at $2 each and sold them all for a total of $100. He was selling each tie for $4, or keystoning ($100/25 ties = $4 per tie).

- David's selling price per unit is $4 for each tie.

- David's unit of sale is one tie.

- David's cost of goods sold per unit is $2.

$4 (Selling Price per Unit) – $2 (Cost of Goods Sold per Unit) = $2 (Gross Profit per Unit)

DAVID'S INCOME STATEMENT

(A)	Sales	$ 100	25 ties x $4/tie = $100
(B)	Less Total Cost of Goods Sold	50	25 ties x $2/tie = $50
(C)	Gross Profit	50	A – B = C
			$100 – $50 = $50
(D)	Less Operating Costs		
	(D1) Fixed Costs	$ 24	$24
	(D2) Variable Costs	0	$0
		24	D1 + D2 = D
(E)	Profit before Taxes	26	C – D = E
			$50 – $24 = $26
(F)	Taxes	6	Taxes = $6
(G)	Net Profit (Loss)	$ 20	E – F = G
			$26 – $6 = $20

David's gross profit per unit is $2.

Gross profit per unit is used to pay the operating costs of a business. From the formula, you can see that gross profit per unit is the result of subtracting the cost of goods sold per unit from the selling price per unit.

Calculating Break–Even Units

Because many small-business operating costs are fixed, break-even is often calculated by assuming that *all* operating costs are fixed. Using gross profit per unit, David can calculate how many units he will have to sell each month to cover his fixed costs. This simple formula divides gross profit per unit into monthly fixed costs to determine break-even units:

$$\frac{\textbf{Monthly Fixed Costs}}{\textbf{Gross Profit per Unit}} = \textbf{Break-Even Units}$$

Break-even units are the number David will have to sell each month to cover fixed costs. His fixed costs of $24 represent the amount of money he spends each month on flyers to advertise his business.

$$\textbf{For David's business: } \frac{\textbf{\$24 (Monthly Fixed Costs)}}{\textbf{\$2 (Gross Profit per Unit)}} = \textbf{12 (Break-Even Units)}$$

David has to sell 12 ties each month to cover the cost of his advertising and stay in business. If he sells fewer than 12, he will suffer a net loss. If he sells more than 12 ties, he will earn a net profit.

DAVID'S INCOME STATEMENT AT BREAK-EVEN		
Sales (12 ties x $4)		$48
Less Total Cost of Goods Sold (12 ties x $2)		24
Gross Profit on Sales ($48 – $24)		24
Less Total Operating Costs		
Fixed Costs	$24	
Variable Costs	0	
		24
Profit on Sales before Taxes		0
Taxes		0
Net Profit/(Loss) on Sales after Taxes		$ 0

David's profit before taxes is zero. David's net profit (loss) when he sells twelve ties is zero. Twelve ties is the break-even point for David's business. Once he has sold twelve ties, he has covered his costs.

Of course, your fixed costs are not usually only for marketing. Operating costs include everything in USAIIRD: Utilities, Salaries, Advertising, Interest, Insurance, Rent, and Depreciation. But, of those costs, the entrepreneur can only completely control advertising because your marketing plan determines how much you will spend. Break-even analysis is a good tool for looking at all your costs and should be performed frequently. It is especially important after you've completed your marketing plan and before you start your business, to see if your plan is realistic.

Including Variable Cost in Break-Even Analysis

If you do want to calculate break-even units, including variable costs, first you must know your estimated variable cost per unit. Then, use this formula to figure break-even units:

$$\frac{\text{Monthly Fixed Costs}}{\text{Gross Profit per Unit - Estimated Variable Cost per Unit}} = \text{Break-Even Units}$$

Let's figure the break-even units for a shoe store with the following figures:

Estimated Variable Cost per Unit: $1.00 (estimated utilities per unit)

Monthly Fixed Costs: $1,100.00

Gross Profit per Unit: $12.00

Break-Even Units: 100

Break-Even Analysis of Jersey Mike's

The National Foundation for Teaching Entrepreneurship owned a student-run fast-food franchise in Newark, called Jersey Mike's. Here is a break-even analysis of the restaurant:

1) Each customer at Jersey Mike's usually bought a sandwich for $4 and a drink for $1, so our average sales per customer were $4 + $1 = $5. Therefore, we defined our unit of sale as $5.

2) The cost of goods sold for each unit was $1 for the sandwich and $.25 for the drink, so the cost of goods sold was $1 + $.25 = $1.25 per unit of sale.

3) Fixed costs for a month at Jersey Mike's were:

Utilities	$1,000
Salaries	3,000
Advertising	1,000
Interest	0
Insurance	1,000
Rent	1,000
Depreciation	+1,000
	$8,000

4) There were no variable operating costs.

5) The store was open twenty days per month. To figure how many units Jersey Mike's would have to sell to break even, divide gross profit per unit into monthly fixed costs.

Gross Profit per Unit = Price of a Unit ($5) – Cost of Goods Sold ($1.25) = $3.75

$$\frac{\textbf{Monthly Fixed Costs}}{\textbf{Gross Profit per Unit - Estimated Variable Cost per Unit}} = \textbf{Break-Even Units}$$

$$\textbf{Break-Even Units} = \frac{\textbf{Monthly Fixed Costs (\$8,000)}}{\textbf{Gross Profit per Unit (\$3.75)}} = \textbf{2,133 Units}$$

Jersey Mike's had to make sales of 2,133 units a month to break even. Since the store was open twenty days a month, to break even the store had to sell:

$$\frac{2,133 \text{ units}}{20 \text{ days}} = 107 \text{ units per day}$$

Chapter 31 Review

N O T E : The exercises printed below can be found in the corresponding chapter of the NFTE MODULE 2 WORKBOOK that came with your textbook. Please write your answers there. If you do not have a workbook, write your answers on a separate sheet of paper.

Critical Thinking about . . . Break-Even

1. Describe how finding your business' break-even point would help you operate your business.

2. Before you can find your break-even point, what other financial statement(s) and information do you need?

3. Figure Gross Profit per Unit:

Selling Price per Unit – Cost of Goods Sold per Unit = Gross Profit per Unit

Item	Selling Price per Unit	COGS per Unit	Gross Profit per Unit
Comb	$ 1.00	$ .50	$ .50

Strategies for Improving Break-Even

Calculate Break-Even Units:

$$\text{Break-Even Units} \;=\; \frac{\text{Monthly Fixed Costs}}{\text{Gross Profit per Unit}}$$

Pretend you have a business selling a product for $10 that you buy at the wholesaler's for $5. The business has $2,000 per month in fixed costs. Last month you sold 300 units. Write a memo analyzing this business from a break-even point of view and discuss three strategies for improving the situation.

Getting the Facts

1. Describe why break-even analysis is the fourth step in the marketing process.

2. What is the formula for calculating break-even for a business with fixed costs only? What is the formula for a business that has variable costs, as well?

Review

Chapter Summary

I. **Break-even analysis is the fourth step of marketing. A business breaks even when it neither earns a profit nor sustains a loss.**

A. Net profit (loss) at the break-even point is zero.

B. A business must break even to survive.

C. A business must earn a profit to survive in the long run.

II. **Break-even analysis helps the entrepreneur determine how many units must be sold for the business to cover its operating costs (USAIIRD).**

A. First the business owner must define one unit of sale.

    1. The unit of sale is typically one item for a product business.

    2. The unit of sale is typically one hour for a service business.

B. Next, gross profit per unit must be determined.

    Selling Price – Cost of Goods Sold per Unit = Gross Profit per Unit

C. Then the number of units needed to be sold to break even must be calculated.

$$\frac{\text{Monthly Fixed Costs}}{\text{Gross Profit per Unit}} = \text{Break-Even Units}$$

III. To include variable costs in break-even analysis, use this formula:

$$\frac{\text{Monthly Fixed Costs}}{\text{Gross Profit per Unit - Variable Cost per Unit}} = \text{Break-Even Units}$$

Michelle Lee Araujo, À La Mode, New Bedford, Massachusetts

"My dream is not to die in poverty, but to have poverty die in me," says Michelle Lee Araujo. Michelle insists that there is always time to start your own business. Even if you're a single mother and a full-time college student. Michelle should know, because at 19 she started her own business while caring for her daughter Angela, 3, and Erica, 18 months, and her newborn son, Kristian — while attending college.

Michelle owns a clothing retail company called À La Mode. She has always loved fashion, so she was excited to visit Manhattan's wholesale clothing district with her NFTE class. Michelle knew there was a demand in her hometown for the latest fashions, but hadn't figured out how to fulfill it.

During her visit to the wholesale district, Michelle realized she could buy clothes wholesale and mark them up for resale to her neighbors in New Bedford. She could even outperform the competition by offering the latest styles at lower prices than the stores in town. Michelle resells the clothes from her home or on visits to customers' houses. Michelle's friends and neighbors were delighted to have an alternative to high prices. Her customers also enjoy shopping in a more intimate setting.

As Michelle says, "Who would ever think a teenage mother living in public housing on public aid with three children could ever own her own business and graduate from college?"

Michelle plans to own her own clothing boutique, but first she wants to finish college. "There are very few small clothing boutiques in New Bedford," Michelle explains. She hopes her success will spark a revival of small business in her community.

My life seems like one long obstacle course, with me as the chief obstacle.

— Jack Paar, entertainer

KEY OBJECTIVES

READING THIS CHAPTER AND DOING THE EXERCISES WILL ENABLE YOU TO:

■ Explain why stocks are traded.

■ Read a daily stock table.

■ Calculate a stock's price/earnings ratio.

■ Calculate a stock's yield.

STOCKS

Businesses come in three basic legal structures: the sole proprietorship, the partnership, and the corporation. Many small businesses have only one owner (the proprietor). Most big businesses are corporations.

A **corporation** is a legal structure that allows for ownership of the business to be bought and sold as stock.

Stockholders actually own a corporation. Each **share** of stock represents a percentage of ownership, with a *stock certificate* representing this "piece of the company." How large a piece depends on how many shares of stock were purchased.

If Street Scooters, Inc. has sold 10 shares of stock, each to a different individual, that means there are 10 stockholders. Each owns 1/10th of the company. If Street Scooters, Inc. sold 100 shares of stock, each to a different individual, there would be 100 stockholders. Each would own 1/100th of the company.

Public corporations offer their stock to the general public on the open financial markets. **Offerings**, as the initial sales are called, raise **capital** (money). The corporation can use the capital to expand or to pay off debts.

Once the stocks are sold, however, the corporations have no control over who owns them. These **securities** can be resold, or *traded* by *brokers* many times. A broker is someone who has access to financial securities, such as stocks and bonds. Look in the *Yellow Pages* or online to find a local stockbroker in your community.

The price of a stock reflects public expectations of how well the company is going to perform. People have different ideas about how well a company will do, however. You might be willing to invest in a company at $50 per share. Your friend might really have confidence in that business and be willing to pay $60. You could sell your share to your friend for $60 and earn a profit of ten dollars ($60 - $50 = $10).

Such trading activity occurs constantly on the stock market. As a result, stock prices change almost continually.

The daily record of trading activity appears in tables published in *The Wall Street Journal* and in the business sections of many other newspapers. These tables allow investors to track the changing value of their investments.

Let's say you own ten shares of a stock you bought at $10 (for a total of $100). You see in the stock table that the price per share has declined to $5.50 that day. Your $100 investment is now worth only $55 (10 shares x $5.50/share = $55). You have three choices:

1. Sell the shares before their value declines further.

2. Keep them, hoping the decline is temporary.

3. Buy more shares at the lower price to increase your profit when the price goes back up (this choice is based on the "buy low, sell high" principle).

Reading Stock Tables*

At first glance, stock tables appear to be written in a foreign language, but they are not hard to read. In this chapter is a sample stock table from *The Wall Street Journal*. Following are explanations of some of the terms you'll see:

52-Week High Low: The first figure in the column is the highest price at which the stock traded over the previous year. The second figure is the lowest. All prices are listed in dollars and fractions of dollars. The fractions are traditionally given in eighths.

---

*Adapted with permission from materials prepared by Dow Jones, Inc.

Stock: The name of the company. *The Wall Street Journal* gives both the company name and its symbol. Every stock has a symbol, usually consisting of one to four letters.

Div (Dividend): Corporations can pay each stockholder a *dividend*, or sum of money proportionate to the number of shares the stockholder owns. A dividend is a return on investment for the stockholder. Corporations pay dividends out of the company's profits.

A figure of 1.00 in this column means a dividend of $1 per share of stock was paid out to the company's stockholders over the course of the year. A stockholder who owned 100 shares was, therefore, paid $100 ($1 x 100) in dividends.

Yld (Yield): The rate of return on the stock expressed as a percentage:

$$\frac{\textbf{Dividend}}{\textbf{Closing Price}} \textbf{ x 100}$$

The yield on a stock is low compared to the ROI on some other investments. Stocks are usually purchased with the expectation that the price will go up, though. Reselling the stock at a higher price is how an investor's ROI is usually made in the stock market.

P/E Ratio (Price/Earnings Ratio): The P/E is the price of one share of stock divided by the earnings per share. If the price of the stock is $28, and the company earned $7 for each share of stock outstanding, the P/E Ratio would be four: 28 ÷ 7 = 4

A P/E of 4 is considered low. A low P/E can indicate a stable company. A high P/E is about 20 and above. A P/E of 8 is more or less average.

In general, the higher a P/E, the greater the risk investors are willing to take. They have confidence that the company is going to make more money in the future. A new industry, like genetic engineering, will often have a high P/E because the future earnings are as yet unknown. If the company makes a scientific breakthrough, its stock prices might soar because investors hope the company will earn lots of money.

vol 100s (Volume of shares traded): The number of shares traded (bought and sold) during the previous day's trading period. (The New York Stock Exchange trades Monday through Friday from 9:30 a.m. to 4 p.m., Eastern Standard Time.)

Volume is given in hundreds of shares. Add two zeros to a number in the Vol 100s column to get the correct figure. When there is a very high volume of stock being traded, it means investors are taking an interest in that stock. Volume does not indicate whether the price will go up or down.

Hi Lo Close: The highest, lowest and last price the stock was traded for during the previous day's trading period. Again, the figures are given in fractions of dollars.

Net Chg (Net Change): The change in price from the close of the previous day's trading period.*

52 Wks												
Hi	Lo	Stock	Sym	Div	Yld	P/E	vol 100s	Hi	Lo	Close	Net Chg
34	$16_{1/2}$	Mattel	MAT	.20	.6	19	4020	$33_{3/4}$	$33_{1/8}$	$33_{1/8}$	. . .
$60_{3/8}$	$37_{3/8}$	MayDeptStrs	MAY	1.62	3.2	13	1595	51	50	$50_{1/2}$	-1/4
23	$13_{3/4}$	McClatchy A	MNI	.20	1.1	21	12	$18_{1/4}$	$18_{1/8}$	$18_{1/8}$	+1/8

Selling Short

Stock traders make money by buying stock and then selling it for a profit when the price of the stock rises. Traders can also make money when a stock is falling, however, selling the stock "short."

Selling short is a way to make money when you expect a stock's price to decline. Let's say you "borrow" a $100 share of stock from a broker with an agreement to give it back at the end of three months. Next, you sell the stock for $100, which is its present market value, to a buyer. At the end of the three months, the price of the share of stock has fallen to $50 in the market. You buy a share for $50 and return it to the broker you borrowed it from. You have earned a $50 profit because you sold the borrowed stock for $100 and replaced it for $50 ($100 − $50 = $50).

As you see, like stock trading in general, short selling is *speculative*. It is a gamble and can be highly risky. If, in the example above, the price of the stock does not go down, as you thought it would, but rises to, say, $150 at the end of the three months, you will have lost $50 on the transaction because it will cost you $50 more than you paid to return it to the broker ($150 − $100 = $50).

In fact, only about 5% of all investors get involved with selling short, and these are usually experts in the financial markets. The point is, though, that there are always ways to make money when the economy as a whole is not doing well. Don't think only in terms of making money in an "up" market.

---

* Note: There are additional special symbols that are explained at the bottom of the published stock tables.

Chapter 32 Review

NOTE: The exercises printed below can be found in the corresponding chapter of the NFTE MODULE 2 WORKBOOK that came with your textbook. Please write your answers there. If you do not have a workbook, write your answers on a separate sheet of paper.

Critical Thinking about . . . Reading a Stock Table

Look up the following stocks in *The Wall Street Journal* and answer the questions.

Ford Motor Co.

J.P. Morgan Chase & Co.

Colgate-Palmolive

Reebok

Disney

1. Which stock is the most expensive?

2. Which stock has the highest dividend?

3. Which stock has the highest yield?

4. Which stock has the lowest P/E ratio?

Using New Words

capital
corporation
offering
securities
share
speculative

On a separate sheet of paper, write the vocabulary term with the letter of its corresponding definition.

a. stock certificates

b. uncertain or risky

c. a public stock sale

d. money raised in a public offering

e. a single piece of stock

f. a business structure that allows for ownership to be sold in shares

Review

Chapter 32 Review

Getting the Facts

1. Why are investors willing to pay different prices for the same stock?

2. What is the return on investment of a stock called? How is it calculated?

Exploring Your Community

True or False?

1. The lower the P/E on a stock, the higher the risk to the investor.

2. Corporations must pay monthly dividends to stockholders.

3. Corporations have no control over the securities they issue.

4. When a share's price declines, you should always sell it.

5. Short selling is best undertaken by financial experts, because it is highly speculative.

In Your Opinion

Discuss with a group:

Based on your knowledge of current events and trends, from which of the three companies below would you buy stock? Write a memo discussing your decision and share it with the class.

(Hint: There is no "right" answer — like any stockholder, your preferences will depend on the acceptable levels of risk and your opinions about the economy.)

Company A makes a vital part for cellular phones.

Company B has just invented a process for cloning cows.

Company C manufactures automobiles.

Monitoring Stock

Pretend you could buy one share of any stock listed in *The Wall Street Journal*. Monitor the stock for one week. Calculate your profit and your return on investment for each day you hold your imaginary investment.

Review

Chapter Summary

I.   Public corporations sell stock to raise capital.

A. Securities can be traded.

B. Daily trading causes stock prices to change.

C. Daily trading is reported in detail in *The Wall Street Journal*.

II. If the price of a stock you own declines, you have three options:

A. Sell.

B. Hold the stock.

C. Buy more at the cheaper price.

III. Stock tables provide the following information:

52-week high/low

name of stock

dividend

yield

price/earnings ratio

trading volume

high/low close

net change in price

IV. Selling short is a high-risk way to make money when a stock price is falling.

Problems are only opportunities in work clothes.

— Henry J. Kaiser,
American industrialist

KEY OBJECTIVES

READING THIS CHAPTER AND DOING THE EXERCISES WILL ENABLE YOU TO:

- Do business math in your head so you can think on your feet.
- Convert bulk prices to per-unit cost quickly during negotiations.
- Read pie charts and graphs.

MATH TIPS TO HELP YOU SELL AND NEGOTIATE

One of the great things about studying entrepreneurship is that it can really motivate you to study subjects — like math — that you might not have found much use for before you became an entrepreneur. To run a business, you need a solid grasp of basic math so you can negotiate the best possible deals for your business. Being able to do math in your head will also help you think on your feet when you are trying to make a sale.

Math In Your Head*

Being able to do simple calculations in your head will allow you to negotiate prices and quantities with much more success. While you are bargaining with a wholesaler, or a supplier, you can be converting the price for large quantities into your per-unit purchase price. This will help you know whether the deal will be profitable or not.

---

* Special thanks to Jack Mariotti for the ideas he contributed to this chapter.

5 per box X $1 each = $5

Sheila sells lipsticks for $1 each. She buys them wholesale in boxes of five. In her head, she calculates:

5 sticks per box x $1 per stick = $5

Sheila can make a profit if the wholesaler will sell her a box for under $5. Before you bargain, know what your limit is (Sheila's is $5). When buying wholesale, your limit is somewhere below your resale price for each item.

Business Math Tips

1. Break down one big math problem into several smaller problems. Solve them one at a time.

Example: A wholesaler says he can sell you a dozen hats for $60. Your *cost of goods sold* (the cost of a single hat) is $60 divided by 12.

Break it down: 12 = 2 x 6, so:

a. $60 ÷ 2 = $30

b. $30 ÷ 6 = $5

Answer: Each hat costs $5.

2. Round off numbers to do easier calculations. Adjust for the rounding off after you have done them.

Example: A wholesaler offers you 10 blank videocassette tapes for $24.50. How much does one cassette cost?

Round off: Round off $24.50 to $25.00

Calculate: $25.00 ÷ 10 = $2.50

Adjust: You rounded off by $0.50 for ten cassettes.

$0.50 ÷ 10 = $0.05

$2.50 – $0.05 = $2.45

The exact cost of one blank videocassette tape is $2.45.

3. If all you need is an approximation to know if you are getting a good deal, just round off and calculate. Skip the adjustment.

4. Approximation is very helpful in translating between hourly and daily rates.

Example: Someone works for you for $10 per hour. How much will he cost per year?

Approximate: He works approximately 40 hours per week.

　　　　　　　　There are about 50 work weeks in a year.

　　　　　　　　40 hours per week x 50 weeks per year = 2,000 hours per year.

Calculate: 2,000 hours per year x $10 per hour = $20,000 per year.

　　　　　　　　OR

Approximate: He works about 8 hours a day.

Calculate: 8 hours per day x $10 per hour = $80 per day.

Approximate: There are 250 work days in a year (5 days per week x 50 weeks).

Calculate: $80 per day x 250 days per year = $20,000 per year.

5. The Rule of 72: 72 divided by ROI = number of years it will take to double the investment.

Example 1: Say you invest $10 in a savings account that pays 5 percent yearly interest. How long will it take, at that rate of return, for your $10 to grow to $20?

Rule of 72:   72 ÷ 5 = 14.4 years

Example 2: You purchase a newsstand that nets 20 percent per year. You paid $20,000 for the stand. How many years will it take to double your investment?

Rule of 72:   72 ÷ 20 = 3.6 years

Practice business math in your head whenever you have the opportunity. For example, apples at your local supermarket cost $1.10 per dozen. How much does one apple cost? Practicing business math will make you a sharper negotiator.

6. Keystoning.

Always remember that many businesspeople routinely double their costs to get their price. This is called keystoning.

Bar Graphs and Pie Charts

Business information is often presented in bar graphs or pie charts because they are easy to read at a glance.

A pie chart shows how parts of a whole are divided. Think of the pie as 100 percent. The wedges of the pie are smaller percentages of the whole.

Example: Let's look at David's Income Statement from Chapter 4 and show it as a pie chart on the following page.

DAVID'S INCOME STATEMENT		
Sales:		$ 100
Less Total Cost of Goods Sold:		50
Gross Profit:		50
Less Operating Costs:		
Fixed Costs:	$ 24	
Variable Costs:	0	
		24
Profit Before Taxes:		26
Taxes:		6
Net Profit/(Loss):		$ 20

David's Income Statement as a Pie Chart

The pie represents what happened with the $100 in sales.

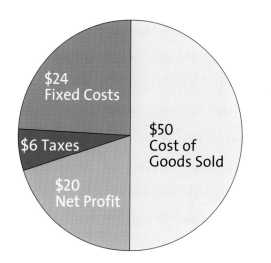

David's Income Statement as a Bar Graph

David could use a bar graph to track his sales over time. A bar graph would show at a glance whether sales are rising or falling.

Let's say David sells $100-worth of merchandise in January, $150 in February, $200 in March, $200 in April — and only $75 in May, because he took a vacation. The bar graph would look like this:

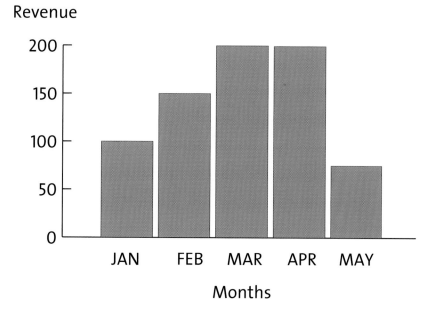

Chapter 33 Review

N O T E : The exercises printed below can be found in the corresponding chapter of the NFTE MODULE 2 WORKBOOK that came with your textbook. Please write your answers there. If you do not have a workbook, write your answers on a separate sheet of paper.

Critical Thinking about . . . Business Math

Try these problems in your head!

1) A wholesaler offers to sell you pens at $1.20 per dozen. You know you can sell pens at school for $.25 each.

   How much will each pen cost?

   Would you make or lose money buying and selling these pens?

   How much would you make or lose on each pen?

2) You want to hire someone to help with your business. The person you want to hire wants to make $12,000 per year.

   How much would you need to offer per hour to equal $12,000 per year?

3) How long would it take to turn $5,000 into $10,000 if you had an investment that yielded a 6 percent return, compounded annually?

4) Figure out the cost of one unit per item.

Example:

Item	Cost per Dozen	Unit Cost
Soda	$ 3.00	$ .25

5) Use the concept of keystoning to calculate the retail price and gross profit of each item.

Example:

Item	Wholesale Cost	Retail Price	Gross Profit
Soda	$ .25	$ .50	$ .25

6) Figure out the cost of one unit for each item.

Example:

Item	Cost per Dozen	Unit Cost
Soda	$ 6.00	$ .50

Chapter Summary

I.   Entrepreneurs need to be able to do simple math in their heads.

A. Figuring unit costs while bargaining with a wholesaler or supplier will help you bargain better.

B. Use the Rule of 72 to figure out how long it will take to double an investment.

II.   Use approximation and adjustment techniques to do quick math.

A. Round off numbers, then adjust after calculating.

B. Break a large math problem into several smaller ones.

III. Business information is often presented in pie charts or bar graphs.

A. They are easy to read at a glance.

B. A pie chart shows how the parts of a whole are divided.

C. A bar graph makes comparison over time easy.

When there's nothing to lose and much to gain by trying, try.

— W. Clement Stone,
master salesman

KEY OBJECTIVES

READING THIS CHAPTER AND DOING THE EXERCISES WILL ENABLE YOU TO:

- Keep your goals in mind when making a sales call.
- Explain the seven steps of a sales call.
- Fill out a receipt.

THE ADVANCED SALES CALL*

A sales call is an appointment with a potential customer to explain or demonstrate your product or service. The goals to keep in mind when making a sales call are:

- Make the customer aware of your product or service.
- Ask questions to uncover the customer's needs and priorities.
- Make the customer want to buy that product or service by demonstrating that it meets their needs.
- Even if you do not make the sale, always ask for referrals.
- Establish a strong relationship with the customer so that you can make future sales.

---

* Special thanks to Sandra Sowell-Scott for the ideas she contributed to this chapter.

Before Your First Sales Call

Before going on any sales call, take the time to get your marketing materials right. These are brochures, order forms, samples, etc. They should be clear and easy to read and use. All marketing materials for your business should reinforce your competitive advantage in the customer's mind.

Good marketing materials accomplish three things:

1. Preparing them forces you to organize your thoughts.
2. You can use them to teach employees about your business quickly.
3. They are very helpful during a sales call.

The Eight-Step Sales Call

1. **Preparation.** Prepare yourself mentally. Analyze both the product/service and the customer. Have the price, discounts, all technical information and any other details "on the tip of your tongue." You don't want to waste your customer's time fumbling for information you should know. Be willing to obtain further information, however, should your customer request it.

2. **Greeting.** Greet the customer graciously. Do not plunge immediately into business talk. The first few words you say can be the most important. Keep a two-way conversation going. Maintain eye contact and keep the customer's attention.

3. **Showing the product/service.** Try to "personalize" it. Point out the benefits for this particular customer. Use props and models (or the real thing) where appropriate.

4. **Listen to the Customer.** After you pitch your product or service once, carefully listen to the customer's reaction. This is how you will get your most valuable information and learn what the customer needs and wants. Your goal here and throughout the sales call is to make the customer believe that you are trying to solve his or her problem, not just make a sale. That's how you establish trust and create a genuine relationship.

   Research has shown that in successful sales calls, the buyer does most of the talking — not the salesperson!

 RULE OF THUMB: If a customer says No three times, you still have a shot at making the sale. If the customer says No a fourth time, he/she means it.

5. **Answering Objections.** During the listening phase, you will hear a customer's objections to your product or service. Always acknowledge these concerns and deal with them. Don't pretend you didn't hear. Don't overreact to objections and don't be afraid to listen. Sometimes objections are simply misunderstandings that, through careful listening, you can clarify for the customer. A famous real estate entrepreneur, William Zeckendorf, said, "I never lost money on a sales pitch when I listened to the customer." Do not hesitate to tell the absolute truth about any aspects of your product or service that do not meet your customer's immediate expectations. Each time you honestly answer a customer's concern, you gain their trust.

6. **Asking for a Commitment.** If concerns have come up, point out that, at this price, the product or service is still an excellent buy. Review the benefits of the product. Narrow the choices the customer has to make. Ask for a commitment. However, if it appears that the product does not match the customer's needs, do not try to make a sale. Don't overstay your welcome. There is a rule of thumb that says: If a customer says No three times, you still have a chance. If he/she says it the fourth time, it's really No. If the answer is No, take it gracefully. You may make a sale to this customer in the future. Also, always remember to fill out a receipt to finalize a successful sale, and keep a record of every sale you make.

7. **Follow-up.** Make regular follow-up calls to find out how the customer likes the product or service. Ask if you can be of any further help. If the customer has a complaint, don't ignore it. Keeping the customer's trust after the sale is the most important part of the whole process because a successful business is built on repeat customers. Plus, every time you talk to a customer you are deepening your friendship. Your best sales prospects in the future are people who have already bought something from you. Keep them posted on your business by sending postcards or flyers.

8. **Ask for references.** If you did a good job for customers who needed your product or service, ask them to refer you to other potential customers. Try to set up a system that encourages others to send sales prospects your way. Offer discounts, gift certificates, or other incentives to customers who refer people to you. Give customers a few business cards to pass on to their friends.

Use Technology to Sell

You can use technology to sell your product, help your customers understand and use it, and to stay in touch with them. Examples include:

- A videotaped demonstration or presentation of your product.

- A website customers can visit for updates or product facts.

- Using e-mail and faxes to stay in touch with customers.

- A customer database — this is a list of all customers and potential customers. The database should include each person's name, e-mail address, phone and fax numbers, and mailing address. Also include the date of your last contact, and a note about what the person bought and said.

Pre-Qualify Your Sales Call

Before calling to make an appointment for any sales call (sometimes called a sales *pitch*), ask yourself these questions: Is this person in my market? Would he/she need my product? Can he/she afford it?

If the answer to any of these questions is No, making a sales call on that person may be a waste of time. Asking these questions is called *pre-qualifying* a sales call.

The Sales Commission

Salespeople often work on *commission*. This means that, for every sale made, they are paid a percentage of the total sale. A car salesman making a 10 percent commission, for instance, would be paid $1,000 if he were to sell a $10,000 car (.10 x $10,000 = $1,000). The owner of the car dealership is paying the salesman a commission to encourage him to sell.

The Sales Receipt

When you make a sale, you should fill out a receipt for the customer in a carbon-copy receipt book. The original is your record of income that you record in your accounting journal.

The receipt must include the date of the sale, the item sold, and its price. It can also include the name and address of the purchaser. The carbon copy of the receipt is the customer's proof that the item or service was purchased.

In the example below "Reg. No." (cash register number) and "clerk" would be applicable to larger stores; #28 is the style number of the T-shirt. This is important to know for purposes of *inventory* (the amount of a product you have on hand).

GINA'S T-SHIRT CO.

Date **June 13**   **1995**

Sold to: **George Braxton**

Address: **123 E. Orange St.**

Reg. No.   Clerk

1	**1 red T-shirt (#28) @**	**$10.99**	**$10.99**
2			
3		Tax	.61
4			
5		Total	$11.60
6			
7			
8			
9			
10			

Paid in Cash

Style 1200   **495-1**

Chapter 34 Review

N O T E : The exercises printed below can be found in the corresponding chapter of the NFTE MODULE 2 WORKBOOK that came with your textbook. Please write your answers there. If you do not have a workbook, write your answers on a separate sheet of paper.

Critical Thinking about . . . Sales Calls

1. What is a sales call? Do you plan to make sales calls for your business? Why or why not?

2. Come up with five sales-call prospects for your business. How would you go about pre-qualifying these sales prospects?

3. Have you created any marketing materials for your business? If so, have three friends and a mentor (someone older that you respect who can give you advice about your business) look at your materials and give you feedback. Write a memo listing their suggestions and what you plan to do to improve your marketing materials.

Making One-Minute Sales Calls

1. Develop a one-minute sales call for three things that you are wearing. Try out a sales pitch for each item on a partner. Have your partner help you time each to one minute.

2. Write a memo to your partner discussing his/her sales calls and how they could be improved. Use the Eight Steps of a Sales Call as your guide when analyzing your partner's efforts.

Review

Chapter Summary

I. The only way to become a good salesperson is to make sales calls.

   A. A sales call is an appointment with a potential customer.

   B. The goal of the call is to make the customer aware of the product or service and make him or her want to buy it from you.

II. Get your marketing materials together before making your first sales call.

   A. Marketing materials include brochures, business cards, order forms, and samples.

   B. You can also use marketing materials to teach employees about your business.

III. The eight steps of a sales call are:

1. Preparation
2. Greeting
3. Showing
4. Listening to the customer
5. Answering objections
6. Asking for a commitment
7. Follow-up
8. Referral

IV. Use technology to help you sell.

   A. E-mail, fax, video brochures, websites are all effective sales tools.

   B. Keep a customer database.

V. Always fill out a sales receipt for the customer.

   A. The receipt is the customer's proof of purchase.

   B. The receipt is your record of income.

The first and best victory is to conquer the self.

—Plato,
Greek philosopher

KEY OBJECTIVES

READING THIS CHAPTER AND DOING THE EXERCISES WILL ENABLE YOU TO:

- List the benefits and drawbacks of franchising.
- Describe the contents of a franchise agreement.
- Contrast licensing with franchising.
- Explore the concepts of synergism and branding.

FRANCHISING AND LICENSING: CAPITALIZING ON YOUR BRAND

The Power of a Great Brand

A brand is a name, term, sign, logo, design, or combination of these that identifies the products or services of a company. The brand represents the company's promise to consistently deliver a specific set of benefits to customers.

One entrepreneur can create a business that grows from a sole proprietorship to an international conglomerate. But there's another way to grow a business — and that's by creating **franchises**, or by licensing a brand.

Franchising

A franchise is a business that markets a product or service developed by someone else in the manner prescribed by the person who developed the business. Once you have developed a strong business and created a brand people recognize, you can consider using franchising to grow.

McDonald's restaurants are examples of a franchise. McDonald's was developed by Ray Kroc, who had persuaded the McDonald brothers to let him become the franchising agent for their highly successful hamburger restaurant. Kroc's great insight was to realize that the **franchisees** — the people who bought a McDonald's franchise — needed extensive training and support to succeed, and that their success would only strengthen McDonald's as a whole.

The McDonald's franchisee owns the restaurant, but has agreed to market the food under the McDonald's name and trademark in the fashion first developed by Kroc. This is spelled out in a franchising contract. This protects the brand so it continues to mean the same positive thing in the mind of the consumer — no matter who is running the business.

The franchisee invests his or her capital in a proven, successful business concept. McDonald's receives a fee and a share of the franchisee's profits. McDonald's provides its trademark, management training, marketing, national advertising, promotional assistance, and standardized operating procedures to the franchisee.

The Franchise Boom

Many different kinds of businesses have been franchised — fast-food restaurants, auto-repair shops, motels, health clubs, insurance agencies, hair salons, and so on.

As an entrepreneur you could develop a brand and a system that can be reproduced. When that happens, you can franchise your business and reap the rewards of all your hard work. You could also decide to buy a franchise if you'd like to be an entrepreneur but you don't want to create a business from the ground up. A franchise may be less risky than starting your own business because it is based on a concept that has been proven successful.

Although franchising has been around since the Singer Sewing Machine Company first developed it in the 1850s, its popularity has exploded in recent years. Over 4,000 companies offer franchises. The number of individual franchises grew to nearly half a million between 1977 and 1997.

Women and minorities have been especially drawn to franchises as a way to enter the business world. Recognizing this, Burger King, Pizza Hut, Taco Bell, Kentucky Fried Chicken, and Baskin-Robbins all offer special financing and other incentives to recruit minority franchise owners. Other franchise programs have focused, with great success, on recruiting women.

A Synergistic Relationship

The exciting thing about franchises is that both parties benefit from the transfer of knowledge. Both parties *must* benefit, in fact, for either to succeed. For the franchisee to succeed, the **franchisor** must do a good job of teaching the business and providing support and supplies. For the franchisor to succeed, the franchisee must do a good job of running the business. This is a *synergistic* relationship: The cooperation of both parties yields a greater whole than either could have achieved alone.

Benefits of Franchising

Franchisor

- Growth with minimal capital investment.

- Lower marketing and promotion costs.

- Royalties.

Franchisee

- Ownership of a business with less risk than is involved in starting a business alone.

- Help with management and training.

- Advertising — the franchise chain can afford television ads, etc., that the small-business owner could not finance alone.

Drawbacks of Franchising

Franchisor

- The franchisee may disregard the training and fail to operate the business properly, tarnishing the reputation of the franchise and the brand.
- It can be difficult to find qualified or trustworthy franchisees.
- Franchisees who do not experience success may try to sue the franchisor.

Franchisee

- Giving up control — much of the franchise's operations are dictated by the franchisor.

- The franchisor may fail to deliver promised training and support.

- The franchisor may engage in poor business practices that affect the earnings or image of the franchise.

The Franchise Agreement

The franchise agreement is the contract between the franchisor and franchisee. The contract establishes the standards that assure uniformity of product and service throughout the chain.

Included in the franchise agreement are:

1. The term of the agreement, or length of time the franchisor and franchisee agree to work together.

2. Standards of quality and performance.

3. An agreement on **royalties** — usually a percentage of the franchise's sales is paid to the franchisor.

4. "Non-compete clauses" stating that, for instance, if you own a McDonald's, you cannot also own a Blimpie's.

5. Territories — franchisees are usually assigned areas in which they can do business. Within the assigned areas no other franchisee from that company will be allowed to compete.

6. Remember, there are many federal and state regulations in franchising. Before you enter a franchise agreement, make sure that you understand these regulations.

Licensing

Licensing is another way to profit from your brand. The difference between **licensing** and franchising is one of control.

- The franchisor controls every aspect of how the franchisee runs the franchise. It is all specified in the franchise agreement.

- The **licensor** grants the **licensee** the right to use the former's name on a product or service but has less control of how the licensee does business.

Many fashion designers and celebrities have made millions by licensing their well-known names for perfume, athletic shoes, and other products. Licensing is also subject to fewer government regulations than franchising.

Ray Kroc: Fast-Food Franchisor

Ray Kroc used franchising to open McDonald's restaurants all over the world. McDonald's was the first franchisor to provide in-depth training to franchises in everything from how to make the perfect french fry to how employees should dress and greet customers. The entire system of cooking and serving the food was timed.

In this way, Kroc guaranteed that the food at all McDonald's restaurants would taste the same and be served quickly in a clean environment.

The first of Kroc's McDonald's opened in Des Plaines, Illinois, in 1955. By 1960 there were 228 McDonald's in the United States. A hundred additional restaurants opened each year until 1968. After 1968, over 200 opened per year. By 1983, McDonald's was a $3 billion company with 7,778 restaurants in thirty countries. Through franchising, Ray Kroc turned a simple idea — the fast production of inexpensive hamburgers — into an internationally recognized symbol of American enterprise.

The Wrong Licensing Can Damage Your Brand

The licensee pays a fee for the license and may pay royalties on sales to the licensor.

Licensing is only effective, though, when the licensor is confident that his or her company name won't be damaged by the licensee's use of it. When Coca-Cola licenses its name to a T-shirt maker, there's not much the T-shirt maker can do to tarnish the reputation of Coca-Cola by making the shirts. Coca-Cola gets free advertising, as well as royalties.

Coca-Cola would be unwilling to license its name to a soft drink manufacturer, however, because the licensing agreement would not guarantee that the manufacturer would make a product of the same quality as Coca-Cola's. If Coca-Cola did want to expand in this fashion, it would be better served by a franchising agreement.

Like franchising, licensing must be done carefully, with respect for the company's brand. Many companies have taken popular brands, such as Adidas athletic shoes, and applied them with disastrous results to products like Adidas cologne. It didn't work very well to apply a brand like Adidas, associated with sneakers (which can smell pretty bad) to cologne! Using an established brand to promote different products is called "line extension" (extending a line of products). It can work if the brand is very strong and the new product the brand is being applied to is similar to the original product. Kraft General Foods successfully applied the Jell-O brand name to a line of puddings after it had established Jell-O as the number one gelatin dessert.

In most cases, however, focusing your brand tightly on your product is a better strategy.

Chapter 35 Review

NOTE: The exercises printed below can be found in the corresponding chapter of the NFTE MODULE 2 WORKBOOK that came with your textbook. Please write your answers there. If you do not have a workbook, write your answers on a separate sheet of paper.

Critical Thinking about . . . Franchising

Franchise	Franchise Fee	Start-up Costs	Royalty Fee
McDonald's	$22,000	Varies	4%
Arby's Inc.	$25,000–$37,500	$550,000–$887,500	4%
General Nutrition Franchising Inc.	$17,500	$58,700–$137,500	5%
Hardee's	$15,000	$699,900–$1.7 million	4%

For each franchise, use this formula to calculate how much you would owe the franchisor in royalties if you made one million dollars in sales:

Royalties = Royalty Fee x Sales

Using New Words

franchise
franchisee
franchisor
licensing
licensee
licensor
royalty

On a separate sheet of paper, write the vocabulary term with the letter of its corresponding definition.

a. person who develops and sells a franchise system

b. an already developed business concept and system

c. person or business that buys rights to a name or trademark

d. person who buys a franchise unit

e. renting one's name or trademark

f. a percentage share of the proceeds of the sale of a product

g. person or business receiving payment for allowing use of name or trademark

Review

Chapter 35 Review

Getting the Facts

1. Why would a franchising agreement include a "non-compete" clause?

2. Write a short essay describing the differences between branding, franchising, and licensing.

3. What did Ray Kroc do with his franchisees that was unique?

Analyzing Franchises and Licenses

1. Would you be interested in running a franchise? Why or why not? Write a memo analyzing the advantages and disadvantages.

2. You probably own some products that involve licensing. Pick one and write a memo analyzing the licensing strategy's weaknesses and strengths.

Chapter Summary

I.   If you create a strong brand, you can grow your business through franchising and licensing.

    A. Franchising reproduces your business system exactly and trains other entrepreneurs to follow it.

    B. Licensing sells your business name and logo to other companies to put on their products.

II.   A franchise is a business that can easily be reproduced.

    A. The franchisee follows production and marketing standards set out in the franchising agreement.

    B. The franchisee pays a share of profits as royalties to the franchisor.

III.   Franchising is a synergistic relationship: the cooperation of franchisee with franchisor creates a greater whole than either could achieve alone.

IV.   Unlike the franchisor, the licensor does not control every aspect of how the licensee does business.

    A. The licensor receives royalties from the sale of items bearing the licensor's name.

    B. The licensor cannot control the quality of the licensee's product.

V.   Focusing on the brand may be a better strategy than using it to extend the line.

    A. The goal is to make sure your brand comes to mean something very specific in the customer's mind.

    B. You can dilute the strength of your brand if you use it on too many products.

KEY OBJECTIVES

READING THIS CHAPTER AND DOING THE EXERCISES WILL ENABLE YOU TO:

- Get your business agreements in writing.

- Use contracts to strengthen your business plan.

- List "The Four A's" of a successful contract.

- Summarize what can be done in case of breach of contract.

CONTRACTS

Getting It In Writing

In Chapter 22, we discussed using a memo as informal proof of an agreement or discussion. A **contract** is a formal written agreement between two or more individuals. A franchise agreement is an example of a contract.

The power of a contract is that, once the individuals involved have signed it, they must stick to its conditions or risk being sued and punished in a court of law. This is why "getting it in writing" is more important than any verbal agreement.

Contracts Allow Planning

Contracts are the building blocks of business. Let's say a department store wants to start selling your customized T-shirts. You work out a six-month contract specifying how many shirts you will supply at what price, and how and when the store will pay you.

With that contract in hand you can call your wholesaler. Because you have an order for six months, you will want to order in bulk. With the contract as written proof of your relationship with the store, your wholesaler may give you credit. You can arrange to buy the T-shirts from the wholesaler you need now to fill the order, and pay for them after you sell them to the store.

You can also plan ahead with your advertisers or work out an advertising plan with the store as part of your contract.

Contracts allow you to sue if the store does not honor the agreement. If the store fails to buy your T-shirts as agreed, you can take it to court and force payment. That way, you can honor your contract with your wholesaler.

See a Lawyer

Never sign a contract without having an attorney examine it for you. Never sign a contract that you yourself have not read from top to bottom, even if your lawyer tells you it's all right. If you are ever taken to court and argue that "I didn't understand that part of the contract," that will not satisfy the judge. Your signature at the bottom tells the court that you read, understood and agreed to every word.

Lawyers typically charge by the hour, so be as prepared and organized as possible before visiting one. Read the contract ahead of time and make a copy of it. Circle sections on the copy that you do not agree to or understand. This will help your attorney advise you efficiently.

Drafting a Contract

If you are consulting your attorney because you need to write, or **draft**, a contract, do as much work as you can in advance. First, determine your needs. What do you need from this contract? What should it say? Make a list.

A successful contract should achieve "The Four A's":

1) Avoid misunderstanding
2) Assure work
3) Assure payment
4) Avoid liability

Avoid Misunderstanding

When putting together a contract, spell out everything that will be done, even what is most obvious. Go into full detail (not just how many shirts you will supply to the store and when, but what types and sizes). If you don't cover all the details, the person with whom you are contracting may add provisions you won't like.

Assure Work

For a contract to be legally binding, both parties must do something or exchange something of value, or agree *not* to do something they were legally entitled to do. You can even exchange one dollar as a token payment to make a contract legal. The contract should assure that you or the other person fulfill some kind of obligation. The exact nature of the obligation, and the time frame for accomplishing it, should then be specified fully.

Assure Payment

A good contract specifies how payment will be made, and when and for what. It should leave no room for misinterpretation.

Avoid Liability

Because this world is full of surprises, your contract should spell out **contingencies** — unpredictable events beyond your control that could cause you to fail to fulfill your responsibilities. The contract should list these contingencies for which you are not *liable* (responsible). Common contingencies are "acts of God" (earthquake, hurricane) or illness.

When you take the draft of your contract to your attorney, ask these two basic questions:

1) Will this agreement protect my interests?

2) What would you add, drop, or change?

Letter of Agreement

Sometimes you won't need a contract, because the relationship is going to be brief or the work and money involved are relatively minor. In such cases, a **letter of agreement** may be enough.

A letter of agreement puts the verbal agreement in writing, in the form of a business letter. The other person must respond to it in writing, either agreeing with it or suggesting changes.

Breach of Contract

A contract is breached when one of the **signatories** (a person who signed the contract), fails to fulfill it. The person injured by the signatory's failure to comply with the contract may then sue for **breach of contract**.

For a contract to be *breached*, it must first be legally binding. Most states require that all signatories be eighteen years of age and that the contract represent an "exchange of value." If a contract is breached, a **lawsuit** must be brought by the injured party within the **statute of limitations** of the state, which limits the time period within which legal action may be taken.

A lawsuit is an attempt to recover a right or claim through legal action. Because lawyers are expensive and court cases time-consuming, lawsuits should be avoided whenever possible. Other options are **small claims court** and **arbitration**.

Small Claims Court

Conflicts involving less than a certain amount of money, which varies by state law, can usually be resolved in a small claims court. In New York State, claims for $2,500 or less can be settled in this manner. In small claims court, *complainants* are allowed to represent themselves before a court official who hears each side's arguments and makes a decision that is legally binding.

Arbitration

Sometimes contracts specify that conflicts may be settled in arbitration, instead of in court. In such cases an *arbitrator* — someone both sides agree to trust — is chosen to act as judge. Both sides agree to abide by the arbitrator's decision.

A Contract Is No Substitute for Trust

A contract is not a substitute for understanding and communication. If you don't like or trust someone, having a contract will not improve the relationship. It could lead, instead, to a lawsuit. *Never sign a contract with someone you don't get along with or trust.*

One good reason never to sign a contract with such a person is that you might need to renegotiate the contract at some point. Running a small business is challenging and unpredictable. Using the example from earlier in the chapter, what if, after you get credit from your T-shirt supplier and make your custom T-shirts, the department store decides not to buy them? How will you pay the T-shirt supplier? You might need more time to find another buyer for your T-shirts. If you have a friendly relationship with your supplier, you should be able to negotiate a longer term for the contract.

Sample Contract

CONTRACT FOR SALE OF GOODS

Agreement made and entered into this ***May 17, 2001***, by and between:

The ***National Foundation for Teaching Entrepreneurship, Inc. (NFTE)***, 120 Wall Street, 29th Floor, New York, NY 10005, referred to as *Seller* , and

John D. Doe, 33 Mockingbird Lane, Smallville, NY 10562, referred to as *Buyer.*

Seller hereby agrees to transfer and deliver to buyer, on or before May 25, 2001, the following goods: ***25 Toshiba laptop computers***.

The agreed upon purchase price is ***$1,000*** per unit.

Goods shall be deemed received by Buyer when delivered to address of Buyer as described above. Until such time as said Buyer has received goods, all risk of loss from any damage to said goods shall be on Seller.

Buyer has the right to examine the goods on arrival and has 10 days to notify Seller of any claim for damages on account of the condition, grade or quality of the goods. That said notice must specifically set forth the basis of his claim, and that his failure to either notice Seller within the stipulated period of time or to set forth specifically the basis of his claim will constitute irrevocable acceptance of the goods. This agreement has been executed in duplicate, whereby both Buyer and Seller have retained one copy each, on May 17, 2001.

_____   _____
             Buyer   ***Seller***

Chapter 36 Review

Critical Thinking about ...
an Entrepreneur's Contracts

Brainstorm a list of types of contracts an entrepreneur might enter into during the course of doing business. Draw up a sample contract between you and a wholesaler for business supplies.

Using New Words

arbitration
breach of contract
contract
contingency
draft
letter of agreement
signatory
statute of limitations
small claims court
lawsuit

On a separate sheet of paper, write the vocabulary term with the letter of its corresponding definition.

a. informal written agreement

b. unexpected event

c. court where minor lawsuits can be settled

d. failure to comply with the contract

e. settling a conflict with the help of another person both parties trust rather than in a court of law

f. limits number of years in which legal action can be taken

g. person who signs a contract

h. an early version of a written document

i. a legally binding agreement

j. attempt to recover a right or claim through legal action

Getting the Facts

1. What two things should you do before signing a contract?

2. What are some alternatives to settling a breach of contract with a lawsuit?

3. Write a letter of agreement between you and a supplier for your business.

4. What does your signature at the bottom of a contract mean in a court of law?

Review

Chapter Summary

I. Contracts are the building blocks of business.

A. A contract is more formal and complex than a memo.

B. Contracts allow a business to plan.

II. See a lawyer when drafting or signing a contract and be sure to ask these two questions:

A. Will this agreement protect my interests?

B. What would you add, drop, or change?

III. A successful contract achieves "The Four A's":

A. Avoid misunderstanding

B. Assure work

C. Assure payment

D. Avoid liability

IV. A contract is breached when one of the signatories fails to comply.

A. Conflicts involving smaller sums can be settled in small-claims court.

B. Some contracts specify arbitration.

V. A contract is not a substitute for trust.

A Business for the Young Entrepreneur: Party Clown

Do you know how to juggle or do magic tricks? Do you enjoy making people laugh? Become a party clown. Parents will hire you to entertain at their children's birthday parties. Hospitals and restaurants also hire clowns.

Make up some short, entertaining clown routines. These might include:

- Mime
- Juggling
- Jokes
- Tumbling
- Balloon tricks
- Silly songs

You Will Need

- Clown costume
- Clown makeup
- A bag with whatever you need for your routines (balloons, balls, etc.); bring some games with you, too, like Pin-the-Tail-on-the-Donkey.

Before Each Job

- Find out the age of the children at the party so you can practice appropriate routines.
- If there is a birthday boy or girl, or a guest of honor, get his or her name in advance. Have this person pointed out to you.
- Discuss how long you are expected to entertain at the party and how much you will be paid.

One great, strong, unselfish soul in every community could actually redeem the world.

— Elbert Hubbard, American lecturer and essayist

KEY OBJECTIVES

READING THIS CHAPTER AND DOING THE EXERCISES WILL ENABLE YOU TO:

- List new sources of capital.
- Consider offering equity to finance your business.
- Manage accounts payable to maximize use of your money.

RAISING CAPITAL: OTHER PEOPLE'S MONEY

Sources of Other People's Money (OPM)

There are many sources of capital for your business. Except for gifts, all come as either debt or equity. One way to finance a business is with Other People's Money. One source of OPM — venture capital — is discussed in detail in the next chapter. Others include:

- Family
- Friends, colleagues, acquaintances
- Accounts payable
- "Angels"
- Minority financing

Family and Friends

Family and friends are obvious sources for loans, but how about offering them equity instead of borrowing money? Unless your business is incorporated,* you cannot officially offer stock in your company, but you can still offer equity ownership:

- Offer a percentage of your business enterprise in exchange for financing.

- Explain that the equity percentage of your profits could end up being a lot more than the original investment.

- Explain to the family member or friend that the risk of equity lending is higher, but so are the potential rewards.

Accounts Payable

You should always negotiate up front the best possible payment terms with your suppliers so that your business can hold on to its cash for as long as possible. This is a source of short-term financing within your company that uses your **accounts payable**. Accounts payable is an accounting term for money a business owes its suppliers.

Let's say you have a telephone bill for $50 due on March 15th. You also have an opportunity to buy merchandise for $50 that you know you can resell in five days for $100. You could call the telephone company and arrange to pay the bill on March 20th instead. You've just arranged an interest-free loan of $50 for five days.

Most corporations postpone payments to suppliers as long as legally acceptable. They use money freed up by these postponements to make short-term investments. This is something you can do, too.

Always call the creditor and request permission to pay a bill late. *Never* just skip a payment and pay a bill late without permission from the creditor.

"Angels"

Angels are people who have money to invest. They are typically private investors worth over $1 million and interested in investing in start-ups — or for a variety of reasons, from friendship to a desire to support entrepreneurship. Bill Gates, for example, has bankrolled several biotechnology start-ups because he is interested in the field.

---

* See chapter 40 for more information about incorporating your business.

If your business has a solid business plan, you might be able to raise angel financing. Typically, start-up financing is in the $100,000 to $500,000 range. Angels tend to seek a return of ten times their investment by the end of five years.

You might meet angels through friends and family. Good contacts are lawyers, accountants, and any clubs for young people in your community that bring in business speakers or introduce you to local businesspeople. Some states also have "angel networks." Call your local Small Business Administration or chamber of commerce for details. Regional networks can be very helpful because angels tend to invest in businesses they can visit frequently.

Online Networking

You can also search for angels — and connect with other young entrepreneurs — online. Websites like the one for the Young Entrepreneurs Organization (www.yeo.org) put young entrepreneurs in touch with each other and with older ones who have established successful businesses. This kind of networking is a great potential source of angel financing.

Minority Financing

If you are African-American, Hispanic, Asian, or belong to any other minority group, look into Minority Enterprise Small Business Investment Companies (MESBICs for short). MESBICs are privately owned and managed investment firms, chartered by the Small Business Administration, that provide debt and equity capital to new, small, independent businesses. To find a MESBIC in your community, try using a search engine such as www.excite.com or www.yahoo.com. Enter MESBIC and your state or city.

The Minority Business Development Centers (MBDC) are another great resource. You should be able to find a center in your area at www.mbda.gov.

Chapter 37 Review

NOTE: The exercises printed below can be found in the corresponding chapter of the NFTE MODULE 2 WORKBOOK that came with your textbook. Please write your answers there. If you do not have a workbook, write your answers on a separate sheet of paper.

Critical Thinking about ... Other People's Money

1. Make a list of friends and family who might be willing to invest in your business in exchange for equity.

2. Do you know any potential "angels"? How do you think you could meet some?

3. Searching on the Web, find a MESBIC in your area.

Using New Words

accounts payable
"angel"

Write a paragraph describing how you could use Other People's Money to help finance your own business. Include the vocabulary terms above.

Getting the Facts

1. What does accounts payable mean?

2. Describe how to manage accounts payable in a way that will give your business short-term financing but won't upset your creditors.

In Your Opinion

Discuss with a group:

1. How much money would you feel comfortable borrowing from friends or family for your new business?

2. Would you rather pay interest or give equity in exchange for business capital?

Review

Chapter Summary

I. Sources of OPM include: friends, family, "angels," and accounts payable.

II. You can manage accounts payable to use your money wisely.

A. Accounts payable means "bills that you owe".

B. Sometimes it makes sense to postpone paying a bill to take advantage of a business opportunity.

C. Never skip or postpone a payment without obtaining permission from the creditor.

III. Angels are successful people (usually worth more than $1 million) who are looking to invest in small businesses.

A. Angels will want to see a business plan.

B. Angels tend to invest in businesses near where they live, so to find them get involved with local organizations, such as the chamber of commerce.

IV. Financing for minority-owned businesses is available from MESBICs, or Minority Enterprise Small Business Investment Companies.

We are not permitted to choose the frame of our destiny. But what we put into it is ours.

— Dag Hammerskjold, Secretary General of the United Nations and Winner of the Nobel Peace Prize

KEY OBJECTIVES

READING THIS CHAPTER AND DOING THE EXERCISES WILL ENABLE YOU TO:

- Learn what a professional venture capitalist is.

- Explain what venture capitalists seek in return for providing capital.

- Determine a company's total value.

- List the elements of a business plan.

VENTURE CAPITAL

There are investors and investment companies who focus on financing new small business ventures that have the potential to earn a lot of money. Because these investors often provide the first cash-for-equity investment that the entrepreneur can use to start his or her business, they are called **venture capitalists**.

Venture capitalists expect a high rate of return on the investment. The rule of thumb is that venture capitalists expect six times their money back over a five-year period. That works out to about a forty percent return on investment. Typically, professional venture capitalists won't invest in a company unless its business plan shows it is likely to generate sales of at least $25 million within five years.

Venture Capitalists Want Equity

Venture capitalists want equity — a piece of the company — in return for their capital. They are willing to take the risk that the venture might fail in order to earn very high returns if the company succeeds. Venture capitalists sometimes seek a **majority interest** in the business. A majority interest means more than fifty percent. A majority stakeholder would have the final word in management decisions.

When he founded the Ford Motor Company in 1903, Henry Ford gave up 75 percent of the business for $28,000 of badly needed capital. Use this formula to determine how much Ford Motor Company was worth at the time:

$$\frac{\text{Amount of Venture Capital Received}}{\% \text{ of Company Sold}} = \text{Total Value of Company}$$

$$\frac{\$28,000}{.75} = \$37,333 = \text{Total Initial Value of Ford Motor Co.}$$

It took Ford many years to regain control of his own company, which is now worth over $100 billion. Still, many small business owners turn to venture capital when they want to grow the business but can't convince banks to lend them money.

Anita Roddick, the owner of the hugely successful The Body Shop (a skin-care and cosmetics chain), opened her first store in 1976 in England (see profile of Anita Roddick in Module 1). Within a few months she was eager to open a second store because the first one was doing so well, but no bank would lend her the money. She borrowed £4,000 (about $7,500) from a friend named Ian McGlinn in exchange for an equity share of 50%. McGlinn became a multimillionaire but Roddick says she does not regret her decision because, without his money, neither of them would have gotten rich.

How Venture Capitalists Get Their ROI

Venture capitalists typically reap the return on their equity investment in one of two ways:

1. The venture capitalist sells his/her percentage of the business to another investor.

2. The venture capitalist waits until the company "goes public" (starts selling stock to the general public) and converts his/her share into stock. The stock can now be traded on the market.

The Business Plan

Both venture capitalists and bankers will want to see a business plan before they will even consider lending money. An entrepreneur may have a brilliant idea, but if it is not set out in a well-written business plan, no potential professional investor will be interested.

Most venture capitalists will reject an incomplete or poorly presented business plan right away.

If you have completed the chapters in Module 1, you will have already written an Basic Business Plan and an Intermediate Business Plan. When you finish this module you will be ready to write the Advanced Business Plan that you will be able to use to raise money for your business.

A good business plan must include:

- Your business idea
- Long- and short-term goals
- Market research
- Your competitive advantage
- Marketing plan
- Philanthropic plan
- Start-up and operating costs
- Management
- Legal structure
- Time management
- Financing plan
- Break-even analysis
- Accounting system
- Projected monthly income statement
- Projected yearly income statement
- Financial ratio analysis
- Balance sheet

The business plan should be no longer than 20 typed pages, because most investors who look at them are "one-hour investors." They don't want to look at something that takes them more than one hour to read.

Chapter 38 Review

N O T E : The exercises printed below can be found in the corresponding chapter of the NFTE MODULE 2 WORKBOOK that came with your textbook. Please write your answers there. If you do not have a workbook, write your answers on a separate sheet of paper.

Critical Thinking about . . . Venture Capital

1. Describe the differences between venture capitalists and bankers. Which type of investor do you think would be better for your company and why?

2. If a venture capitalist invests $5 million to help you start your company, how much money is he or she hoping to earn on the investment over the next five years?

3. What are two ways that a venture capitalist who invested in your company can attempt to cash in his or her investment?

4. Have you written a business plan yet? How many business plan parts do you know how to write? Which ones do you still need to learn?

Using New Words

majority interest
venture capital

On a separate sheet of paper, write the vocabulary term with the letter of its corresponding definition.

a. money invested by a venture capitalist

b. largest share of ownership in a company

Chapter 38 Review

Getting the Facts

1. What rewards do venture capitalists seek for the risks they take with their money?

2. What will a venture capitalist want to see before financing a business?

3. What does "majority interest" mean? Would you be willing to give someone a majority interest in your company in exchange for financing? Under what circumstances?

Analyzing the Value of a Business

How much is a company worth?

Formula: $\dfrac{A}{B} = C$

Example:

A	B	C
AMOUNT OF VENTURE CAPITAL RECEIVED	% OF COMPANY SOLD	TOTAL VALUE OF COMPANY
$ 1,000	20%	$ 5,000

In Your Opinion

Discuss with a group:

1. To finance your business, would you be willing to give up as much as Henry Ford and Anita Roddick did?

2. Anita Roddick says she doesn't hold a grudge against the man she made a multimillionaire. Would you feel the same way?

Review

Chapter Summary

I. **Venture capitalists expect six times their money back over five years.**

   A. Venture capitalists want equity in exchange for capital.

   B. Venture capitalists sometimes seek a majority interest.

II. $$\frac{\textbf{Total Value of Company}}{\textbf{\% of Company Sold}} = \textbf{Amount of Venture Capital Received}$$

III. **Venture capitalists and bankers both want to see thorough business plans.**

A Business for the Young Entrepreneur: Used CD's

The nice thing about CD's is that people get tired of listening to them before they wear out. There's a strong market, therefore, for used CD's. Your parents, their friends, and your own friends probably have CD's they don't really want anymore. Offer to buy their unwanted CD's for a dollar apiece. You could sell these to people who do want them for as much as they are willing to pay — from two dollars on up! Use part of your profits to buy more CD's to keep your business going.

To Get Started

- Make business cards and flyers advertising that you buy and sell used CD's.

- Decorate the boxes you keep them in with paint or stickers.

- Make cards to divide your CD's into categories, such as "Classical," or "Rap." This will make it easy for your customers to look through them for those they might want.

Tips

- Don't just buy CD's you like. Try to stock different types of music.

- If possible, arrange with the school authorities to sell your CD's in the cafeteria during lunch hour, or at school events.

- Sell your CD's at a local flea market.

You can get everything in life that you want . . . if you'll just help enough other people get what they want.

— Zig Ziglar,
sales expert

TAXATION FOR THE ENTREPRENEUR

Your Legal Obligation as a Small Business Owner

Once you start a small business, you will probably have to pay **taxes**. A tax is a percentage of your gross profit that the government takes. The government uses taxes to support schools, the military, police and fire departments, and many other public services.

States usually raise money from a **sales tax** on the sale of goods, and sometimes services. The sales tax is a percentage of the cost of the item sold and is added to its price. If a state charges 8% sales tax on a $10.00 item, the sales tax would be 80 cents. The customer would pay a total of $10.80. If you sell a product, you will have to collect sales tax from your customers and pay it to the state. In this case, you would collect $10 from the customer for your business and 80 cents for the state. Businesses are typically required to pay the collected sales tax to the state four times per year. Most states also impose an income tax. Sales taxes are taxes on *consumption*.

City and other local governments are supported primarily by taxes on property. The federal government is financed by personal and corporate income taxes.

A Sole Proprietor Pays Two Kinds of Taxes to the Federal Government

INCOME TAX — You must **file** an income-tax return if you are earning money above a minimum of $5,500, which can go up each year based on inflation. Income taxes fund the federal government's operations and the various services it provides.

SELF-EMPLOYMENT TAX — **Self-employment tax** is for people who work for themselves. Entrepreneurs must pay self-employment tax if they earn more than $400 per year. So must others who work for themselves, such as doctors, lawyers, and writers.

Entrepreneurs pay self-employment tax because they don't have an employer who contributes to **Social Security** for them. Self-employed tax covers the Social Security obligation for self-employed people. The federal government's Social Security program pays benefits to retired people and the families of dead or disabled workers. People who are employees have taxes for Social Security withheld from their paychecks. The amount withheld from paychecks of employees is half the total — the other half is contributed by the employer. A total of 15.3% of the employee's income goes to Social Security — 7.65% from the employee and 7.65% from the employer.

Forms to File

Income-tax returns, which include self-employment tax forms, must be filed (mailed) by midnight on April 15th of each year. If you file late, you may have to pay penalties and interest. Failure to file your tax returns can lead the **Internal Revenue Service** (IRS) — the government bureau in charge of federal taxation — to charge you penalties, and even put you in jail for **tax evasion**.

Income tax is filed using the basic 1040 U.S. Individual Tax Return, and Schedule C — Profit or Loss from Business. Self-employment tax is filed using Schedule SE. Tax forms are usually available at your local post office or bank. Forms can also be ordered from the IRS by calling 1-800-829-3676. We have included some sample forms for you to look at later on in this chapter.

The tax code is very complex. The IRS offers booklets and telephone service to help answer questions. Help with the 1040 form is available at 1-800-424-1040. You can also go to the local IRS office and meet with an agent who will guide you through the forms for free. It's important to get new forms and booklets each year, as rules, rates and forms change from one year to the next. You may want to have your taxes prepared by a professional accountant (CPA — Certified Public Accountant).

Help Yourself by Keeping Good Records

You will make filing your taxes easier by keeping good records throughout the year. You will have to determine your net income (gross income minus expenses). If you have kept track of income and expenses in your ledger, this should not be too difficult.

If you are in doubt, call the IRS or visit an accountant or tax-preparation office, such as H&R Block. Mistakes on your tax return could cause the IRS to **audit** you. That means they will send an agent to your business or home to examine your ledgers and receipts and invoices thoroughly to make sure your taxes were filed correctly. This is another excellent reason to keep good records and file all your invoices and receipts in a safe place.

Evaluating Taxes

As a taxpayer, you have the right to ask these questions:

- Where are my tax dollars going?
- Are they supporting services that will benefit me and my community?
- Am I paying taxes to support services that could be better supplied by private industry instead of the government?
- Are the tax rates fair?

Taxpayers demand answers to these questions from the politicians who represent them in city councils, state legislatures, and the United States Congress. One of the most important jobs politicians do each year is figure out government budgets and then determine how much tax money will be needed to finance them. They also pass laws that change the tax code.

Remember always to:

- Keep good records
- File your returns
- Pay your taxes on time

Sample U.S. Individual Income Tax Return: Form 1040

This is the form that you would use to report your income tax to the IRS.*

---

* Note: Tax forms can change from year to year. Call the IRS at 800.829.3676 or visit www.irs.gov to obtain the most recent forms so that you can file your tax return properly.

Sample Profit or Loss From Business (Sole Proprietorship): Schedule C (Form 1040)

This is the form that you would use to report the profit or loss from your sole proprietorship business to the IRS.*

SCHEDULE C
(Form 1040)

Department of the Treasury
Internal Revenue Service (99)

Profit or Loss From Business
(Sole Proprietorship)

▶ Partnerships, joint ventures, etc., must file Form 1065 or Form 1065-B.

▶ Attach to Form 1040 or Form 1041.   ▶ See Instructions for Schedule C (Form 1040).

OMB No. 1545-0074

2000

Attachment
Sequence No. **09**

Name of proprietor | Social security number (SSN)

A Principal business or profession, including product or service (see page C-1 of the instructions) | B Enter code from pages C-7 & 8 ▶

C Business name. If no separate business name, leave blank. | D Employer ID number (EIN), if any

E Business address (including suite or room no.) ▶ ....
City, town or post office, state, and ZIP code

F Accounting method: (1) ☐ Cash (2) ☐ Accrual (3) ☐ Other (specify) ▶ ....

G Did you "materially participate" in the operation of this business during 2000? If "No," see page C-2 for limit on losses . ☐ Yes ☐ No

H If you started or acquired this business during 2000, check here . . . . ▶ ☐

Part I Income

1	Gross receipts or sales. **Caution.** If this income was reported to you on Form W-2 and the "Statutory employee" box on that form was checked, see page C-2 and check here . . . . . . ▶ ☐	1
2	Returns and allowances	2
3	Subtract line 2 from line 1	3
4	Cost of goods sold (from line 42 on page 2)	4
5	**Gross profit.** Subtract line 4 from line 3	5
6	Other income, including Federal and state gasoline or fuel tax credit or refund (see page C-2) . . .	6
7	**Gross income.** Add lines 5 and 6 . . . . ▶	7

Part II Expenses. Enter expenses for business use of your home **only** on line 30.

8	Advertising	8	19	Pension and profit-sharing plans	19
9	Bad debts from sales or services (see page C-3) . .	9	20	Rent or lease (see page C-4): a Vehicles, machinery, and equipment .	20a
10	Car and truck expenses (see page C-3)	10		b Other business property . .	20b
11	Commissions and fees . .	11	21	Repairs and maintenance . .	21
12	Depletion	12	22	Supplies (not included in Part III) .	22
13	Depreciation and section 179 expense deduction (not included in Part III) (see page C-3) . .	13	23	Taxes and licenses	23
			24	Travel, meals, and entertainment: a Travel	24a
14	Employee benefit programs (other than on line 19) . . .	14		b Meals and entertainment	
15	Insurance (other than health) .	15		c Enter nondeduct- ible amount in- cluded on line 24b (see page C-5) .	
16	Interest:			d Subtract line 24c from line 24b	24d
	a Mortgage (paid to banks, etc.) .	16a	25	Utilities	25
	b Other	16b	26	Wages (less employment credits) .	26
17	Legal and professional services	17	27	Other expenses (from line 48 on page 2)	27
18	Office expense	18			

28	**Total expenses** before expenses for business use of home. Add lines 8 through 27 in columns . . . ▶	28	
29	Tentative profit (loss). Subtract line 28 from line 7	29	
30	Expenses for business use of your home. Attach **Form 8829**	30	
31	**Net profit or (loss).** Subtract line 30 from line 29. • If a profit, enter on **Form 1040, line 12,** and **also** on **Schedule SE, line 2** (statutory employees, see page C-5). Estates and trusts, enter on Form 1041, line 3. • If a loss, you **must** go to line 32.	31	
32	If you have a loss, check the box that describes your investment in this activity (see page C-5). • If you checked 32a, enter the loss on **Form 1040, line 12,** and also on **Schedule SE, line 2** (statutory employees, see page C-5). Estates and trusts, enter on Form 1041, line 3. • If you checked 32b, you **must** attach Form 6198.	32a ☐ All investment is at risk. 32b ☐ Some investment is not at risk.	

For Paperwork Reduction Act Notice, see Form 1040 instructions. | Cat. No. 11334P | **Schedule C (Form 1040) 2000**

---

* Note: Tax forms can change from year to year. Call the IRS at 800.829.3676 or visit www.irs.gov to obtain the most recent forms so that you can file your tax return properly.

Sample New York State and Local Quarterly Sales and Use Tax Return Form

This is the form that you would use to report sales and use tax to the State Department of Taxation and Finance.*

New York State Department of Taxation and Finance

Quarterly   ST-100

1st Quarter

New York State and Local Quarterly Sales and Use Tax Return

March	April	May

Tax Period
March 1, 2001 – May 31, 2001

Sales tax identification number ▶

Legal name *(if no label, print legal name as it appears on the Certificate of Authority.)*

dba (doing business as) name

Number and street

City, state, ZIP code

Place address label here

June 2001

S	M	T	W	T	F	S
					1	2
3	4	5	6	7	8	9
10	11	12	13	14	15	16
17	18	19	20	21	22	23
24	25	26	27	28	29	30

102

Due date:
20 **Wednesday, June 20, 2001**
You will be responsible for penalty and interest if your return is not postmarked by this date.

No tax due? Check the box to the right and complete Step 1; in Step 3 on page 3, enter *none* in boxes 13, 14, and 15; and complete Step 9. You **must** file by the due date even if no tax is due. **There is a $50 penalty for late filing of a no-tax-due return.** See ❶ in instructions. ...☐

Multiple locations? If you are reporting sales tax for more than one business location **and** your identification number does not end in *C*, check the box to the right and attach a list of your locations. ....☐

Final return? Check the box to the right if you are discontinuing your business and this is your final return; complete this return and the back of your *Certificate of Authority*. Attach the *Certificate of Authority* to the return. See ❷ in instructions. ....☐

Has your address or business information changed? If so, check the box to the right and enter new mailing address on preprinted label above. See ❸ in instructions. ☐

Step 1 of 9   **Gross sales and services** | Enter total gross sales and services in box 1 .... ➔ | **1** | .00

Do not include sales tax in the gross sales and services amount. See ❹ in instructions.

Step 2 of 9   **Identify required schedules** | Check the box(es) on the right below, then complete the schedule(s) if necessary and proceed to Step 3. **Need to obtain schedules?** See *Need help?* on page 4 of this form.

Quarterly schedule	Description	Check the box for each schedule you are attaching
SCHEDULE A	Use Form ST-100.2, *Quarterly Schedule A,* to report tax and taxable receipts from sales of food and drink (restaurant meals, takeout, etc.) and from hotel occupancy **in Nassau or Niagara County,** as well as admissions, club dues, and cabaret charges in Niagara County.	☐
SCHEDULE B	Use Form ST-100.3, *Quarterly Schedule B,* to report tax due on **utilities (residential/nonresidential), transportation and delivery of gas and electricity, and residential energy sources and services,** including school district utility taxes. Reminder: You must report sales of nonresidential utility services made to QEZEs on Form ST-100.3-ATT, *Quarterly Schedule B-ATT.*	☐
SCHEDULE FR	Use Form ST-100.10, *Quarterly Schedule FR,* to report **retail sales of motor fuel or diesel motor fuel,** and fuel taken from inventory, as explained in the schedule's instructions.	☐
SCHEDULE H	Use Form ST-100.7, *Quarterly Schedule H,* to report **sales of clothing and footwear that were eligible for exemption** from New York State and some local sales and use tax.	☐
SCHEDULE N	Use Form ST-100.5, *Quarterly Schedule N,* to report taxes due and sales of certain **services in New York City.** Reminder: Providers of parking services must also file Form ST-100.5-ATT, *Quarterly Schedule N-ATT.*	☐
SCHEDULE Q	Use Form ST-100.9, *Quarterly Schedule Q,* to report **sales of tangible personal property or services to Qualified Empire Zone Enterprises (QEZEs) eligible for exemption** from New York State and some local sales and use tax.	☐
SCHEDULE T	Use Form ST-100.8, *Quarterly Schedule T,* to report taxes due on **telephone services, telephone answering services, and telegraph services** imposed by certain counties, school districts, or cities. Reminder: You must report sales of these services made to QEZEs on Form ST-100.8-ATT, *Quarterly Schedule T-ATT.*	☐

Schedules CT and NJ: For reciprocal tax agreement filing requirements, see ❺ instructions.

Refer to instructions (Form ST-100-I) if you have questions or need help. | *For office use only*
Please be sure to keep a completed copy of your return for your records.
See the bottom of page 4 for informational telephone numbers.

Page 1 of 4   ST-100 (3/01) | Proceed to Step 3, page 2 ▶

---

* Note: Every state has its own state and local tax forms. Contact your State Department of Taxation and Finance or visit your local library to obtain the correct forms for your state.

Chapter 39 Review

Critical Thinking about . . . Taxes

1. Why does the government ask self-employed people to pay self-employment tax in addition to income tax?

2. Do you earn any money from self-employment? Do you earn enough to pay self-employment tax? What tax form would you use to report self-employment income?

3. When you visit a wholesaler to buy products for your business, the wholesaler will not charge you sales tax. Why?

4. How can you help reduce the chance that the IRS will choose to audit your business?

5. How much income tax would you owe given the following tax rates and net incomes?

Tax Rate	Net Income
25%	$65,000
30%	$100,000

Getting the Facts

True or False?

1. You have to pay self-employment tax even if your business only earns $200 the first year.

2. If you file your tax return after April 15, you may have to pay a fine.

3. States raise money from property taxes.

4. If you order tax forms from the IRS this year, you won't need to order them next year.

Analyzing Public Service

1. In a group, choose a public service you think could be provided more efficiently by private business. Develop an argument for replacing this service with a private business and present it to the class. Have the class vote on your proposal.

2. Fill out tax forms provided by your teacher.

Review

Chapter 39 Review

Using New Words

audit
file
incentive
Internal Revenue Service
sales tax
self-employment tax
Social Security
tax
tax evasion

On a separate sheet of paper, identify the correct definition for each vocabulary term.

1) audit
   a) financial statement
   b) formal investigation of a tax-payer's accounts by the IRS
   c) business tax on auditory equipment

2) file
   a) to send one's tax return to the IRS
   b) to file one's tax return in a filing system
   c) to fill out one's tax return

3) incentive
   a) lack of motivation
   b) a motivating factor
   c) a non-motivating factor

4) Internal Revenue Service
   a) state taxation bureau
   b) federal taxation bureau
   c) local government board in charge of taxation

5) sales tax
   a) tax on profit
   b) tax on manufacturing
   c) tax on consumption

6) self-employment tax
   a) a tax on earnings from self-employment
   b) a substitute for Social Security tax for self-employed people
   c) a) and b) are both correct

7) Social Security
   a) a federal program that provides benefits to elderly and disabled people
   b) a federal program that provides business insurance
   c) a federal program that provides employment security

8) tax
   a) the percentage of sales taken by the government
   b) the percentage of net profit taken by the government
   c) the percentage of gross profit taken by the government

9) tax evasion
   a) late filing of a tax return
   b) inability to pay tax bill
   c) deliberate failure to pay taxes

Review

Chapter Summary

I. City, state, and federal governments use taxes to fund public services.

   A. States use a sales tax (tax on consumption).

   B. Cities use a property tax.

   C. Federal and state governments use income taxes from individuals and businesses.

II. A sole proprietor pays income and self-employment taxes.

   A. You owe self-employment tax if you earn over $400 in a year from your business.

   B. Failure to pay taxes can lead to penalties and jail.

III. Many Americans think taxes are unfair and too high.

   A. Taxpayers complain to politicians, who pass budgets and change tax codes.

   B. High taxes can remove the incentive to work, start new businesses or get off welfare.

   C. Some people believe public services funded by taxes could be better provided by private business.

IV. Self-employed people must send the federal government money for their Social Security benefits in the form of self-employment tax.

   A. Self-employed people must pay self-employment tax if they earned more than $400 per year through self-employment.

   B. Self-employment tax is 15.3% of net earnings.

V. Self-employment tax is a proportional tax.

   A. As an example, a self-employed person earning $40,000 per year will pay double the self-employment tax of someone earning $20,000 per year.

VI. Income tax is a progressive tax: it takes a larger percentage of larger incomes and a smaller percentage of smaller incomes.

Great works are performed not by strength, but perseverance.

— Samuel Johnson,
English author

KEY OBJECTIVES

**READING THIS CHAPTER AND DOING
THE EXERCISES WILL ENABLE YOU TO:**

- Explain the corporate structure.

- Discuss how a corporation is treated by business and tax laws.

- Evaluate the pros and cons of different types of corporations.

CORPORATIONS: LIMITING LIABILITY*

A **corporation** is a legal "person," or *entity*, composed of stockholders under a common name. A legal corporate entity has a separate, independent existence apart from its owners and employees. It is treated as an individual under business law. It incurs expenses and earns income. A corporation may be a small "privately held" business or a large "publicly held" company like General Motors or IBM. The shares of stock of public companies are often traded on the stock market. Whether large or small, corporations:

- Issue stock, representing shares of ownership.
- Elect officers and a **board of directors**. The board is a group of people chosen by the stockholders to manage the company.

Shares of stock represent a percentage of ownership of a corporation. If privately held, the shares are owned by only a few. In a "public" corporation, such as General Motors

---

* Thanks to Gary Castle, of Anchin, Block & Anchin, for the ideas he contributed to this chapter.

or Microsoft, the company's stock is offered for sale to the general public and anyone may purchase it at the market price. Stockholders are paid **dividends** when the company's profits are good. Dividends are part of the stockholders' return on their investment in the company.

Corporate Legal Responsibility

As we have said, under the law a corporation is a legal "person." It is the corporation that is liable, not the corporation's officers or board of directors. If General Motors is sued because of a defect in an automobile, it is the corporation and its resources that may be used to pay any court settlement. The private assets of the company's officers or stockholders are shielded. Corporations can also buy and sell property and enter into legal contracts.

When the abbreviation "Inc." (for "Incorporated"), "Corp." (for "Corporation"), or "Ltd" (for "Limited") appears after a company's name, it means it has been legally incorporated.

Advantages of Corporations

- Limited legal liability; the personal assets of the officers or stockholders cannot be used to pay corporate debts.
- Money can be raised through the issuing of stock.
- Ownership can be transferred easily, because the new owner does not have to become personally responsible for the corporation's debts.

Disadvantages of Corporations

- Corporations are often more heavily taxed than sole proprietorships or partnerships. Their profits are often taxed twice: first, as the income of the corporation, and again as dividends to stockholders, who must include such dividends as personal income on their tax returns.
- The founder of a corporation (the original entrepreneur) can lose control to the stock holders and board of directors if he or she no longer owns more than half the stock. This happened to Steven Jobs, the co-founder of Apple Computer, who was fired by his own company's board of directors (although he was later invited back to run the company again).
- It is more expensive to start a corporation.
- Corporations are subject to many government regulations.

Four Kinds of Corporations

#1: Subchapter-S Corporation

To qualify as a Subchapter-S type of corporation, the company must have fewer than 75 stockholders, no corporate, partnership or non-resident alien shareholders, and no shareholders who are not U.S. citizens. This corporate structure offers most of the legal protection of a C Corporation (see below), without the double taxation on income. Subchapter-S corporate income is only reported by the stockholders as personal income — it is usually not also taxed as corporate income.

#2: Professional Corporation

Doctors, lawyers, architects, and other professionals can also incorporate themselves. The initials P.C. ("Professional Corporation") after a doctor or lawyer's name means the individual has incorporated his or her practice.

#3: Nonprofit Corporation

Nonprofit corporations (also called 501(c)(3) corporations, from the tax-code regulation pertaining to them) are corporations that aim to contribute to the greater good of society and are not seeking to make a profit. Churches, museums, charitable foundations, and trade associations are all examples of nonprofit corporations.

Nonprofit corporations are **tax-exempt**. They do not pay taxes because their income is being used to address society's problems. The government closely monitors nonprofit corporations to make sure they are really using their income to benefit society.

For the same reason it doesn't pay taxes, a nonprofit corporation may not pay out dividends or bonuses. It cannot issue stock. It raises money instead through **donations** (gifts) of money or through charging dues to members. Donors to nonprofits can usually use such donations as tax deductions.

As with other corporations, it is possible for the founder of a nonprofit to lose control of the company to the board of directors. People who create nonprofit corporations typically do so because they are deeply committed to a social cause such as education, the environment, or human rights. In starting an organization as a nonprofit, you should know that you will probably not make as much money as you would running a successful for-profit company. However, some people find that they get just as much, if not more personal satisfaction from their work in nonprofit organizations because they are actively helping to improve a social problem that they care about. This is really a personal decision that each entrepreneur needs to make for her/himself when the time is appropriate.

#4: C Corporation

Most big companies are C Corporations. They sell ownership as shares of stock. Stockholders may vote on important company decisions. To raise capital, the C Corporation can sell more stock.

Limited Liability Companies

A newer business structure, that has now been approved in all 50 states and the District of Columbia, is the **limited liability company**. It seems to combine the best features of partnerships and corporations. It is a good choice for many small businesses:

- As in a partnership, income is taxed only once, as the personal income of the members.

- As in a corporation, personal assets are protected from creditors and lawsuits.

The advantage of the LLC over the Subchapter-S is that many of the restrictions (number and type of shareholders) of Subchapter-S corporations do not apply to LLC's. The person who has the largest percentage of the membership interests will, in general terms, control the LLC.

This development of a relatively new legal business structure underscores the main point of this chapter: Consider the needs and goals — both short- and long-term — of your business carefully. Study what's available before you choose a legal structure for your business.

Think Ahead

Think ahead to your long-term goals. If you are starting a small T-shirt design business while you are in high school to make money for college, for example, you do not need to incorporate. A sole proprietorship will serve you very well. On the other hand, if your goal is to develop a clothing-design firm that will eventually place your designs in every

department store in the country, you might consider incorporating from the start.

Never go into a business where your product or service could hurt someone without incorporating. You will need the limited liability offered by a corporation to protect your personal assets from potential lawsuits.

When it comes time to choose a legal structure for your business, make the decision carefully, with a lot of thought and some advice from an attorney. As your business develops, however, you can always reevaluate your decision and change your legal structure.

COMPARISON OF LEGAL STRUCTURES

	Sole Proprietorship	General or Limited Partnership	C Corporation	Subchapter-S Corporation	Nonprofit Corporation	Limited Liability Company
Ownership	The proprietor	The partners	The stockholders	The stockholders	No one	The members
Liability	Unlimited	Limited in most cases	Limited	Limited	Limited	Limited
Taxation issues	Individual* (lowest rate)	Individual* (lowest rate)	Corporate rate; double taxation on individual	Individual (lowest rate)	None	Individual rate
How profits are distributed	Proprietor receives all	Partners receive profits according to partnership agreement	Earnings paid to stockholders as dividends in proportion to the number of shares owned	Earnings paid to stockholders as dividends in proportion to the number of shares owned	Surplus cannot be distributed	Same as partnership
Voting on policy	Not necessary	The partners	Common voting stockholders	Common voting stockholders	The board of directors/trustees agreement	Per operating
Life of legal structure	Terminates on death of owner	Terminates on death of partner	Unlimited	Unlimited	Unlimited through trustees	Variable
Capitalization	Difficult	Better than sole proprietorship	Excellent — ownership is sold as shares of stock	Good — same as partnership	Difficult because there is no ownership to sell as stock	Same as partnership

* When the double taxation of corporations is taken into account.

Raúl Hernandez: Nurturing Latino Culture and Hispanic-American Businesses

When Hispanic-American Raúl Hernandez noticed how nonprofit corporations such as the YMCA and the Red Cross raised millions for their causes, he said to himself, "Why can't Latinos do the same for their causes, their programs?"

In 1985, at the age of 29, Hernandez founded the Mission Economic and Cultural Association (MECA) in San Francisco. His first goal was to build the economic base of San Francisco's Spanish-speaking community. He also wanted to promote needed services, such as child care. His third goal for MECA was to help preserve the cultural traditions of people from all over South and Central America.

MECA has held three major festivals each year: a re-creation of Brazil's *Carnival*; the *Festival de las Américas*, which celebrates the independence of eight Central and South American countries from colonial rule; and *Cinco de Mayo*, which celebrates the Mexican army's defeat of a would-be French occupation. Together, the festivals are attended by millions of people and help Hispanic businesses network, promote, and advertise their products and services. MECA evolved from a $3,200 organization in 1985 to a nonprofit corporation with a budget of $1.2 million by 1990. It supports itself and has stimulated the Hispanic-American economy in many ways. The enterprising Hernandez has realized his dream, which was to have a financially self-sufficient business that would help his community.

Chapter 40 Review

NOTE: The exercises printed below can be found in the corresponding chapter of the NFTE MODULE 2 WORKBOOK that came with your textbook. Please write your answers there. If you do not have a workbook, write your answers on a separate sheet of paper.

Critical Thinking about ... Legal Structures

Entrepreneurs can choose from many legal structures for their businesses — from sole proprietorships to partnerships to a variety of corporations. Choose the best legal structure for each business below and explain your choice:

1. A DJ who already owns the equipment she needs to entertain at parties.

2. Someone who wants to start his own record company and has several artists but no money.

3. A jewelry designer whose work is wanted by a national department-store chain.

4. A social worker who wants to start a program to bring meals to housebound senior citizens.

5. Several doctors who want to go into practice together.

Using New Words

board of directors
corporation
dividend
donation
limited liability company
tax-exempt

On a separate sheet of paper, write the vocabulary term with the letter of its corresponding definition.

a. a gift to charity

b. corporate payment to stockholders

c. sheltered from tax

d. a legal "person" (entity) composed of people appointed to direct or advise a corporation

e. a partnership offering limited liability

Getting the Facts

1. Write a business letter to a mentor requesting donations to a nonprofit corporation that you are starting to help solve a social problem.

2. Write a memo to a mentor explaining the advantages and disadvantages of incorporating and how these apply to your business.

Review

Chapter Summary

I. **A corporation is a legal "person," or entity, composed of stockholders.**

    A. Corporations issue stock.

    B. Stockholders elect officers and a board of directors.

II. **Corporations offer these advantages:**

    A. Limited legal liability

    B. Raising capital by issuing stock

III. **Corporations have these disadvantages:**

    A. Double taxation (corporate income and dividends to shareholders)

    B. Danger that original owner could lose control

    C. Expenses and government regulations

IV. **Other types of corporations:**

    A. Subchapter-S

    B. Professional Corporation

    C. Nonprofit Corporation [or 501(c)(3)]

V. **Some states have approved Limited Liability Companies (LLC's).**

A Business for the Young Entrepreneur: Consignment Shop

Do you ever throw out clothes because you're tired of them? Maybe someone else would buy the clothes you don't want anymore. Maybe you would like to buy clothes one of your friends doesn't want anymore.

This is the idea behind the clothing-resale or "consignment" shop which sells used clothing. People bring in clothes they don't need and the shop sells them. In return, the clothing consignor receives a percentage of the sale, usually 30% to 50%. Consignment shops are becoming more popular as people search for ways to stretch their clothing dollar. You could run a consignment shop from your house (in your garage or basement) after school, or on weekends.

How to Buy and Sell Clothes on Consignment

- Decide how much commission you will pay on each sale.

- Have each person who brings you clothing fill out a tag with his or her name, address and phone number. Put in writing how much commission you will pay.

- When you sell a piece of clothing, take the tag and write on it the amount for which you sold the garment.

- At the end of the day, make a list of whose clothes you sold and for how much.

- Let each person know how much money you owe them. Let's say Daphne brought you a dress that you sold for $15. If you have agreed to pay a commission of 30%, you owe Daphne $15.00 x .30 = $4.50. You make $15.00 – $4.50 = $10.50.

Tips

- Only take articles of clothing on consignment that you really think you can sell. Don't take clothes that aren't in good condition or unsaleable.

- Wash or dryclean all clothing before selling it or make a rule that you'll only take cleaned clothing.

- Create a fun atmosphere when your shop is open. Play your friends' favorite music. You can even sell lemonade and cookies.

*The first and best victory
is to conquer the self.*

—Plato,
Greek philosopher

KEY OBJECTIVES

**READING THIS CHAPTER AND DOING
THE EXERCISES WILL ENABLE YOU TO:**

- Manage your time more efficiently.
- Hire employees.
- Build a management team.

PUTTING THE RIGHT MANAGEMENT TEAM IN PLACE

Most small businesses start out as sole proprietorships, operated by one very busy person. Just getting a business up and running requires a tremendous amount of time and energy. One of the most important things you can do when you start your first business is learn how to manage your time more efficiently. Getting more done in less time is the name of the game.

The "PERT" Chart

You may not have employees to manage yet but you can manage yourself better. Here's a tool called the PERT Chart (**P**rogram **E**valuation and **R**eview **T**echnique) that you can use when you feel overwhelmed by the many things you need to do when starting up your first business. As your venture grows, you can use the PERT Chart concept to manage more and more complex tasks.

Sample PERT Chart

SAMPLE PERT CHART						
Task	**Week 1**	**Week 2**	**Week 3**	**Week 4**	**Week 5**	**Week 6**
Befriend banker	X	X	X	X	X	X
Order letterhead		X				
Select location	X					
Register business	X					
Bulk mail permit			X			
Select ad agency	X					
Meet with lawyer				X		
Meet with accountant				X		
Meet with suppliers					X	
Utilities deposits					X	
Promotional material					X	
Phone system			X	X	X	
Website designed						X
Database set up						X
Network computers						X

Adding Employees to the Mix

As your business grows, you can begin to add employees. At first these might just be friends or family members who help you with deliveries or boxing up shipments. But eventually you will need to hire real employees. Once you do, you will have to become aware of the laws and tax issues affecting hiring. These include:

- Payroll taxes — if you hire employees, you will have to deduct payroll taxes from their earnings. Your accountant can advise you in more detail when you get to this point. For now it's important that you know you will be responsible for contributing to Social Security on their behalf.

- Fair Labor Standards Act — this law, passed in 1938, requires you to pay employees at least minimum wage. It also prohibits you from hiring anyone under age 16 full time.

- Equal Pay Act of 1963 — this law requires employers to pay men and women the same amount for the same work.

- Anti-discrimination laws — there are other laws that protect employees against discrimination on the basis of age, race, religion, national origin or color, gender, or physical disabilities.

Getting the Best Out of Your Employees

When you do hire people, treat them fairly and with respect. This approach will get you the best results. Many companies make their employees part owners by giving shares that entitle them to a portion of company profits. Wouldn't you work harder if you knew your efforts would make a difference in your wallet?

Follow these guidelines and you should be a terrific boss:

1. Get the right people. Putting the right people in the right job is half the battle. This means getting to know each employee's strengths and weaknesses.

2. Provide a fair salary and good working conditions.

3. Share your vision for the company.

4. Give employees incentives to work hard — start a profit-sharing plan, for example.

5. Give them control over their work.

6. Give them definite responsibilities and areas of control.

Firing Employees

Sometimes you hire someone and it just doesn't work out. Can you fire that person? Yes, but protect yourself by documenting reasons when you fire someone. You can be sued for *wrongful termination* if an employee thinks he or she was fired for no good reason. If an employee is violating rules, notify him or her in writing (and keep a copy for your records) before terminating employment. If things still don't improve and you have to fire him or her, you will have proof that there were problems with that employee's performance.

Corporate Management — Building a Team

As a small business grows, it will reach a point where the entrepreneur and a few employees cannot handle the business efficiently. At that stage, the business will need managers. These are people who specialize in running business operations. Many successful entrepreneurs are creative people who tend to get bored with the everyday details of running a large business. The best entrepreneurs recognize this about themselves and hire managers.

Much of an entrepreneur's job will be to build a team of people, treat them well, and give them a vision for meeting a consumer need.

An entrepreneur with a growing corporation can raise capital by selling stock. Some of the capital can be used to hire managers to operate the business more efficiently. The entrepreneur may be the president and hire managers to handle the daily operations of each important department. This will free the entrepreneur to spend less time managing and more time thinking up new ideas for the business.

A management organizational chart for a small business might look like this:

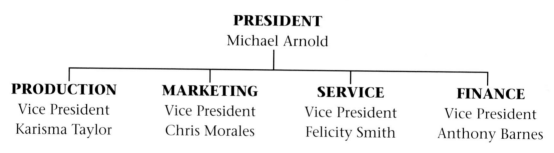

FRED'S CITY RECORDS, INC.

PRESIDENT
Michael Arnold

PRODUCTION	**MARKETING**	**SERVICE**	**FINANCE**
Vice President	Vice President	Vice President	Vice President
Karisma Taylor	Chris Morales	Felicity Smith	Anthony Barnes

Management Functions

But what do managers do? Ideally, they perform the functions that will help a small business grow into a very successful company.

1. **PLANNING –** This function includes deciding on the company's long-term goals and creating strategies to help achieve them.

2. **ORGANIZING –** This includes everything from hiring to buying or leasing equipment and resources. It includes setting up an organizational chart and defining each person's responsibilities.

3. **LEADING –** Managers lead the company's employees through the execution of its strategies.

4. **DIRECTING –** After the entrepreneur and the managers have made the plans and organized the employees and resources, managers have to motivate the employees to perform the work that will move the company toward its strategic goals.

5. **STAFFING –** This function involves hiring and firing and making sure employees are placed in the positions that best utilize their skills and experience.

6. **CONTROLLING –** This step involves measuring the business' performance and figuring out how to improve it. Is the budget actually being followed? Are products achieving the level of quality set? How about customer service?

7. **COORDINATING –** Coordinating includes creating in-house communications, telephone and e-mail systems, teaching everyone to use them, scheduling regular meetings and updates, and making sure managers are using appropriate styles and working toward the same goals.

8. **REPRESENTING –** Managers represent a company to its people and its people to the company; they also represent the company to the outside world. Managers need to dress and behave in a way that accurately reflects the "company culture."

9. **INNOVATING –** Managers should always be thinking about and creating new ways to help the company meet its goals. The entrepreneur may be the guiding creative force behind the company, but managers should also be problem-solvers.

10. **MOTIVATING –** Each decision managers make will affect how employees feel about working for the company. If a manager assumes that people need to be pushed to work, for example, and treats employees that way, he or she will incur resentment. A manager who assumes that employees want to do their best will be more successful. Some ways managers can motivate employees include: involving employees in decisions, recognizing outstanding contributions, and rewarding achievement.

Chapter 41 Review

N O T E : The exercises printed below can be found in the corresponding chapter of the NFTE MODULE 2 WORKBOOK that came with your textbook. Please write your answers there. If you do not have a workbook, write your answers on a separate sheet of paper.

Critical Thinking about . . . Management

1. Write an essay describing how you could find five more hours in your weekly schedule to manage your business.

2. Create a weekly time-management schedule for yourself.

3. Fill out a PERT Chart for your business.

4. Do you have any employees for your business yet? If so, describe how much you pay them and how this is working out. If not, describe your ideal employees, what you would pay them and what their jobs would be.

Getting the Facts

1. How old does someone have to be before they can work full time?

2. What is one kind of tax employers have to pay for employees?

3. Can you fire an employee if you have an argument about religion?

4. How does incorporating help an entrepreneur to put management into place?

5. Write an essay on what you would do to develop teamwork for your management and employees.

In Your Opinion

Discuss with a group:

Should an employer be able to fire an employee if he or she finds out the employee is often ill? Before the discussion, prepare by searching the Internet to find out what legal issues exist in firing employees.

Chapter Summary

I.   You can learn how to manage your time more efficiently.

A. Use a PERT chart.

B. Getting more done in less time will help you be a more successful entrepreneur.

II. If you take on employees, you must learn about laws and taxes affecting hiring, including:

A. Payroll taxes

B. Fair Labor Standards Act

C. Equal Pay Act of 1963

D. Anti-discrimination laws

III. Guidelines for hiring.

A. Put the right people in the right job.

B. Give employees a fair salary and good working conditions.

C. Share your vision for the company with your employees.

D. Give employees incentives to work hard — start a profit-sharing plan, for example.

E. Give employees control over their work and well-defined responsibilities.

IV. Managers can run the day-to-day operations of a business, allowing the entrepreneur more time to create new business ideas.

A. Some management functions are: planning, organizing, leading, directing, staffing, controlling, coordinating, representing, innovating, motivating.

B. An incorporated business can sell stock to raise capital to hire managers.

KEY OBJECTIVES

READING THIS CHAPTER AND DOING THE EXERCISES WILL ENABLE YOU TO:

- Explain how bonds differ from stocks.
- Summarize how bonds work.
- Discuss the effect inflation has on the value of a dollar.
- Read a bond table.

BONDS AND OTHER DEBT-BASED FINANCING STRATEGIES

The Differences between Bonds and Stocks

Bonds are interest-bearing certificates that corporations and governments issue to raise capital. Bonds are loans; the original amount borrowed, plus interest, must be paid by the corporation. For this reason bonds are considered a **debt** form of financing.

In contrast, stocks are a form of **equity** financing. Equity is ownership in a company, received in exchange for money invested. A person who buys stock is buying a piece of the company. Unlike the bondholder, the stockholder is not paid interest and is never paid back. The stockholder, however, is entitled to share in the company's profits. These are paid as *dividends*. The company may choose when to pay dividends and whether or not to pay them at all.

Stockholders can also profit by selling stock for more than they bought it for — if the stock's price rises in the market.

Stockholders never know if they are going to be paid dividends or if the value of their stocks are going to increase. They may make or lose money. The risks, and therefore the rewards, can be high. Bondholders, on the other hand, are guaranteed a specific return on the investment (the interest rate on the bond) and will get their investment back eventually. The issuing company must pay interest to the bondholder on a precise *schedule*. The risks of holding bonds are lower, but typically so are the returns.

How Bonds Work

Bonds are issued at a declared rate of interest paid each year to the holder of the bonds until their **maturity**. On the maturity date the investor returns the bonds to the corporation to be **redeemed**. The investor gets his/her original investment back on that date.

Until maturity, bonds may be traded publicly, with their price going above or below their **face value**. Face value is the original amount the purchaser paid ("loaned" to the corporation) for the bonds. The face value of a single bond, also referred to as **par**, is usually $100.

When the bond's market value rises above par, it means the bond is being traded for more than $100 — perhaps someone purchased it for $102. A bond trading above par is trading at a **premium** — in this case, the premium is $2. A bond trading below par is trading at a **discount**. If the above bond were trading at $94, the discount would be $6.

Bonds and Inflation

The value of bonds is affected by *inflation*. Inflation is a continuous increase in the prices of products and services in an economy. When prices rise, money isn't worth as much. When the cost of a loaf of bread rises from one dollar to two dollars, the dollar you earn can only buy half a loaf of bread instead of a whole loaf. Over time, inflation reduces the value of money.

A $100 bond bought today will only pay the bondholder back $100 at maturity. The bond offers no protection against inflation because, no matter what happens to the value of a dollar, the bond will still only be redeemable for $100. When investors hear economic news that makes them worry about inflation, therefore, bond prices usually decline. No investor wants to pay $100 for a bond that may only be worth $70 at maturity.

Until the maturity date, the bonds are traded, like stocks, on the open market. If more people want to buy the bond than sell it, the price will rise.

Reading Bond Tables

Current bond prices can be found in *The Wall Street Journal* and other newspapers on a daily basis.

Bonds		Cur Yld	Vol	Close	Net Change
ATT	4 3/4 98	5.0	5.6	94 3/8	- 1/2
DukeEn	6 1/4 04	6.3	2	100	- 1 7/8
Dole	7 7/8 13	7.2	6	97 1/8	- 2
Lucent	7 1/4 06	7.5	1099	96 3/4	- 3/4

Bonds are discussed in lots of $100. In the example above, AT&T has issued bonds that pay 4 3/4 dollars interest on every $100 each year until maturity. This bond issue becomes due in the year 1998 (indicated by the "98"), at which time the bonds are *redeemed*, or turned in, for their face value.

The Remainder of the Abbreviations Are Explained Below:

CUR YLD. (Current Yield): The yield is the interest divided by the price you paid for the bond. If the bond price declines, the yield rises. This means that the bond is trading at a discount. If the bond is trading at a premium, the yield declines.

VOL. (Volume of bonds traded): The numbers are given in thousands. As with stocks, when there is a great deal of volume in a given issue, it means that investors are taking an interest but does not indicate whether the price will go up or down.

CLOSE: The price in dollars at the end of the last day of trading.

NET CHG. (Net Change): The change in price from the close of the previous day's trading period.

Chapter 42 Review

N O T E : The exercises printed below can be found in the corresponding chapter of the NFTE MODULE 2 WORKBOOK that came with your textbook. Please write your answers there. If you do not have a workbook, write your answers on a separate sheet of paper.

Using New Words

bond
debt
discount
equity
face value
maturity
par
premium
redeem

On a separate sheet of paper, identify the vocabulary term that completes each sentence.

1) The _____ of a bond appears on it but does not necessarily reflect its market value.

2) A bond may change owners many times as it is traded on the open market, but whoever owns it at _____ may redeem it at the issuing company.

3) A bond trading at a _____ has lost some value.

4) A bondholder may _____ the bond at maturity.

5) A bond trading at _____ is worth the same amount of money as it was the day it was issued.

6) A bond trading above par is trading at a _____.

7) Bonds are considered a _____ form of financing a business.

8) A corporation that offers stock in return for money is financing the business through _____.

9) A _____ is an interest-bearing certificate issued by a corporation or government.

Review

Chapter 42 Review

Use the table below to answer the following questions.

Bonds		Cur Yld	Vol	Close	Net Change
ATT	4 3/4 98	5.0	5.6	94 3/8	- 1/2
DukeEn	6 1/4 04	6.3	2	100	- 1 7/8
Dole	7 7/8 13	7.2	6	97 1/8	- 2
Lucent	7 1/4 06	7.5	1099	96 3/4	- 3/4

1) Which bond has the highest current yield?

2) Which bond had the highest volume in trading?

3) Which bond closed at the lowest price?

4) Which bond increased in value?

Getting the Facts

Identify the phrase that best completes each sentence.

1. High volume in a bond issue means that
   a. the price of the bond is going to rise.
   b. investors are actively trading the issue.
   c. the price of the bond is going to fall.

2. A $100 bond bought today will pay
   a. $100 at maturity.
   b. $98 at maturity.
   c. $100 minus the market discount.

3. Bonds differ from stocks in that
   a. dividends must be paid.
   b. interest must be paid.
   c. ownership is offered.

4. A bond trading above par is trading
   a. at a discount.
   b. at maturity.
   c. at a premium.

5. Bonds are discussed in lots of
   a. $1,000
   b. $100
   c. $10

Review

Chapter Summary

I. Bonds are a form of debt financing.

A. The original amount of the bond plus interest is paid by the borrower.

B. Until maturity, bonds trade publicly.

C. Stock is a form of equity financing.

II. Bond prices tend to reflect inflation expectations.

A. Inflation is a continuous increase in prices.

B. Inflation reduces the value of money.

C. Bond prices fall when inflation is expected to rise.

III. Prices for bonds traded on the market are found in bond tables in newspapers.

A Business for the Young Entrepreneur: Pet Care

If you love animals, there are lots of money-making services you can offer. It would be best to pick one and stick with it. Here are some ideas:

Dog Walker

Many people are too busy to walk their dogs every day. But you could walk several at one time! Is there a dog run in your neighborhood park? Arrange to take several dogs to the dog run each afternoon. This is a good way to meet other dog owners who might need your service!

Cleaning Aquariums

Fish tanks are beautiful but require regular cleaning and care. This service requires some knowledge about caring for fish. The fish tank is a delicate environment. If disturbed by the wrong chemicals, fish can die. This is a good business idea, therefore, only if you already love fish and understand how to take care of them. You will need to know how to clean both freshwater and saltwater tanks. You will also need cleaning supplies and fish food.

Pet Sitter

You can take care of pets for people who are on vacation. Before accepting a job, though, go to the home and meet the pet. Make sure it's an animal you feel comfortable handling yourself. Before the owners leave, ask how to contact them in an emergency. You should also get the phone number and address of the family veterinarian.

Pet Grooming

If you really like to play with animals, pet grooming can be lots of fun. Cats and dogs need regular baths and flea treatments. If you have a good pair of clippers, you can also offer haircuts for dogs. Veterinarians usually offer free booklets on care and grooming of pets and the necessary expertise. A veterinarian or pet store can direct you to the safest bath and flea product use.

There is a tide in the affairs of men, which, taken at the flood, leads to fortune; omitted, all the voyages of their life are bound in shallows and in miseries.

— William Shakespeare, English poet and playwright

KEY OBJECTIVES

READING THIS CHAPTER AND DOING THE EXERCISES WILL ENABLE YOU TO:

- Explain how insurance protects business.

- Determine when a business owner needs liability insurance.

- Summarize how insurance companies profit.

- List different types of insurance.

INSURANCE AND OTHER OPERATING COSTS

Insurance Protects Your Business from Disaster

Insurance is provided by companies to protect people and businesses from having property or wealth stolen, lost, or destroyed. There are many kinds of insurance, and almost anything can be insured by **insurance agents**.

Insurance is one of a business owner's operating costs. It is the second "I" in USAI-IRD (Utilities, Salaries, Advertising, Interest, Insurance, Rent, Depreciation). If you owned a restaurant, for example, you would need fire insurance. Your insurance agent would help you calculate how much money it would take to replace everything in the restaurant and rebuild if a fire were to destroy it.

Let's say rebuilding your restaurant would cost $150,000. You would need an **insurance policy** that will guarantee you $150,000 in case of fire. Your insurance agent will figure out how much you must pay for this policy. You might pay $100 per month, for instance. This monthly payment is your **premium**.

As long as you paid the premiums on your fire-insurance policy, you would not have to worry about losing your restaurant to a fire. If it burned down, you would have the money to rebuild and continue the business. Insurance prevents random events from destroying you financially.

Liability Insurance

Business owners also need insurance to protect their businesses from the risk of injury to the customer.

Liability insurance pays the expenses of anyone who is injured while on your property or using your product or service.

If a customer proves that you *knew* your product or service was dangerous but you didn't inform him/her, you could be sued, and forced by a court to pay *damages*. Failure to inform a customer of potential danger from your product or service is called **fraud**.

The entrepreneur has a moral duty to inform customers of possible danger. The best idea is not to sell a product or service that could harm anyone. Even if you're selling something as harmless as ties, make sure they are not made of flammable material!

Before you decide to sell a product or offer a service, think about it. Try to imagine how your product or service could cause injury to someone. *If you think it might cause injury, don't sell it.*

How Insurance Companies Make Money

By now you may be wondering, "How can an insurance company afford to pay $150,000 to a restaurant owner whose place has just burned down, if the restaurant owner has only been paying the insurance company $100 a month?"

The answer is that insurance companies employ experts who calculate the odds of a particular event actually happening. Insurance companies keep statistics and study demographics.

An insurance company that specializes in fire insurance, for example, will have information about fires in restaurants going back many years. Analysts at the insurance company study this information and figure out how often fires tend to occur and how much they cost.

Analysts then determine how much to charge for premiums to guarantee that, even if some fires do occur, the cost of insurance paid out to one policyholder has been covered by the premiums paid by the many other policyholders.

Basic Coverage for Small Business

You won't need insurance if you are simply selling ties on the street or at school, but *the moment you move your business into a building, you will need coverage.*

You will need to choose an affordable **deductible**. The deductible is the amount of loss or damage you agree to cover before the insurance takes over. In the restaurant example, the owner might feel confident that he or she could cover $5,000 in damages from a fire without going bankrupt. The insurance company would have to pay $145,000 if a fire gutted the restaurant. It would charge a lower premium of, say, $90 per month. The policyholder pays a lower premium in return for a higher deductible.

Lower deductible = Higher premium

Higher deductible = Lower premium

Although state laws vary, most require business owners who have people working for them to carry:

WORKERS' COMPENSATION — covers employees for loss of income and medical expenses due to job-related injuries.

DISABILITY INSURANCE — covers employees for loss of income due to a disabling injury or illness.

If you have a car or truck, you must carry:

AUTO INSURANCE — covers your liability for personal injuries in an accident as well as damages to any vehicle involved, and injuries to other persons.

Other Important Types of Insurance

PROPERTY INSURANCE — provides for the replacement of any property damaged by fire, flood, vandalism, or other types of damage as specified in the policy.

CRIME INSURANCE — protects against robberies as well as theft by employees. The federal government has a program that provides crime insurance for small businesses located in high-crime areas where insurance companies don't want to provide coverage.

There are many other types of insurance available that can be tailored to the needs and resources of your business that are not mentioned here.

Chapter 43 Review

N O T E : The exercises printed below can be found in the corresponding chapter of the NFTE MODULE 2 WORKBOOK that came with your textbook. Please write your answers there. If you do not have a workbook, write your answers on a separate sheet of paper.

Critical Thinking about ... Insurance

1. Imagine that a small hardware store with several employees is destroyed by fire. What types of insurance should the store owner have carried?

2. Explain how insurance companies make money, even though they sometimes have to make very large payouts.

Getting the Facts

True or False?

1. The higher the deductible, the higher the premium.

2. Small-business owners should avoid selling products that could cause customer injury.

3. Businesses that sell dangerous products must carry disability insurance.

4. Insurance protects wealth and property from random events.

5. Insurance companies carefully calculate the odds of disaster striking.

Chapter 43 Review

Using New Words

deductible
fraud
liability insurance
insurance
insurance agent
insurance policy
premium

On a separate sheet of paper, identify the vocabulary term that best completes each sentence.

1) _____, or the failure to inform a customer of potential damage from a product or service, is one of the most unethical things a business owner can do.

2) To keep your insurance policy active, you must always pay your _____.

3) An _____ can help you determine your insurance needs.

4) If you have an accident that causes $2,000 worth of damage to your car, but your _____ is $500, your auto insurance policy will pay you $1,500.

5) If you are selling anything that could injure a customer, you will need _____.

6) Business owners protect their businesses from disaster with _____.

7) The _____ is a contract between you and the insurance company that obligates you to pay a premium in return for coverage.

Exploring Your Community

Ask an entrepreneur how he or she decided how much insurance to carry and whether to have a large or small deductible. Write about your interview. Present a report on your entrepreneur's insurance plan to the class.

Review

Chapter Summary

I.   **Insurance protects your business from disaster.**

II. **Business owners also need protection from liability.**

   A. A business must carry liability insurance if the product or service can injure its customers.

   B. A business must inform customers whether a product or service can cause injury. Failure to inform is fraud.

   C. Small businesses should avoid risky products because liability insurance is expensive.

III. **Insurance companies are experts at calculating odds.**

   A. They study statistics and demographics to evaluate risks.

   B. They charge premiums high enough to cover payouts.

   C. The size of the deductible determines the premium:

      1. Higher deductible = Lower premium

      2. Lower deductible = Higher premium

IV. **You'll need insurance once you move your business into a building.**

   A. Businesses with employees require workers' compensation and disability insurance.

   B. If you have a car, you must carry auto insurance.

A Business for the Young Entrepreneur: Photography

Is photography one of your hobbies? You might turn it into a profitable business by taking pictures of groups or special events. Here are some opportunities:

MUSICIANS — Rock bands, rappers, solo artists all need photos to send to clubs, newspapers, music magazines and record companies. Most artists need lots of copies of their photos. You can get paid for taking the photo and for supplying the prints, too!

SPORTS TEAMS — Little League teams, high school teams, adult softball teams, all need photos to send to newspapers, put on posters, or have as souvenirs.

- Graduation parties
- Anniversary parties
- Weddings

Tips

- Very important: Always insure your photography equipment. Get insurance that protects it not only in your home but while you are using it at different locations.

- Get on the staff of your school yearbook as a photographer. You will gain experience and take photos you can show customers.

- Start a portfolio. A *portfolio* is a portable case with pages inside for mounting photographs and artwork. It also means the work you have to show. Customers will want to see "your portfolio." Mount your best photos in the portfolio and show it to potential customers. You can also post photos on your website.

- Put up flyers advertising your business in music stores, sporting goods stores, and party supply stores.

> *Your life is a work of art. A craft to be most carefully mastered. For patience has replaced time and you are your own destination.*
>
> —Rick Jarow, professor and author

KEY OBJECTIVES

READING THIS CHAPTER AND DOING THE EXERCISES WILL ENABLE YOU TO:

■ Locate manufacturers in your community.

■ Have a prototype made.

■ Investigate zoning laws that might affect your business.

MANUFACTURING: FROM IDEA TO PRODUCT

To **manufacture** an item means to make it from raw materials. Many entrepreneurs create successful businesses by selling products that other businesses manufacture. To manufacture a product in large quantities can be very expensive because it requires machinery and factories. Also, in most communities, manufacturers can only operate in areas that have been set aside for *industrial* use.

What if you have an idea for a product, though, that no one else is has thought of? If you can't buy it from a wholesaler, you will need either to make it yourself or find a manufacturer to make it for you.

Making It Yourself

If you decide to manufacture the product yourself, the first thing you should do is call your local chamber of commerce and ask about zoning laws and licensing requirements. Some towns prohibit manufacturing in residential areas, for example.

One NFTE student, who sold birdcages that he made in his parent's garage, found out that this was illegal. He moved his operation to his uncle's garage because his uncle lived in a neighborhood that didn't prohibit manufacturing in a residence.

Manufacturing a product yourself is fine for a small business that sells products locally. But if you intend to sell them nationwide someday, you could be limiting your growth by manufacturing the products yourself. If you have something you think could sell nationwide, or worldwide, it might be wiser to develop your product and then hire a manufacturer to make it.

How Henry Ford Changed Manufacturing

Some entrepreneurs have become successful manufacturers. But this can be an undertaking that may require raising large amounts of capital to buy machinery and build factories. Still, sometimes manufacturing is the only way an entrepreneur can control the price of his or her product and make it affordable for the consumer.

Back in the late 1800s, automobiles existed but were very expensive to produce. Cars were considered novelties for the wealthy. Car manufacturers didn't think the middle class would need or want cars, so manufacturers didn't try to cut the costs of producing them.

In contrast, Henry Ford believed that every American would buy a car if they were affordable. He realized that only the manufacturing cost stood in his way.

Ford was determined to build an automobile that almost anyone could afford. But, to do this, he would have to change how cars were made.

Ford Invents the Assembly Line

To cut costs, Ford invented the "**assembly line**." He set up a line of workers and built a conveyer belt that would carry the unfinished automobiles past them. Each worker was responsible for attaching one item to each car. In this way, cars could be built much more quickly and less expensively.

Ford's assembly line revolutionized manufacturing. Other companies had to change their factories over to assembly-line production just to compete.

The assembly line made it possible for companies to lower their manufacturing costs enough to sell products to the average consumer that previously were unaffordable. This improved the American standard of living enormously.

By inventing a new way to manufacture cars, Ford cut costs enough to be able to sell his automobiles cheaply and still make a profit. The Ford Motor Company became one of the largest companies in the world. Ford revolutionized industry by introducing the concept of mass production.

Step One: Make a Model

If you don't want to become a manufacturer, but you have created a product that will need to be manufactured, the first step is to make a model of the product. As we discussed in Chapter 6, a model can be rough and made from inexpensive materials, such as paper, wood, paint, cloth, or plaster of paris. Don't be afraid to experiment or to show your design to friends. Now is the time to make changes — while they are inexpensive to make.

Step Two: Have a Prototype Made

Once you have perfected your model, you are ready to find a company that makes *prototypes*. A prototype is an exact model of the item made by the manufacturing process that would be used in actual production.

There are many ways to find prototype manufacturers. As mentioned in Chapter 6, you can check the *Thomas Register*, which lists all U.S. manufacturers. You can also check the ads in trade publications for your industry. If you have designed something fashionable — a unique kind of handbag, for example — look in the back pages of *Women's Wear Daily*. Companies that make prototypes for fashion items advertise there.

Prototypes can be quite expensive, especially if machinery needs to be created to make your product. For a manufacturing business, developing a prototype for the item being manufactured would probably be a major start-up cost.

Step Three: Set Up Manufacturing

Many companies that make prototypes can also help you set up your manufacturing operation because they have contacts at factories around the world. The company that makes the prototype for your handbag, for example, might have the prototype made at a factory in Costa Rica that could also become your manufacturer.

Distributors and *publicists* are also good contacts for manufacturers. Distributors are companies that arrange to have your product sold in stores around the country. They also advertise in trade publications for your industry.

You can also connect with distributors, publicists and manufacturers in your industry by showing your prototype at a trade fair.

Chapter 44 Review

NOTE: The exercises printed below can be found in the corresponding chapter of the NFTE MODULE 2 WORKBOOK that came with your textbook. Please write your answers there. If you do not have a workbook, write your answers on a separate sheet of paper.

Critical Thinking about ... Manufacturing

1. Write an essay discussing the advantages and disadvantages of choosing to manufacture your product yourself.

2. Call your local chamber of commerce and find out about manufacturing laws in your neighborhood. Write a memo describing these zoning laws and how they will affect your business.

3. Conduct research at the library or online to find an important trade publication or website for your industry. Find three advertisements from prototype makers, manufacturers, publicists or distributors who could be helpful to your business and share the ads with the class.

Getting the Facts

1. What are "raw materials"? Pick a product you use often and list all the materials that went into its manufacture.

2. Think of a product that has dropped significantly in price in your lifetime. Write an essay explaining why you think this price drop occurred.

Using New Words

assembly line
manufacture

Using the vocabulary terms, write a paragraph explaining why Ford's use of the assembly line was an important breakthrough for manufacturing.

Exploring Your Community

Is there an area zoned for manufacturing in your community? Contact your chamber of commerce and do research online to learn more.

Review

A Business for the Young Entrepreneur: Button Manufacturing

About three years ago, 11-year-old Daniel Trainor was diagnosed with a brain tumor. By January of 1999, he had finished his cancer treatment and was scheduled for an internship at NFTE. Daniel had seen ads for NFTE in *Boy's Life* magazine and was very excited about becoming an entrepreneur. "It's very cool. In all those TV sitcoms, I see people with tyrannical bosses; and I don't want to end up like that."

Sadly, Daniel had a recurrence of cancer. Since he had received a laptop computer for his birthday and was missing a lot of school due to his cancer treatments, Daniel decided to take advantage of NFTE's online curriculum, BizTech™, a program sponsored by Microsoft. Using BizTech, Daniel created a business plan for making and selling buttons. In the back of a magazine, he saw an ad for a button machine, which he bought for $100.

His first buttons were for the new millennium — "Peace on Earth."

"I already learned what a business is — getting receipts, keeping records. Once I understood it, it was pretty simple," says Daniel. He sells the buttons for $1.00 and has orders from some of the staff at the hospital where he's being treated.

Starting his own business has not only given Daniel something to do that is worthwhile, it has helped take his mind off the side effects of his cancer treatment, which has kept him out of school for long periods of time.

One of Daniel's plans is to establish a website for his business with help from his brother. "I expect to be able to make $40 or $50 a week once it's up and running. It only takes 15 seconds to make a button."

Daniel's advice to other kids: "You need to do something that you like doing. I thought making buttons would be really cool, and I'm excited about it. It's really fun." With his enthusiasm and creativity, Daniel is sure to succeed.

There is no security on this earth; there is only opportunity.

— Douglas MacArthur,
American General

KEY OBJECTIVES

READING THIS CHAPTER AND DOING THE EXERCISES WILL ENABLE YOU TO:

- Explain compound interest.

- Read the present and future value of money from a chart.

- Summarize the difference between the present and future value of a dollar.

- Use the "Rule of 72" to calculate how long it takes for an investment to double.

FUTURE AND PRESENT VALUE OF MONEY

Future Value of Money

The future value of money is the amount it will **accrue** (increase) over time through investment. If you invest $100 at 10% interest for one year, you will have $110 at the end of that period. If you let the accumulating interest and the original $100 remain in this investment for ten years, it will grow to $259 (look up ten periods at 10% in the **Future Value** n-chart in this chapter).

COMPOUND INTEREST — that is, money making money — is the essence of investment.

This insight comes to many entrepreneurs, just as it did to John D. Rockefeller when he was still a teenager (back in the mid-19th century). He had lent $50 to a neighboring farmer. A year later the farmer paid him back the $50 plus $3.50 interest on the loan. Around the same time, Rockefeller had made $1.12 for thirty hours of back-breaking work hoeing potatoes for another neighbor. "From that time on," he said in his biography, "I was determined to make money work for me."

Money grows on its own through wise investments. You are not doing physical labor but mental labor, when you invest, by determining the best place to put your money.

There are a wide variety of investment opportunities in a free-market society. Many *instruments* — bonds, stocks, certificates of deposit, mutual funds and the like — are offered in the marketplace. These instruments offer different interest rates, or rates of return, depending on the risk factor. As you've learned, a higher interest rate implies a greater amount of risk.

For the investor willing to accept a high risk, small business can be an excellent investment opportunity. The ROI of a successful small business can be thousands of percent, but risk of business failure is also high.

The Future Value n-chart can help you figure out how much one invested dollar will be worth over time at a given interest rate.

The Present Value of Money

The concept of the **present value** of money is based on the old saying, "A bird in the hand is worth two in the bush."

The Rule of 72

Using simple arithmetic, one can calculate how long it would take for one dollar to double. Just take the return on investment and divide it into 72. This will give you the number of years it will take for the investment to double.

$$\frac{72}{\text{ROI}} = \text{number of years for investment to double}$$

You want to have your money *now*. If you can't have it now, you want to be compensated with a return. Three reasons money in the hand is worth more are:

1. Fear of **inflation**. (A dollar tomorrow will buy less than a dollar does today.)
2. Risk of the investment not being paid back.
3. Loss of the opportunity to use the money for a better investment now.

The Present Value n-chart shows what a promise of future money is worth now, based on:

1) How many years you must wait for it.
2) Your next-best investment opportunity.*

For Example:

A client agrees to pay you, three years from now, $100 for services you render today. Your next-best opportunity for investment is 10% ROI. Look at the Present Value n-chart under period 3 (for three years) and 10%. The present value of $1.00 at three years and 10% is $0.75. The present value of the agreement of $100, therefore, is $75 ($100 x 0.75 = $75).

Your client's agreement is worth only $75 now. Anytime you are asked to wait for payment, you should be compensated, because money in your hand now is worth significantly more than money received in the future.

---

* Technically, this discount rate is a subjective combination of risk, inflation, and potential loss of investment. Each person would have an individual "next-best" investment opportunity.

N-CHART

THE FUTURE VALUE OF MONEY

Future Value of $1 After "n" Periods

Periods (in years)	1%	2%	3%	4%	5%	6%	7%	8%	9%	10%	11%	12%
1	1.0100	1.0200	1.0300	1.0400	1.0500	1.0600	1.0700	1.0800	1.0900	1.1000	1.1100	1.1200
2	1.0201	1.0404	1.0609	1.0816*	1.1025	1.1236	1.1449	1.1664	1.1881	1.2100	1.2321	1.2544
3	1.0303	1.0612	1.0927	1.1249	1.1576	1.1910	1.2250	1.2597	1.2950	1.3310	1.3676	1.4049
4	1.0406	1.0824	1.1255	1.1699	1.2155	1.2625	1.3108	1.3605	1.4116	1.4641	1.5181	1.5735
5	1.0510	1.1041	1.1593	1.2167	1.2763	1.3382	1.4026	1.4693	1.5386	1.6105	1.6851	1.7623
6	1.0615	1.1261	1.1941	1.2653	1.3401	1.4185	1.5007	1.5869	1.6771	1.7716	1.8704	1.9738
7	1.0721	1.1487	1.2299	1.3159	1.4071	1.5036	1.6058	1.7138	1.8280	1.9487	2.0762	2.2107
8	1.0829	1.1717	1.2668	1.3686	1.4775	1.5939	1.7182	1.8509	1.9926	2.1436	2.3045	2.4760
9	1.0937	1.1951	1.3048	1.4233	1.5513	1.6895	1.8385	1.9990	2.1719	2.3580	2.5580	2.7731
10	1.1046	1.2190	1.3439	1.4802	1.6209	1.7909	1.9672	2.1589	2.3674	2.5937	2.8394	3.1059
11	1.1157	1.2434	1.3842	1.5395	1.7103	1.8983	2.1049	2.3316	2.5084	2.8531	3.1518	3.4786
12	1.1268	1.2682	1.4258	1.6010	1.7959	2.0122	2.2522	2.5182	2.8127	3.1384	2.4985	3.8960
13	1.1381	1.2936	1.4685	1.6651	1.8057	2.1329	2.4098	2.7196	3.0658	3.4523	3.8833	4.3635
14	1.1495	1.3195	1.5126	1.7317	1.9799	2.2609	2.5785	2.9372	3.3417	3.7975	4.3104	4.8871
15	1.1610	1.3459	1.5580	1.8009	2.0789	2.3966	2.7590	3.1722	3.6425	4.1773	4.7846	5.4736

To find the future value, take a given interest rate, go down column to correct number of periods, then multiply by the number you find.

* If you invest $1 at 4% for two years, it will be worth $1.08 at the end of that period.

N-CHART

THE PRESENT VALUE OF MONEY

Lost Investment Opportunities
Present Value of $1 after "n" periods

Periods, (in years)	1%	2%	3%	4%	5%	6%	7%	8%	9%	10%	11%	12%
1	.99010	.98039	.97087	.96154	.96238	.94340	.93458	.92593	.91743	.90909	.90090	.89286
2	.98030	.96117	.94260	.92456*	.90793	.89000	.87344	.85734	.84168	.82645	.81162	.79719
3	.97059	.94232	.91514	.88900	.86384	.83962	.81630	.79383	.77218	.75131	.73119	.71178
4	.96098	.92385	.88849	.85480	.82379	.79209	.76290	.73503	.70843	.68301	.65873	.63552
5	.95147	.90573	.86261	.82193	.70363	.74726	.71299	.68058	.64993	.62092	.59345	.56743
6	.94204	.88797	.83748	.79031	.74622	.70496	.66634	.63017	.59627	.56447	.53464	.50663
7	.93272	.87056	.81309	.75992	.71068	.66506	.62275	.58349	.54703	.51316	.48166	.45235
8	.92348	.85349	.78941	.73069	.67404	.62741	.58201	.54027	.50187	.46651	.43393	.40388
9	.91434	.83675	.76642	.70259	.64461	.59190	.54393	.50025	.46043	.42410	.39092	.36061
10	.90529	.82035	.74409	.67556	.61391	.56839	.50835	.46319	.42241	.38554	.35218	.32197
11	.89632	.80426	.72242	.64958	.58468	.52679	.47509	.42888	.38753	.35049	.31728	.28748
12	.88745	.78849	.70138	.62440	.56684	.49697	.44401	.39711	.35553	.31683	.28584	.25667
13	.87866	.77303	.68095	.60057	.53932	.46884	.41496	.36770	.32618	.28966	.25751	.22917
14	.86996	.75787	.66112	.57747	.50607	.44230	.38782	.34046	.29925	.26333	.23199	.20462
15	.86135	.74301	.64186	.55526	.48102	.41726	.36245	.31524	.27454	.23939	.20900	.18270

To find the present value, take a given interest rate, go down column to correct number of periods, then multiply by the number you find.

*If it will be two years before you receive the dollar, and you could have invested it at 4%, you are actually receiving 92 cents.

441

Chapter 45 Review

NOTE: The exercises printed below can be found in the corresponding chapter of the NFTE MODULE 2 WORKBOOK that came with your textbook. Please write your answers there. If you do not have a workbook, write your answers on a separate sheet of paper.

Critical Thinking about . . . Present and Future Value of Money

1. Using the charts in this chapter, write an essay discussing whether you would rather have $5 now or $10 a year from now, if your opportunity cost is 10%.

2. Pretend you have a graphic design business. A client agrees to pay you $500 after one year if you create illustrations for his website now. Meanwhile your next-best opportunity would be to invest in a one-year CD at your bank that pays 10% per year. How much extra should you ask your client to pay in return for allowing him to wait one year to pay you?

3. If you want to have $100,000 fifteen years from now, how much money do you need to invest today, assuming an interest rate of 12%?

Getting the Facts

1. What determines stock prices?

2. What is the Rule of 72?

3. List three reasons why you might choose not to invest your money in a given instrument.

In Your Opinion

Investing is a balancing act between risk and return. "Conservative" investors prefer low risk and low return. "Aggressive" investors are willing to accept high risk for the possibility of a high return. If someone gave you $50 to invest, would you be conservative or aggressive? Mark your position on the line below. Make another mark to show where you would stand if you were investing $3,000 and it was all the money you had.

1　2　3　4　5　6　7　8　9　10

Conservative　　　　　　Aggressive

The Rule of 72

How long would it take an investment of $1.00 to double?

Chapter 45 Review

Using New Words

accrue
future value
inflation
present value

On a separate sheet of paper, identify the correct definition for each vocabulary term.

1) future value

   a) a good deal on an investment

   b) the cheaper of two stock prices

   c) how much an investment is worth in the future if invested at a given rate of return

2) present value

   a) a good deal on an investment

   b) the cheaper of two stock prices

   c) how much an investment is worth today

3) accrue

   a) to figure accurately

   b) to grow

   c) to pay interest

4) inflation

   a) economic growth

   b) a continuing increase in prices of goods and services

   c) improvement in the stock market

Review

Chapter Summary

I. The future value of money is the value it gains over time when invested.

A. Money grows through wise investing.

B. A future value chart can show the value of an investment.

II. The Rule of 72: Divide the return on investment into 72 to figure how many years it will take an investment to double in value.

III. The present value of money is how much a given amount of money in the future is worth today.

A. You want to receive your money now for three reasons:

1. Fear of inflation.
2. Risk of the investment not being paid back.
3. To take advantage of a better investment.

B. The present value chart shows what the value of future money is now, based on:

1. How many years you must wait for it.
2. Your next-best investment opportunity.

A Business for the Young Entrepreneur: Messenger Service

If you're fast on your feet or your bicycle and know your way around town, you could start a messenger service. Offer your service to local businesses and offices. Let them know what hours you can be available, from 3:30 to 6 p.m. on weekdays, for example.

What You'll Need to Get Started

- A bicycle helmet — riding a bicycle can be risky. You should always wear a helmet and observe all traffic laws.

- Knapsack for carrying items to be delivered.

- Receipt book — when you deliver an item, always have the person who takes it sign for it. Bring the receipt back to the person who ordered the delivery. It is proof that you made the delivery.

- Maps — carry street maps, subway maps, etc., in your knapsack.

- A watch.

- If you're using a bicycle, don't forget to keep any necessary licenses current.

- Insurance — make sure you have insurance so that you are protected in case you get into an accident.

Tips

- Make flyers advertising your service. Put them up in office buildings, gyms, and stores.

- Start looking for customers by asking your family's friends if they work somewhere that might need a messenger service.

All businesses were launched by entrepreneurs, and all were once small.

— Nat Shulman,
family business owner
and columnist

KEY OBJECTIVES

READING THIS CHAPTER AND DOING THE EXERCISES WILL ENABLE YOU TO:

- Explain the value of treating customers and employees ethically.
- Analyze the importance of repeat customers.
- Recognize ethical business behavior.

ETHICAL BUSINESS BEHAVIOR

Business Ethics

Ethics are the standards and rules that help one determine right from wrong. The Golden Rule, "Do unto others as you would have others do unto you," is a well-known *ethic*. The Golden Rule will help you "do the right thing" in many situations. A behavior may be legal and still not be ethical. For example, it is not illegal to be rude to your customers and employees, but it is unethical.

Ethical business behavior is not only moral, it makes good business sense. Have you ever bought something from a store and felt you were cheated? How did you react? Did you ever go back to that store again? Probably not. You may have even told your friends about the experience, so the store lost more than just one customer.

Repeat Customers

Business success is not built on drawing in a customer just once and taking his or her money. Success is based on **repeat business** — building up a satisfied group of customers who not only buy your product or service again, but recommend it to their friends and relatives.

Ethical Employer/Employee Relationships

It's important to treat your employees well, too. Aside from the fact that it is morally right to treat people ethically, it is in your best interest as an employer to do so. As the entrepreneur, your values will set the ethical tone for your company. If you think it's okay to cheat a customer, your employees will sense that it is okay to cheat customers — and then they will probably try to cheat you!

Employees who feel "used" by their employers will not do their best work. The most successful companies are those in which the employees' interests correspond with what is best for the company.

Many large companies offer their employees stock at low prices, or give generous bonuses at the end of the year based on how well the company does. In this way, the employees know that they will profit from the company's success. This motivates them to care about the company they work for.

Wise employers treat employees as the employers themselves would want to be treated.

Ethical Business Behavior

One can think of a successful business as a house. Good business ethics represent the foundation (what the house or business is based on), and good business behavior forms the floor (where everything takes place). Good business is based on a *fair trade* — the exchange of products or services for money — and a sense of responsibility toward one's fellow human beings.

To get ahead in business, lay the following principles (business behavior) over your foundation (ethics).

1) **PUNCTUALITY** — Be on time for business appointments. If you are late for meetings, you could lose customers and clients — and eventually your business. If, for reasons beyond your control, you are ever late or miss an appointment, apologize immediately and graciously.

2) **RELIABILITY** — Just as your customers must be able to count on you to arrive on time, they need to count on your product or service to perform properly. A successful business is built on customers who keep coming back because the product or service is reliable.

3) **COURTEOUSNESS** — If you are not courteous and polite, you will turn off customers and business contacts. Advice and support are extremely important to the new business owner, but you will not get them if you are rude.

4) **RESPECT** — Show respect for your customers and other businesspeople by being punctual, reliable, and courteous.

5) **COMMUNICATION** — Show respect for others and for yourself by how you speak. Don't use slang or obscenities.

6) **CLOTHING** — From the moment they first meet you, customers are deciding whether or not they should trust you with their money. Before your product or service can prove itself, you are already being judged by what you are wearing. Choose clothes that project the image you want customers to associate with your business.

7) **NEATNESS** — Make sure you always look clean and neat. Customers are very quick to judge people by appearance. Accept this as part of doing business.

8) **DIET** — Eat good food instead of junk food. Candy, soda, and other junk foods make you hyperactive at first and depressed later. If you are moody because of the food you eat, it will show in your business behavior. Drink juice or water instead of soda. Eat fruit, crackers, nuts, or yogurt instead of candy and chips.

Without good business behavior you will alienate customers and employees, and your business will suffer. In addition, other entrepreneurs and businesspeople do not share information with someone who is perceived as doing "bad business." This cuts you off from valuable networking.

If you are lacking in any of these good business principles, don't try to develop them all at once. Choose one and work at developing it. Changing one's habits takes time — that is why they are called habits. A lot of people have found that you must practice a new habit for about 90 days before it becomes something you do naturally.

Chapter 46 Review

N O T E : The exercises printed below can be found in the corresponding chapter of the **NFTE MODULE 2 WORKBOOK** that came with your textbook. Please write your answers there. If you do not have a workbook, write your answers on a separate sheet of paper.

Critical Thinking about . . . Ethical Behavior

1. Write a paragraph about a time when someone was late, unreliable, or rude to you. How did being treated like that make you feel?

2. Write an essay describing how you would handle the following situations if you were an employer:

   Situation #1: An employee repeatedly hands in sloppy paperwork.

   Situation #2: After the introduction of a new computer system to your office, one employee seems to be avoiding his work because he's unsure of how to use the new equipment.

3. It's important in business to know how to apologize if you offend a client, supplier, or business contact. Write a letter apologizing for something you did or said that you regret. Offer to do something to make amends for your behavior.

4. Think of a behavior that is legal but that you do not consider ethical. Write a paragraph explaining why you feel it is not ethical.

Getting the Facts

Identify the phrase that best completes each sentence.

1. Repeat customers are customers who
   A. repeatedly complain.
   B. buy your product or service more than once.
   C. know about your business from an ad.

2. Many companies offer stock or bonuses to employees to
   A. make them care about the company's success.
   B. get them to spend more money.
   C. encourage them to start their own businesses.

3. Customers want to be able to count on your product or service; they want it to be:
   A. reliable.
   B. fairly priced.
   C. both of the above.

Review

Chapter 46 Review

Discuss . . . Your Diet

Write down everything you eat for one day. Share your list with a partner in class. Discuss how you could each improve your diets to become better entrepreneurs. After your discussion, make a list of changes you intend to make to your diet.

Exploring Your Community

Find a charity in your community and call or visit to learn how you could get involved. Make a commitment to this charity to give time or money that you can honor every month. Write a memo to your teacher describing your commitment.

Chapter Summary

I.   **Ethical business behavior is good for business.**

     A. Cheated customers don't return.

     B. Satisfied customers come back and recommend your business to others.

     C. Employees who are treated ethically work harder.

II.   **Ethical business behavior is based on fairness and responsibility.**

     A. Show respect for others by being punctual, reliable, and courteous.

     B. Show respect for yourself by how you communicate, dress, and eat.

III. **Ethical business behavior encourages networking.**

     A. Networking is a source of valuable information, contacts, and services.

     B. Business owners don't like to network with unethical businesspeople.

KEY OBJECTIVES

READING THIS CHAPTER AND DOING THE EXERCISES WILL ENABLE YOU TO:

- Explain the importance of establishing a personal credit history.

- List The "Four C's" of business credit.

- Recognize your rights in dealing with credit-reporting agencies.

- Describe how to use charge accounts and layaway plans.

BUILDING GOOD PERSONAL AND BUSINESS CREDIT

Good Credit

In Chapter 9 we discussed *credit* as a ledger entry designating income. In this chapter we will look at the wider definition of credit: "Integrity in money matters and the ability to make payments when due."*

Great fortunes have been built on good credit. It is one of your most important intangible assets. A good credit rating will increase your financial options dramatically.

How to Establish a Personal Credit History

To establish credit you must show that you are capable of making regular payments on a *debt*. Most banks and other lending institutions do not like to lend money to

---

* *Webster's New World Dictionary of the American Language*, Ed. D.B. Guralnik, 2nd ed. Simon and Schuster, 1986.

people who have never borrowed, because they have no "credit history." Most department stores, on the other hand, are willing to open a **charge account** for customers with no credit history.

Charge accounts enable customers to make purchases without paying cash at the time of purchase. By the end of the month, you will be expected to pay either the balance or a portion of it ("minimum amount due"). Sometimes you will not be charged interest if you pay for the purchase by the end of the month. Otherwise, you will be charged interest on the remaining balance. Most major credit cards will require you to be at least 18 years old before they will issue you a charge account.

When you are old enough to get your first charge account, make a few small purchases and pay for them right away. This is a good way to establish a credit record. Never miss a payment or pay later than the "date due."

Another option is to buy something from a store on **layaway**. Layaway plans allow you to make a down payment on an item and then pay monthly installments until you pay it off. Making payments on time will prove that you know how to manage your money.

The Cost of Credit

The most important thing to remember about credit is that it *costs money*. It costs more to buy on credit than to buy with cash. Whether you are borrowing from a bank, a business associate or through a credit card, you will be paying not only the **principal** (original amount borrowed) but a *finance charge* (interest on the original amount) as well.

Credit-Reporting Agencies

Before a banker lends you money or a credit card company grants you a card, they will investigate your credit history. There are several agencies that keep credit reports on individuals or businesses. The personal credit agencies are Equifax, Experian, TRW, and TransUnion. The best known business agencies are Dun & Bradstreet and NCR Corp.

These agencies gather information given to them voluntarily by bankers, suppliers, and other creditors.

Credit agencies can make mistakes. They do not always verify the information they receive; they just record it. For this reason, you should run credit checks on yourself periodically. Contact the four main agencies to see if they have reports on you or your business. Ask them for a copy of your reports, which they are required by law to supply.

Clearing Up Negative Credit Reports

You may have a negative comment on your report because you failed to pay a bill on time for some reason. But your reason may be legitimate and you can have it cleared. Perhaps you failed to pay because you moved and the bill did not come to your new address. You can then pay it and have it erased from the report.

You can also have disputes recorded as "disputed," not as bad credit. If you are refusing to pay for your new refrigerator because it is not working properly, for example, and the store has reported you as a bad credit risk, you can contact the reporting agency and have the debt designated as "disputed" instead of "unpaid."

Finally, you can file reports on yourself with a credit agency. Give them information that will make your credit report stronger.

Business Credit

It is hard for a business to grow without the use of credit. At some point, the typical small-business owner will be sitting across from a banker and asking for a loan so it is very important that you have excellent credit.

As a small-business owner, you are going to need the help and support of bankers. It is in your long-term interest to learn how to work with them. You will be asking for money for your business, so think of the banker as your potential friend. Be sure to call around to different banks and compare the interest rates they charge on loans.

The "Four C's"

You can shop for the best deal on a loan just as on anything else. Bankers care most about The Four C's:

1) **Collateral**
2) **Cash flow**
3) **Commitment**
4) **Credit history**

Collateral

The banker wants to know what you own that can be pledged against the loan. In other words, what item or property can the bank take if you fail to repay? Examples of **collateral** include a house, a car, or business assets, such as a silk-screening machine or an oven.

Cash Flow

Most small-business loans are repaid from cash generated by the business. Your business plan must include a cash-flow statement that proves to the banker that your business will generate enough cash to pay back the loan.

Commitment

How much of your own money have you invested in your business? Have you gotten friends and family to invest? What about venture capital? The banker wants to see that others have confidence in your business, too.

Credit History

As we have discussed, your credit history is crucial. A banker will not lend money to someone with bad credit and almost never to someone with no credit.

Risks of Credit

Don't forget that borrowing money can be risky and expensive. Once you have a bad credit rating, it can take many years to become creditworthy again.

Chapter 47 Review

NOTE: The exercises printed below can be found in the corresponding chapter of the NFTE MODULE 2 WORKBOOK that came with your textbook. Please write your answers there. If you do not have a workbook, write your answers on a separate sheet of paper.

Critical Thinking about . . . Credit

1. Write a memo explaining why you would qualify for a $500 loan for your business. Describe the purpose of the loan and the "Four C's", as they apply to you and your business.

2. Write a memo describing your plan for establishing good personal credit.

Getting the Facts

In your NFTE Module 2 Workbook, or on a separate sheet of paper, identify the best answer for each question.

1. An example of collateral is
   A. your business idea.
   B. your cash flow.
   C. your car.

2. The cost of credit is
   A. the finance charge.
   B. the principal.
   C. 10%.

3. Someone who has never borrowed money has
   A. good credit.
   B. no credit.
   C. average credit.

4. To use a layaway plan you must first
   A. run a credit check.
   B. make a down payment.
   C. supply collateral.

Review

Chapter 47 Review

Using New Words

charge account
collateral
installment
layaway plan
principal

On a separate sheet of paper, write the vocabulary term with the letter of its corresponding definition.

a. periodic loan payment

b. a store credit policy requiring a down payment

c. amount of a loan before interest

d. anything used to secure a loan

e. store credit allowing purchasing without cash

Exploring Your Community

Visit a local bank and ask for a personal-loan application. Fill it out and bring it to class. Write an essay analyzing whether you think the questions on the application are fair and fully capture a person's creditworthiness.

Chapter Summary

I.   A good credit rating will help you finance your business.

II. Charge accounts, credit cards, and layaway plans can help entrepreneurs to start establishing credit.

   A. Never miss a payment.

   B. Never miss a "due date."

III. Using credit may cost more than paying cash.

IV. Credit-reporting agencies file information on you from creditors.

   A. Credit agencies can make mistakes. Check your record periodically.

   B. Have bad debts removed after you pay them, and debts you disagree with marked "disputed."

   C. Make your report stronger by sending credit agencies information yourself.

V.   Business credit is often obtained from a bank.

   A. Bankers care most about the "Four C's:"

      1. Collateral

      2. Cash flow

      3. Commitment

      4. Credit history

VI. Using credit is a big responsibility.

   A. Most creditors will require that you be at least 18 years old before they will issue you a charge account or a credit card.

   B. Consult with a parent, relative or adult mentor to make sure that you are ready for this responsibility.

   C. Once you do begin using credit, start by borrowing a small amount.

Money is better than poverty, if only for financial reasons.

— Woody Allen,
American comic and film maker

KEY OBJECTIVES

READING THIS CHAPTER AND DOING THE EXERCISES WILL ENABLE YOU TO:

■ Read a balance sheet.

■ Use ratios to analyze a company's balance sheet.

THE BALANCE SHEET: A SNAPSHOT OF YOUR BUSINESS

A Snapshot of the Business

A **balance sheet** is a financial statement showing the **assets**, **liabilities** (debts) and **net worth** of a business. The net worth is the difference between assets and liabilities and is also called **owner's equity**.

Monthly income statements track a business's performance over time. The balance sheet is more like a snapshot of the business.

The audited balance sheet is typically prepared at the end of the **fiscal year***. This is the twelve-month accounting period chosen by the business. The fiscal year may differ from the calendar year (January 1 to December 31). A business that uses the calendar year as its fiscal year would prepare its balance sheet in December.

For various reasons, many businesses find it more convenient to close their ledgers and prepare their balance sheets in a different month. A business might choose a fis-

---

* Most entrepreneurs also prepare a balance sheet every month.

cal year of October 1 to September 30, for example, and prepare its balance sheet in September. Once a business chooses a fiscal year, it cannot change it without approval from the Internal Revenue Service.

Assets

Assets are all items of worth owned by the business, such as cash, inventory, furniture, machinery, etc.

- "Current" assets are those that could be sold for cash within one year.
- "Long-term" assets are those that would take more than a year to turn into cash.

Liabilities

Liabilities are debts owed by the business, such as bank loans, mortgages, credit-card purchases, and loans from family or friends.

- Current liabilities are those that must be paid within one year.
- Long-term liabilities are those that will be paid over a period of longer than a year.

Owner's Equity/Net Worth/Capital *

The terms owner's equity, **capital,** and net worth mean the same thing — what's left after liabilities are subtracted from assets. Owner's equity is the value on the balance sheet of the business to the owner.

Assets – Liabilities = Net Worth (or Owner's Equity, or Capital)

- If assets are greater than liabilities, net worth is positive.
- If assets are less than liabilities, net worth is negative.

The Financial Equation

The balance sheet is divided into two columns. All business assets are listed in the left column. All liabilities are listed in the right column, along with the business's debt and equity.

---

* Material in this section has been derived from *Modern Bookkeeping and Accounting,* by Morris Miller and Arthur Janis (Fearon-Pitman Publishers, Inc., 1973).

Every item a business owns was bought with either debt or equity. If an item was financed with debt, the loan is a liability. If an item was purchased with the owner's own money, it was financed with equity.

Say a restaurant owns its tables and chairs and has $10,000 in cash, but took out a loan to buy its stove. If the tables and chairs are worth $3,000, then the business has a $3,000 asset. If the stove cost $5,000, and the business had borrowed $5,000 to buy it, then the business has a $5,000 asset (the stove) and a $5,000 liability (the loan).

Cash	$ 10,000
Tables and Chairs	3,000
Stove	5,000
TOTAL ASSETS	$ 18,000

The balance sheet would look like this:

BALANCE SHEET CARLA'S RESTAURANT JAN. 2001

Assets		Liabilities	
Cash	$10,000	Loan	$ 5,000
Tables and Chairs	3,000		
Stove	5,000	Owner's equity	13,000
Total Assets	$18,000	Total Liabilities & Owner's Equity	$18,000

The equity ($13,000), on the right side, is equal to the total of the cash owned by the business ($10,000) and the tables and chairs ($3,000) owned by the business. The stove is financed with a ($5,000) loan (debt financing). The cash and tables and chairs are financed by $13,000 of the owner's money (equity financing).

On a balance sheet, both sides must show the same total.

The Financial Equation: Total Assets = Total Liabilities + Owner's Equity.

If your balance sheet total on the asset side doesn't add up to the total on the liability side, you've made a mistake somewhere.

Financial Analysis

The balance sheet is an especially good tool for looking at the relationship between debt and equity financing. As we discussed in Chapter 7, sometimes businesses make the mistake of relying too heavily on one form or the other. An entrepreneur who relies too much on equity can end up losing ownership of the company to the shareholders. An entrepreneur who takes on too much debt can lose the business to a bank or other creditors if he or she becomes unable to meet the loan payments.

All the information you need to analyze a company's financing strategy — total debt, equity, and assets — is in its balance sheet. Looking at ratios is helpful.

Debt Ratios

$$\text{Debt ratio: } \frac{\textbf{Total Debt}}{\textbf{Total Assets}}$$

The debt ratio describes how many of the total dollars in your business have been provided by creditors. A debt ratio of 55% means you are in debt for 55% of your assets.

Entrepreneurs like to have a fairly high debt ratio, because it means they aren't financing the business with their own money but are using the money of creditors and suppliers. On the other hand, bankers don't like to lend money to businesses with high debt ratios. If you need to go to a bank to borrow money or to a supplier to establish credit, keep your debt ratio fairly low.

$$\text{Debt-to-Equity ratio: } \frac{\textbf{Total Debt}}{\textbf{Equity}}$$

A debt-to-equity ratio of 100% would mean that for every dollar of debt the company has a dollar of equity. Equity is ownership that is either kept by the entrepreneur or given out in pieces in return for investment in the company. Too much equity can be dangerous if the equity is largely in the hands of investors, as they might take over control of the company.

Whether a ratio is good or bad depends on the amount of debt considered acceptable in your industry. In general, however, companies with lower debt ratios are considered more financially stable because they will owe fewer creditors if they go bankrupt.

Quick and Current Ratios

You can also analyze a business's *liquidity*, or ability to convert its assets into cash, using the balance sheet and the following ratios:

$$\text{Quick Ratio: } \frac{\textbf{Cash plus Marketable Securities}}{\textbf{Current Liabilities}}$$

This "quick" ratio tells you whether you have enough cash to cover your current debt. (Marketable securities are investments that can be sold for cash within 24 hours.) The quick ratio should always be greater than 1. This means that you have enough cash at your disposal to cover all your current short-term debts. If you had to pay all your bills tomorrow (not loans, just bills), you know you would have enough cash to do so.

$$\text{Current Ratio: } \frac{\textbf{Current Assets}}{\textbf{Current Liabilities}}$$

It's also good to try to maintain a current ratio greater than 1. A number greater than 1 indicates that, if you had to, you could sell some assets to pay off your debts.

Depreciation

As you learned in Chapter 10, **depreciation** is a certain portion of an asset that is subtracted each year until the asset's value reaches zero. Depreciation reflects the wear and tear on an asset over time. This reduces the value of an asset. A used car, for example, costs less money than a new one.

More complex balance sheets show depreciation as a subtraction from long-term assets. Most youth businesses have minimal or no depreciation and do not need to show it on the balance sheet.

Chapter 48 Review

NOTE: The exercises printed below can be found in the corresponding chapter of the NFTE MODULE 2 WORKBOOK that came with your textbook. Please write your answers there. If you do not have a workbook, write your answers on a separate sheet of paper.

Critical Thinking about ... Financial Ratios

Using the balance sheet of Jay's T-Shirt Company below, calculate all four financial ratios (quick, current, debt, and debt-to-equity) for Jay's business. Write a memo analyzing the financial strengths and weaknesses of Jay's venture.

Assets

Cash	$ 1,000
Inventory	1,000
Other Current Assets	1,000
Total Current Assets	$ 3,000
Long-Term Assets	7,000
Total Assets	$10,000

Liabilities and Owner's Equity

Accounts Payable	$ 1,000
Short-Term Loans	500
Total Current Liabilities	$ 1,500
Total Long-Term Liabilities	1,500
Total Liabilities	$ 3,000
Owner's Equity	7,000
Total Liabilities and Owner's Equity	$10,000

Preparing a Balance Statement

Suppose you have started a small business making and selling silk-screened T-shirts. You borrowed $100 from your parents and used $200 in savings to buy a $200 silk-screening machine to make your shirts. You buy 10 shirts wholesale at $2.50 each. Call these shirts "inventory," which is an asset. The money used to purchase them is owner's equity. Prepare your balance sheet.

Chapter 48 Review

Using New Words

assets
balance sheet
capital
depreciation
fiscal year
liabilities
net worth
owner's equity

On a separate sheet of paper, identify the vocabulary term that completes each sentence.

Unlike the income statement, which is typically prepared once a month, the _____ is a financial statement that is usually prepared at the end of the _____. The balance sheet shows the relationship between _____, which are items owned by the business, _____, which are business debts, and _____.

The terms _____ and _____ mean the same thing as owner's equity. Most youth businesses do not show _____ on the balance sheet.

Getting the Facts

True or False?

1. Owner's equity is the same thing as the cash in a business.

2. Current assets are assets that can be sold for cash within a year.

3. If assets are greater than liabilities, net worth is negative.

4. Every item in a business is financed with either debt or equity.

5. If the totals on each side of the balance sheet do not match, you've made an accounting error.

Exploring Your Community

Look up your local Merrill Lynch office in the phone book. Call and request a copy of their free booklet, "Understanding Financial Statements," which explains balance sheets and income statements in detail.

Review

Chapter Summary

I. **A clear picture of a business's financing strategy can be obtained from its balance sheet.**

A. The balance sheet is typically prepared at the end of the fiscal year.

B. The balance sheet shows the relationship between assets, liabilities, and net worth (also called owner's equity, or capital).

II. **Assets are all items owned by a business.**

A. Current assets can be sold for cash within a year.

B. Long-term assets would take more than a year to turn into cash.

III. **Liabilities are all debts owed by the business.**

A. Current liabilities are debts that must be paid within one year.

B. Long-term liabilities are debts that take longer than a year to pay.

IV. **Owner's equity and net worth mean the same thing — what's left after liabilities are subtracted from assets.**

Assets – Liabilities = Owner's Equity (Net Worth, or Capital)

V. **The total for the left, or "assets," side of the balance sheet must match the total for the right, the "liabilities and owner's equity."**

VI. **Four ratios are used to analyze balance sheets:**

A. Debt ratio

B. Debt-to-Equity ratio

C. Quick ratio

D. Current ratio

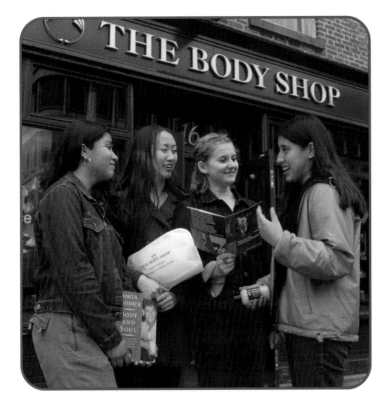

Never doubt that a small group of concerned citizens can change the world — indeed it is the only thing that ever has.

—Margaret Meade,
American anthropologist

KEY OBJECTIVES

READING THIS CHAPTER AND DOING THE EXERCISES WILL ENABLE YOU TO:

- Be able to describe "socially responsible business."

- Determine how to use your business to help people in your community.

- Develop "cause-related marketing" for your business.

SOCIALLY RESPONSIBLE BUSINESS AND PHILANTHROPY: GIVING BACK TO YOUR COMMUNITY

Socially Responsible Business

As you have learned throughout this course, there are many ways that entrepreneurs can use their businesses to help their communities and contribute to society. By being an entrepreneur, you already make an important contribution by providing goods and services to consumers who need them. As well, you can use your entrepreneurial skills, talents, and business venture to support social issues that are important to you. By running your business in a way that is consistent with your ethics and core values, you can start a **socially responsible business.**

Anita Roddick, who founded The Body Shop is a good example of an entrepreneur who has used her company as a force for social change very effectively. Her first big campaign came in 1985. Roddick let Greenpeace, an environmental preservation group, put up posters in Body Shop stores to educate people about the dumping of hazardous waste into the North Sea.

In the 1990s, 15 political prisoners were released due to the volume of letters that Body Shop customers wrote. Another Body Shop campaign raised public awareness about the destruction of the Brazilian rainforest.

"Trade Not Aid"

While traveling in Brazil, Roddick met with some of the tribal leaders in the Amazon region to figure out how the forest could produce income without cutting down trees. The Body Shop began buying Brazil nut oil and vegetable-dye beads from some of the tribes. This helped tribe members establish their own small businesses without destroying the rainforest. Roddick believes that helping poor people start their own business ventures is an effective way to address the negative effects that poverty can have on people's lives.

Cause-Related Marketing

Roddick's social and environmental campaigns created tremendous publicity for The Body Shop. Roddick would have had to spend millions of dollars to buy so much exposure for her company.

This kind of success has inspired other companies to get involved in **cause-related marketing**. This is marketing inspired by a commitment to a social, environmental, or political cause.

A great thing to do for your business is to associate it with a cause that you believe in — but make sure you do your research first. It is important that you understand the activities and purpose of any organization you choose to support through your business. Encourage your employees to participate, too. Corporate volunteerism is a great way to improve morale and make a difference. AT&T, for example, announced in 1998 that it would pay employees to devote one day a month to doing community service.

Gaining Goodwill

Many entrepreneurs try to make a difference in their communities by giving money and time to organizations that help people. Microsoft, for example, made it possible for NFTE to develop an Internet-based curriculum, BizTech (www.nfte.com). Microsoft has donated both money and computer programming experts to this project.

Why would Microsoft do this? For two reasons:

- First, Microsoft's founder, Bill Gates, believes in NFTE's mission and wants to help young people learn about business. The Internet-based program makes it much easier to teach entrepreneurship to greater numbers of young people around the world.

- Second, supporting this program is an intelligent business move for Microsoft. Microsoft gains publicity and **goodwill**. Goodwill is composed of intangible assets, such as reputation, name recognition, and customer relations. Goodwill can give a company an advantage over its competitors, especially when their products and services are similar.

Nonprofit Organizations

Nonprofit organizations are corporations that aim to contribute to the greater good of society and are not seeking to make a profit. The Internal Revenue Service classifies nonprofits under "501(c)(3)" in the tax code. As discussed in Chapter 36, these are corporations that are **tax exempt**. This means they do not have to pay federal or state taxes, and they are not privately or publicly owned. Essentially, a board of directors controls the operations of a 501(c)(3) nonprofit organization.

Such well known institutions as the Boys and Girls Clubs of America, the YMCA, the Girl Scouts, the Red Cross, and Big Brothers/Big Sisters are all examples of nonprofit organizations. Their founders were social entrepreneurs and, although they did not necessarily earn large sums of money personally, and could not sell the organization for a profit, they received great satisfaction and made a difference. Wendy Kopp, of Teach for America, and Michael Bronner of Upromise, are two recent examples of social entrepreneurs who founded innovative and successful nonprofit organizations described below.

Teach for America and Upromise

Founded in 1991, Teach for America recruits recent college graduates to become public school teachers. Operating with a budget of over $11 million, the organization trains thousands of young teachers and then places them in two-year teaching positions in schools where teachers are badly needed. Each year they select 1500 new teachers who reach over 100,000 students across the United States.

Michael Bronner, a former marketing executive who became a social entrepreneur, started Upromise in 2001. Bronner felt strongly that the cost of sending a child to college had become much too expensive for most families. He believed that there needed to be a better way of helping families save money for college. He came up with the idea that a portion of the money that families already spend on popular goods and services, such as groceries and toys, could go into a college savings account for their children. This idea led Bronner to start Upromise. Upromise works with established corporations, such as AT&T, America Online, and Toys "R" Us. Every time a registered family makes a purchase from one of these companies, a percentage of their spending automatically goes into a special college savings account. Both Wendy Kopp and Michael Bronner are examples of creative and successful entrepreneurs who implemented innovative ideas for promoting social change.

What Is Philanthropy?

There is a long, established connection in the United States between entrepreneurs and **philanthropy**. As we discussed in Chapter 46, philanthropists express their concern for social issues by giving money, time, or advice to charities they support. Philanthropists often give their money through **foundations**. A foundation is a nonprofit organization that passes on donated money, through grants, to other nonprofit organizations that help people and social causes.

The Bill and Melinda Gates Foundation, which was started by Microsoft's founder, Bill Gates, is one of the world's largest foundations, with over $23 billion in capital. This money comes from the personal wealth that Gates earned from Microsoft. As a private foundation, it is required by the federal government to give away 5% of the fair market value of its assets every year. The Bill and Melinda Gates Foundation provides an extremely large amount of money annually to other charities. These charities in turn use the money to finance social and community programs that the Gates Foundation supports, such as education and healthcare.

What Entrepreneurs Have Built

Many philanthropic foundations in this country were created by entrepreneurs who wanted to give some of the wealth that they earned back to the public. Entrepreneurs have financed great museums, libraries, universities, and other important institutions. Some foundations created by famous entrepreneurs include the Rockefeller Foundation, the Coleman Foundation, the Charles G. Koch Foundation, the Ford Foundation, and the Goldman Sachs Foundation.

Some of the most aggressive entrepreneurs in American history, such as Andrew Carnegie, have also been the most generous. In 1901, after a long and sometimes ruthless business career, Carnegie sold his steel company to J.P. Morgan for $420 million. Overnight, Carnegie became one of the richest men in the world. After retiring, he spent most of his time giving away his wealth to libraries, colleges, museums, and other worthwhile institutions that still benefit people today. By the time of his death from pneumonia in 1919, Carnegie had given away over $350 million to philanthropic causes.

You Have Something to Contribute

You may not have millions of dollars to contribute to your community . . . yet. But there are many ways you can be philanthropic that will be helpful, get your employees excited, and create goodwill in your community:

- Pledge a percentage of your sales to a nonprofit organization you have researched, believe in, and respect. Send out press releases announcing your pledge.

- Become a mentor to a younger entrepreneur. Help that person by sharing your contacts and expertise.

- Volunteer for an organization that helps your community. Find out how you can serve on their board of directors.

- Sell your product to a charity that you support at a discount. The charity can then resell it at full price to raise money.

- When you give it a little thought, you'll realize that you have a lot to give. Remember, making a contribution doesn't necessarily mean giving money. You can donate your time, advice, and moral support!

Chapter 49 Review

N O T E : The exercises printed below can be found in the corresponding chapter of the NFTE MODULE 2 WORKBOOK that came with your textbook. Please write your answers there. If you do not have a workbook, write your answers on a separate sheet of paper.

Critical Thinking about . . . Socially Responsible Business and Philanthropy *

1. If your business made a net profit of $10,000 this year, to which charity would you donate $100? Choose one of those below. On a separate piece of paper, write a paragraph explaining your choice.

    a) A community garden

    b) A local arts club

    c) A cancer-research lab

    d) An environmental group

    e) Other (create your own suggestion)

2. Write a business letter to another entrepreneur in your class asking him or her to also donate $100. (Explain the purpose of the organization and how it will benefit from the money. Also, explain how contributing the money will benefit your classmate who is making the donation.)

3. If you could create your own foundation, what would it do? Whom would it help? What would you name it? Write a short mission statement for your foundation.

4. Make a list of social issues you think are important. Find at least five non-profit organizations that address the social issues you selected. Conduct research on each one. What are their mission statements? How do they make a difference?

5. Do you think the founders of tax-exempt 501 (c) (3) organizations would have the same incentives as founders of for-profit companies? Discuss and explain.

---

* The authors would like to thank Vicki Kennedy for the idea behind this exercise.

Chapter 49 Review

Getting the Facts

1. How does philanthropy differ from socially responsible business?

2. Find a company you like that uses cause-related marketing. Describe how it is used and why you think it is effective.

Using New Words

foundation
cause-related marketing
goodwill
socially responsible business
philanthropy
tax exempt
nonprofit organization

Use the vocabulary terms to write a paragraph about how you plan to use your business to help others.

Exploring Your Community

1. In Chapter 46 you were asked to make a monthly commitment to a charity in your community. Write a memo to your teacher describing what you have done so far.

2. Write a short essay describing what you think is the most important social or environmental problem in your community. Discuss how you think entrepreneurship could help solve it.

Review

Chapter Summary

I. Running a socially responsible business means that your business practices are consistent with your ethics and core values.

II. You can use cause-related marketing to associate your business with a social cause or issue that you support.

A. Cause-related marketing can raise public awareness about important social, political, and environmental issues.

B. It can also generate free publicity and media attention for your business.

III. Before you associate your business with a charity, do research to make sure that you understand the activities and purpose of the organization or cause you are supporting.

A. Encourage your employees to volunteer and get involved in community service.

IV. When entrepreneurs contribute to social causes, they generate goodwill.

A. Goodwill is composed of intangible assets, such as reputation, name recognition, and consumer relations.

V. One way to contribute to your community is to start or support a nonprofit organization.

A. Nonprofit organizations are corporations that aim to contribute to the greater good of society and are not seeking to make a profit.

B. Nonprofits are classified under 501 (c) (3) in the tax code and are tax-exempt.

VI. Entrepreneurs have been practicing philanthropy for a long time.

A. Some of the great libraries, museums, and universities in the United States were financed by philanthropic entrepreneurs.

B. Philanthropists express their concern for social issues by giving money, time, or advice to charities that they support.

C. Philanthropists often give money to foundations, who then donate the money to other charities.

VI. It is never too early to start being a philanthropist.

A. Even if you don't have a lot of money, you can contribute by giving advice, volunteering, or by donating your services to a charity or cause that you believe in.

B. Think about how you can use entrepreneurship to practice philanthropy.

A Business for the Young Entrepreneur: Sporting Goods Store

Even if your business is small, you can do a lot that will be beneficial for your business as well as your community. Frank Alameda ran a sporting goods store on Manhattan's Lower East Side called East Side Sports. He purchased ads in the *Yellow Pages* but believed his most valuable promotion was community service. Each year Frank sponsored 22 local baseball and basketball teams in the area by providing them with uniforms and balls. This filled his store with kids and made him very popular with the parents in the neighborhood, too!

Frank says he knew his business would succeed because of his location in a neighborhood full of young people. He made it even more popular by getting involved with his community.

Support a Cause that Makes Sense for Your Business

Frank found a cause — sponsoring local teams — that worked with the competitive advantage of his business, which was his location in an urban neighborhood where a lot of young people lived. This made more sense for his particular business, than giving his time and some of his profits to an organization or charity that did not relate to his business. Find a cause that reflects what you care about and use your business to raise people's awareness and make a difference.

Where there's a will, there's a way.

— Anonymous

KEY OBJECTIVES

READING THIS CHAPTER AND DOING THE EXERCISES WILL ENABLE YOU TO:

- Explain how banks can afford to pay interest on deposits.
- Apply for a bank account.
- Befriend your banker.

BUILDING LIFELONG FINANCIAL RELATIONSHIPS

Put Your Money in a Safe Place

Earlier in this course your class probably took a field trip to open a bank account. Once you have a bank account, you will have a safe place to keep your money. People who do not have bank accounts need to carry all their money around at all times or hide it somewhere. This is both risky and dangerous. Your money is safer in a bank, whose deposits are insured by the federal government.

Most banks have their deposits protected by the Federal Deposit Insurance Corporation (FDIC). Individual accounts are protected up to $100,000 — even if the bank fails.

Banks offer two basic kinds of accounts — savings and checking.

Since banks are a major source of business capital through their lending, it is a good idea to begin a relationship with a bank early in your business career.

Savings Accounts

When you put money in a **savings account**, not only is it safe, but the bank pays you interest. It is a low rate of return compared to some other investments, but there is virtually no risk that you will lose your money. A savings account is a "low-risk, low-yield" investment.

Banks make their profit by taking the money of individual depositors and lending it. The banks receive a higher interest rate on the money they lend out than they pay on the deposits.

Checking Accounts

Paying by check, not cash, is the professional way to do business. It is safer than carrying around large sums of cash, and the cancelled checks provide proof that you paid your bill. When you write a check, you are authorizing the bank to pay someone from your account.

Shop around before you decide where to keep your **checking account**. Different banks have different fees and requirements. With some accounts it is necessary to maintain a minimum balance. Others require a minimum balance for you to write checks for free; if your balance is lower, the bank will charge you a small amount for each check you write. Look into what different banks offer. Choose the checking account that best suits your needs.

Sample Check

	1898
July 12, 19 97	55-57 212 **453**

Atlantic Youth Center $16.00

Sixteen dollars and 00/100 ———————— DOLLARS

MAINSTREET
MAINSTREET NATIONAL BANK
HOBOKEN OFFICE, HOBOKEN, N J 07030
MEMO *choir dues*

Theresa Moore

|: 012034 067453 |: || 0036208345 || 1898

Technology Tip: 24-Hour Banking

Banks are using technology to make themselves available to customers 24 hours a day — good news for busy entrepreneurs! You can use your ATM (Automatic Teller Machine) card anytime. More banks are issuing check cards (also called debit cards) that you can use at the ATM and that also let you make purchases from your checking account without the hassle of writing a check and presenting identification. You can even arrange to have payment of monthly utility bills made automatically from your account.

Touch-tone phones have made banking by phone easy and convenient. You can call for automated information about your account balances or recent activity. Or, you can use your bank's website. Many banks now allow you to download information from your bank statements directly into financial software like Microsoft Money, or Quicken. This makes bookkeeping easy.

Befriend Your Banker

At some point in your career as an entrepreneur, you will find yourself sitting in a banker's office asking for a loan. Wouldn't it be better if that banker were already your friend?

As soon as you start your first business, introduce yourself to a loan officer at your bank. People are usually nice to young entrepreneurs and like to hear about their businesses. You can make friends with this banker by showing him or her your business plan. Ask if he or she would be willing to read it and make suggestions for improving it.

As your business grows, keep your banker informed about how you are doing. Take him or her to lunch and talk about your business. If you are involved in social enterprise, involve your banker, too. Perhaps the bank would also be willing to contribute time or money to the charity you are helping.

 RULE OF THUMB: Develop the habit of always depositing 10% of your income into a savings account.

By the time your business needs a loan, you will have a friend at the bank. As your business grows, so will your relationship with your banker. Your banker can be a great source not only of loans, but of contacts with other financial institutions, venture capitalists, and advisors. This could become one of your most important friendships, so nurture it carefully.

Reginald F. Lewis: Billion-Dollar Businessman*

Reginald F. Lewis was born in Baltimore, Maryland, in 1942. When he died in 1993, he was one of the nation's wealthiest entrepreneurs and among the richest African-Americans in The United States. Much of his fortune was created by his wise use of bank financing.

Showing his entrepreneurial drive early on, Lewis grew his first paper route from 10 to 100 subscribers. Lewis acknowledged no racial boundaries as he worked his way through high school and Virginia State University. He was determined to enter Harvard Law School, and was accepted in 1965.

Being a successful lawyer might have satisfied most people, but Lewis was eager to move into the world of high finance. In 1983 he assembled financing from Wall Street investment banks to buy McCall Pattern for $22.5 million. To incentivize McCall's management team, Lewis offered them equity in return for investments. This kept them in the company and highly motivated to make it succeed. Together, in two years, they doubled the company's revenue and Lewis sold it in 1987 for $65 million. This provided a 90 to 1 return for investors. Next, Lewis bought Beatrice International for $950 million. This deal made him one of the biggest financiers in the world.

By the time Lewis died of brain cancer in 1993 at age 50, he was worth $400 million, putting him on the *Forbes* magazine list of the 400 wealthiest Americans. You can read more about Lewis in his book *"Why Should White Guys Have All the Fun?": How Reginald Lewis Created a Billion-Dollar Business Empire,* by Reginald F. Lewis and Blair S. Walker (John Wiley & Sons, Inc., 1995).

---

* Special thanks to NFTE board member Loida Lewis.

Sample Bank Account Application

MAINSTREET
MAINSTREET NATIONAL BANK

PERSONAL ACCOUNT SIGNATURE CARD

Type and Account Number

A	_____
	Name of Primary Account Holder

_____ Checking/Money Market
Investor

_____

B	_____
	Name of Co-Account Holder (Only if Joint Account)

_____ Certificate of Deposit

_____

C	_____
	Name of _____ Custodian _____ "In Trust For" (Beneficiary) _____ Power of Attorney _____

Form of Account   _____ Individual   _____ Joint

_____ Custodial   _____ "In Trust For"   _____ Other _____

_____ Savings _____ Br No. _____

Customer Acknowledgement: By signing this card, I acknowledge that I have received a copy of and accept the rules and regulations on this account which also contain the New Jersey Multiple Party Deposit Account rules and regulations and understand that the right of survivorship will apply to this account. (Does not apply to an individual account). In addition, I have received a copy of MainStreet's Funds Availability Policy.

Primary Account Holder Signature	Date of Birth	Social Security No. or Tax ID No.	Date
Co-Account Holder Signature	Date of Birth	Social Security No. or Tax ID No.	Date
Signature of: _____ Power of Attorney _____ Custodian _____ Other	Date of Birth	Social Security No. or Tax ID No.	Date

Taxpayer Certification: Under penalties of perjury I certify that:

a. The number shown on this form is my correct Social Security Number or Tax ID No.

AND _____ b. I am not subject to backup withholding either because I have not been notified that I am subject to backup withholding as a result of failure to report all interest or dividends, or the Internal Revenue Service has notified me that I am no longer subject to backup withholding.

OR _____ c. I am subject to backup withholding because I have been notified by the IRS that I am subject to backup withholding because of failure to report all interest or dividends or the IRS has not notified me that I am no longer subject to backup withholding.

A	_____	Date
	Primary Account Holder Signature	

B **For Primary Account Holder**
Home Address/No. and Street

Home Telephone _____

Business Telephone _____

City _____ State ___ Zip Code ___

Mother's Maiden Name_____

Employer's Name/Address

For Joint Accounts Only

Mother's Maiden Name_____   Business Telephone _____

Co-Account Employer's Name/Address

For Individual and "In Trust For" Accounts Only
Power of Attorney's/Address

Beneficiary's/Address

For All Accounts

Accounts With Other Banks

For Bank Use Only Opened by	Approved by	
Initial Deposit and Source of Funds	Remarks	Date

Chapter 50 Review

NOTE: The exercises printed below can be found in the corresponding chapter of the NFTE MODULE 2 WORKBOOK that came with your textbook. Please write your answers there. If you do not have a workbook, write your answers on a separate sheet of paper.

Critical Thinking about ... Banking

1. Make a list of the bank accounts and services that you will need to use for your business.

2. Write a memo describing your plan for befriending a banker. Think about everything you've learned in this course — any business plans you've written, your commitments to philanthropy, your personal background, and anything else that would make you an interesting young person that a banker might want to meet.

Getting the Facts

True or False?

1. Savings accounts offer low return for low risk.

2. Your bank account is protected by government insurance.

3. Banks are required by law to offer all consumers the same rates and balance requirements.

Using New Words

checking account
savings account

Using the vocabulary terms, write a paragraph about how you will use each type of bank account in your business.

Exploring Your Community

Visit three banks in your neighborhood and collect information about the checking and savings accounts they offer. Write a memo explaining which bank you would choose and why.

Chapter Summary

I.   **Put your money in a bank account where it will be safe and earn interest.**

II. **Banks pay interest on savings accounts because they profit by lending the deposits out at a higher interest rate.**

III. **Paying by check, not cash, is more professional.**

   A. Cancelled checks provide proof of payment.

   B. Checks are safer to carry than cash.

   C. Shop around for the best deal before choosing a bank for your checking account.

A Business for the Young Entrepreneur: Selling Candy or Soda

Candy and soda are both products that can be bought in bulk and sold as individual items for a profit. Grocery clubs or warehouses offer especially good prices on cases of soda or boxes of candy. If you can sell your product at a lower price than vending machines or stores near your school, your success is guaranteed.

Tips

- Get written permission from school authorities before trying to sell candy or soda in school or at sports events.

- A good rule of thumb is to "keystone" (double) the price of the product you are selling. If you can buy a can of soda for $.50, for example, try to sell it for $1.00.

ADVANCED BUSINESS PLAN REVIEW

NOTE: A complete version of the Advanced Business Plan can be found after Chapter 50 in the NFTE Module 2 Workbook that came with this textbook. Please complete your Plan there. Use the Review Pages below to familiarize yourself with the topics covered in the Advanced Business Plan.

Advanced Business Plan

Now you are ready to write a more detailed plan for your business venture. If you are satisfied with your Intermediate Business Plan, use those worksheets to help you fill out your Advanced Business Plan. This will be an opportunity, however, to improve on your Intermediate Business Plan or even change it entirely. Maybe you have decided to start a different business, for example, or perhaps you have done more research on your costs or market and can create a more accurate Plan now. In addition, this Advanced Business Plan includes a Projected Balance Sheet, Financial Ratio Analysis, and Break-Even Analysis, which will make your planning more accurate and professional.

Part One: Business Description

Your Business Idea
(See Chapter 8)

1) Describe your business idea and why you think it is a business opportunity.

2) What is the name of your business?

3) What is the competitive advantage of your business?

4) What problem or need does your product/service meet?

5) What education, experience, skills, hobbies or interests do you have that will help you make this business successful?

Owners

1) Provide contact information for each principal in the company.

2) Describe each owner's relevant experience, credentials, and percentage of ownership.

Business Goals

1) What are your short-term business goals? (less than one year)

2) What are your long-term business goals? (from one to five years)

3) What are your educational and training goals? (from one to five years)

4) What are your personal (lifetime) goals?

5) How will your business help you to contribute to your community?

Part Two: Marketing
(See Chapters 11, 14, and 18)

Draw Your Logo

Provide a graphic example of your logo and any trademarked slogans.

Step One: Consumer Analysis

Ask three people the following questions about your business. Make sure that they explain the reasons for their answers.

1) Do you like the name of my business? Why or why not?

2) What do you think of my logo?

3) Where would you want to go to buy my product?

4) Do you think my product has value?

5) How much would you pay for my product?

6) How would you improve my business idea?

7) Who is my closest competitor(s)?

8) Do you think my product is better or worse than that offered by my competitor(s)?

Step Two: Market Analysis

1) Analyze your market segment by location, population, personality, and behavior.

2) Describe your targeted market segments and how you intend to reach them with maximum impact for each marketing dollar you spend.

3) What percentage of the market do you feel you need to capture for your business to be profitable?

4) Who are the potential customers you plan to approach in the first two months of business?

5) Provide a profile of your target customer.

6) How do you plan to distribute your product to your target market?

7) Describe your packaging materials. How do they fit into your marketing plan?

8) Develop a mission statement for your business.

9) Do you use cause-related marketing?

Step Three: The Marketing Mix
Price

1) Describe your pricing strategy.

2) Are your prices competitive? Do a comparison.

3) Will you accept personal checks from customers? Credit cards? Will you offer charge accounts or customer credit?

Place

1) Describe your business location and its competitive advantages.

2) What are the zoning laws in your location? Does your business comply?

Promotion

How do you intend to get publicity for your business?

Marketing Plan

Complete your marketing plan in your NFTE Module 2 Workbook.

Sales

1) Describe the benefits of your product (or service) and how they arise from its features.

2) Will you make sales calls? If so, write a four-sentence sales presentation.

Marketing Materials

What marketing materials will you develop? List materials and development costs.

Part Three: Competition
(See Chapter 15)

1) List your closest competitors.

2) Describe the strengths and weaknesses of your competitors.

3) Describe how the market is divided among your competitors and how you intend to develop your market share.

4) Describe your competitive advantage in detail. How does your business differ from your competitors?

5) In what ways do you intend to beat the competition? Price? Service? Quality? New technology? Location?

Part Four: Economics of One Unit
(See Chapter 10)

- **Service Business** (Note: A service unit is typically defined as one hour of service or one job.)
  Define your unit.

- **Retail Business**
  Define your unit.

- **Wholesale Business** (Note: A wholesale unit is typically defined as one hour of service or one job.)
  Define your unit.

- **Manufacturing Business**
  Define your unit.

Part Five: Management
(See Chapter 41)

Consultants

Are you planning to use one or more consultants? If so, name them and describe their qualifications and how they will help your business.

Employees

Will you be hiring employees? If so, name them and describe their qualifications, their salaries, and how they will help your business.

Mentors/Advisors

Provide information for each of your mentors or advisors. If there is a board of advisors, list each member and describe their commitments to the board.

Advanced Business Plan Review

Professional Relationships

Provide contact information for your accountant, attorney, banker, and insurance agent.

Part Six:
Organizing Your Business
(See Chapter 39)

1) Do you have a bank account? Where? What type of account (checking or savings) do you have?

2) Are you planning to fill out a 1040 tax form?

3) Are you planning to fill out quarterly sales tax forms?

Business Ethics and Philanthropy
(See Chapters 46 and 49)

1) What do you consider to be the most important needs in your community? How do you plan to use your business to make a difference?

2) What are your personnel policies? How do you plan to make your business a positive and rewarding place to work?

Business Technology
(See Chapter 21)

Indicate which technology tools you plan to use for your business.

Record Keeping
(See Chapter 16)

1) Describe your accounting system.

2) Describe your filing system.

Part Seven: Legal Structure
(See Chapter 40)

1) Is your business a Sole Proprietorship, a Partnership, a C Corporation, a Subchapter–S, a Limited Liability Corporation, or a Not-for-Profit Corporation?

2) Why did you choose your legal structure?

3) What permits and/or licenses will you need?

Part Eight: Start-Up Costs and Financing Strategy
(See Chapter 7)

1) Itemize your estimated start-up costs.

2) List your sources of financing. Identify whether each source is equity, debt, or a gift.

3) If you are receiving equity financing, what percentage of ownership will you give up?

4) If you are receiving debt financing, what is the maximum interest rate you will pay?

Part Nine: Operating Costs and Break-Even Analysis
(See Chapters 10 and 31)

Monthly Fixed Costs: Utilities, Salaries, Advertising, Interest, Insurance, Rent, and Depreciation (USAIIRD).

1) Type of Fixed Costs

2) Total Monthly Fixed Costs

Variable Costs: Operating Costs that fluctuate with Sales, estimated as a percentage of Sales.

1) Type of Variable Costs

2) Total Monthly Variable Costs

Break-Even Analysis

Calculate the break-even point for a business with no Variable Costs.

Monthly Budget: Projected Income Statement
(See Chapter 4)

Complete the monthly projected budget in your NFTE Module 2 Workbook.

Part Thirteen: Financial Ratio Analysis
(See Chapter 5)

Calculate Return on Investment (ROI), Return on Sales Revenue (ROS), and Payback using numbers from your Projected Income Statement.

Part Fourteen: Cash Flow Statement
(See Chapter 24)

Use the Cash Flow chart in your NFTE Module 2 Workbook to create a Projected Cash Flow statement for your business.

Part Fifteen: The Balance Sheet
(See Chapter 48)

Create a Projected Balance Sheet for your business using the chart in your NFTE Module 2 Workbook.

Advanced Business Plan Review

Resources for the Young Entrepreneur
How to Read The Wall Street Journal *

The Wall Street Journal is read daily by American business — over two million people a day! But even *The Wall Street Journal* began as a small, entrepreneurial venture.

In 1882, Charles Dow and Edward Jones started a service for people working in New York City's financial district. Their service provided handwritten, up-to-the-minute financial news to subscribers. Dow and Jones's first office was in a room behind a soda fountain, in a building next to the New York Stock Exchange on Wall Street. By 1889, *The Wall Street Journal* was being sold as a newspaper for two cents.

Since then, the *Journal* has become the largest daily newspaper in the United States. When you pick up the *Journal,* you are reading the same paper as the world's most successful entrepreneurs. *The Wall Street Journal* is available on newsstands and by subscription. To have it mailed or delivered to you, call: (800) 628-9320 or visit http://www.wsj.com.

The Journal's Three Sections

Breaking the paper down into its three main sections, Front Page, The Marketplace, and Money & Investing will make it much easier to read.

Section A, "Front Page"

1. **What's News** is a brief description of the major stories of the day.
2. At the bottom of the front page is **Today's Contents.** This will help you find the page numbers of other features and departments.
3. Columns 1 (far left) and 6 (far right) are the spots for in-depth articles on a wide range of business topics and for profiles of business and political leaders
4. Column 5 is reserved for what the *Journal* calls its **"Newsletter."**

---

* Adapted with permission from materials prepared by Dow Jones, Inc.

The front page is the first page of Section A. Here is what you'll find in the rest of the section.

1. On page A2 is the latest economic news.
2. The middle part of Section A is generally composed of the stories listed in **What's News**.
3. The daily **Industry Focus** spotlights one company or one industry.
4. Near the back of Section A are two pages devoted to **International Reports** — business and political news from other countries.
5. In its **Leisure & Arts** section, the *Journal* reviews books and music and covers sports news.
6. The two facing pages at the end of Section A are the **editorial pages**.

Section B, "The Marketplace"

This section contains the important business stories of the day. On the first page of the section, look for:

1. The **lead story**, given the most prominent spot at the top of the page.
2. **"The orphan"** — a short, amusing, true story.

Here is what you will find in the rest of Section B:

1. **Index to Business** (page B2). This is a list, by page number, of the businesses written about in that day's issue.
2. The **Enterprise** feature is about smaller, entrepreneurial companies.
3. **Technology** reports on high-tech businesses.
4. **Marketing & Media** covers advertising and the media.
5. **The Law** reports on legal issues affecting business.
6. **The Mart** appears in Business Opportunities at the end of Section B, and consists of classified pages that list employment opportunities and businesses for sale.

Section C, Money & Investing

Activity on the five major financial markets during the previous eighteen months and the previous week is represented through **graphs**. The markets are:

- Stocks
- Bonds
- Interest (rates)
- U.S. Dollar (compared to five foreign currencies)
- Commodities

In the rest of Section C, you will find:

1. An important financial market column, **Heard on the Street**.
2. Reports on how various financial markets, including the stock market, are performing.

Back in 1889, *The Wall Street Journal* started reporting the Dow Jones Industrial Average (DJIA), an average of the prices of eleven major stocks, to indicate how the economy in general is doing. Today, Dow Jones reports price averages for three types of stock and includes many more companies.

The price movements of these stocks are averaged at the end of each day. These averages are called the "Dow Jones Averages." You've probably heard them announced during the business news on television or on the radio.

Other financial markets covered in Section C of the *Journal* are:

- Mutual Funds
- International Stocks
- Foreign Currencies
- Credit Markets
- Futures & Options

Resources

For a more detailed look at *The Wall Street Journal*, see *The Dow Jones-Irwin Guide to Using the Wall Street Journal,* by Michael B. Lehmann (Homewood, Illinois: Dow Jones-Irwin, 1987).

Resources for the Young Entrepreneur
Important Math Equations

1. Return on Investment:

$$\frac{\text{Ending Wealth} - \text{Beginning Wealth}}{\text{Beginning Wealth}} \times 100$$

2. Rule of 72: How many years it takes for money to double in value:

$$\frac{72}{\text{ROI}}$$

3. Break-Even (in units):

$$\frac{\text{Fixed Costs}}{\text{Gross Profit per Unit}}$$

4. Intellectual Property Symbols:

Trademark: ™

Copyright: © or Copyr. or Copyright

Registered (as in Trademark): ®

Service Mark: ℠

5. Debt-to-Equity Ratio:

$$\frac{\text{Debt}}{\text{Equity}} \times 100$$

6. Debt Ratio:

$$\frac{\text{Debt}}{\text{Assets}} \times 100$$

7. Markup Percentage:

$$\frac{\text{Markup}}{\text{Wholesale Cost}} \times 100$$

8. Gross Profit Margin per Unit:

$$\frac{\text{Gross Profit per Unit}}{\text{Retail Price}} \times 100$$

9. Profit Margin:

$$\frac{\text{Profit}}{\text{Sales}} \times 100$$

10. Quick Ratio:

$$\frac{\text{Cash} + \text{Marketable Receivables}}{\text{Current Liabilities}}$$

11. Current Ratio:

$$\frac{\text{Current Assets}}{\text{Current Liabilities}}$$

Glossary

accounts payable *n.* money a business owes its suppliers.

accrue *v.* to increase or grow because interest is being added periodically.

angel *n.* a potential investor who might invest in your business and would not demand as high a rate of return as a venture capitalist or a bank.

arbitration *n.* settling a conflict with the help of another person both parties trust rather than in a court of law.

assembly line *n.* continuous moving line in a factory where parts are put together.

attitude *n.* a way of acting, thinking or feeling that expresses one's opinion.

assets *n.* any item of value owned by a business. Cash, inventory, furniture, and machinery are all examples of assets.

audit *n.* a formal study of accounts conducted by the Internal Revenue Service to determine whether the tax-payer being investigated is paying appropriate taxes.

balance *n.* 1. the difference between the credit and the debit side of a ledger; also, the difference between the assets and liabilities of a financial statement.

2. to calculate such differences; to settle an account by paying debts; to keep books properly so credits and debits in an account equal each other.

balance sheet *n.* a financial statement summarizing the assets, liabilities and net worth (or owner's equity) of a business, so called because the sum of the assets equals the total of the liabilities plus the net worth (or owner's equity).

benefit *n.* an improvement in one's condition; an advantage of doing or accepting something.

board of directors *n.* a group of persons who manage or control a business. The board of directors of a corporation is chosen by the stockholders. Unincorporated business owners sometimes appoint a board of directors to advise the business.

bond *n.* an interest-bearing certificate issued by a government or business that promises to pay the holder interest as well as the value of the bond at maturity.

brand *n.* a name (sometimes with an accompanying symbol or trademark) that distinguishes a business from its competition and makes its competitive advantage instantly recognizable to the consumer.

breach of contract *n.* failure by a person who signed a contract to comply with its provisions.

budget *n.* a plan to spend money.

burn rate *n.* negative cash flow; cash on hand divided by monthly operating costs, which is a ratio that indicates how many months a business can cover its overhead without making a profit.

business *n.* the buying and selling of goods and services in order to make a profit.

business card *n.* a small, rectangular card imprinted with a business's name, logo and contact information (and, often, a slogan).

capital *n.* money or property owned or used in business.

cash flow *n.* cash receipts less cash disbursements over a period of time. Cash flow is represented by the cash balance in an accounting journal or ledger.

cause-related marketing *n.* marketing that is tied to a social, political, or environmental cause that the entrepreneur wants to support.

charge account *n.* credit extended by a store allowing qualified customers to make purchases up to a specified limit without paying cash at the time of purchase.

checking account *n.* a bank account against which the account holder can write checks.

collateral *n.* property or assets pledged by a borrower to a lender to secure a loan.

competition *n.* rivalry in business for customers or markets. Competition in a free market leads to lower prices and produces better quality goods and services for consumers.

competitive advantage *n.* a benefit that you can deliver to the consumers in your market better than any of your competitors.

compromise *n.* a settlement in which each side in a negotiation has given in on some demands.

consumer *n.* a person or business that buys goods and services for its own needs, not for resale or to use to produce goods and services for resale.

contingency *n.* an unforeseen or unpredictable event.

continuous improvement *n.* the idea that constantly seeking to improve quality and efficiency within a business will increase profits.

contract *n.* a formal written agreement between two or more people legally binding each party to fulfill his or her obligations as specified.

core competency *n.* a fundamental knowledge, ability, or expertise in a special subject area or skill set which is critical to the success of a business; another term for "competitive advantage."

corporation *n.* a legal "person" or "entity," composed of stockholders, that is granted the right to buy, sell, and inherit possessions, and is legally liable for the "its" actions.

cost *n.* an expense; the amount of money, time, or energy spent on something.

cost of goods sold *n.* the cost of selling "one additional unit."

cost/benefit analysis *n.* a decision-making process in which the costs of taking an action are compared to the benefits; if the benefits outweigh the costs, the action is taken.

creativity *n.* the ability to invent something using your imagination or perceive an already existing thing or situation in a new way.

credit *n.* in bookkeeping, a recording of income.

cyclical *adj.* occurring in cycles, which are periods when something happens again.

data *n.* information, such as customer addresses, stored in a computer.

debit *n.* in bookkeeping, a recording of an expense.

debt *n.* an obligation to pay back a loan; a "liability."

debt ratio *n.* the ratio of debt (liabilities) to assets.

debt-to-equity ratio *n.* a comparison that expresses financial strategy by showing how much of a company is financed by debt and how much by equity.

deductible *n.* the portion of an insured loss or damage not covered by the insurance; the higher the deductible, the lower the insurance premium.

deduction *n.* expenses incurred during the course of doing business. A business owner may subtract deductible amounts from income when figuring income tax due.

demand *n.* the willingness and desire for a commodity together with the ability to pay for it; the amount consumers are ready and able to buy at the price offered in the market.

demographics *n.* population statistics.

depreciation *n.* the amount of value of an asset subtracted each year until the asset value becomes zero; reflects wear and tear on the asset.

discount *n.* (referring to bonds) the difference between a bond's trading price and par when the trading price is below par.

dividend *n.* each stockholder's portion of the profit per share paid out by a corporation to its stockholders.

donation *n.* a gift or contribution to a charitable organization.

draft *v.* to write a version of a contract or agreement with the understanding that it will probably need to be developed and rewritten further.

economy *n.* the financial structure of a country or other area that determines how resources and wealth are distributed.

electronic rights *n.* protection of a creator's intellectual property (writing, art, music, etc.) from being used on a website without payment to the creator.

electronic storefront *n.* a website set up as a store where consumers can see and purchase merchandise.

e-mail *n.* short for electronic mail; messages sent between computers using the Internet.

employee *n.* a person hired by a business to work for wages (salary) or commission.

entrepreneur *n.* a person who organizes and manages a business, assuming the risk for the sake of the potential return.

equity *n.* ownership in a company received in exchange for money invested. In accounting, equity is equal to assets minus liabilities.

ethics *n.* a system of morals or standards of conduct and judgment.

fax *n.* short for facsimile, a machine that electronically sends printed material over a telephone line; v. to use a fax machine.

face value *n.* the value printed on a bill or bond; not necessarily its market value.

file *v.* (referring to taxes) to fulfill one's legal obligation by mailing a tax return, and any taxes due, to the Internal Revenue Service or state or local tax authority.

fiscal year *n.* a twelve-month period between settlements of financial accounts.

fixed costs *n.* business expenses that must be paid whether or not any sales are being generated; USAIIRD: utilities, salaries, advertising, insurance, interest, rent, and depreciation.

foundation *n.* an organization that manages money donated to it by philanthropists.

franchise *n.* a business that markets a product or service developed by the franchisor, in the manner specified by the franchisor.

franchisee *n.* owner of a franchise unit or units.

franchisor *n.* person who develops a franchise or a company that sells franchises.

fraud *n.* intentional failure by a business owner to inform a customer that he or she could be hurt in some way by the business's product or service.

free enterprise system *n.* economic system in which businesses are privately owned and operate relatively free of government interference.

future value *n.* the amount an investment is worth in the future if invested at a specific rate of return.

goodwill *n.* an intangible asset generated when a company does something positive that has value — goodwill can include the company's reputation, brand recognition, and relationships with the community and customers.

Gross Domestic Product (GDP) *n.* the annual estimated value of all products and services produced within a country.

Gross National Product (GNP) *n.* the annual market value of all products and services produced by the resources of a country.

gross profit *n.* total sales revenue minus total cost of goods sold.

hyperlink *n.* a highlighted or underlined word, phrase, or icon on a website that, when clicked on, leads to a new document page anywhere on the Internet.

immigrant *n.* a person who settles in a new country or region, having left his or her country or region of birth.

incentive *n.* something that motivates a person to take action — to work, start a business, or study harder, for example.

income statement *n.* a financial statement that summarizes income and expense activity over a specified period and shows net profit or loss.

inflation *n.* a continuous increase in the prices of products and services, usually resulting from an increase in the amount of money in circulation in an economy.

infringe *v.* to violate a copyright, trademark, or patent.

installment *n.* payment on a loan or debt made at regular intervals.

institutional advertising *n.* advertisements placed by large corporations to keep the name of the company in the mind of the public, not to promote a specific product or service.

insurance *n.* a system of protection provided by insurance companies to protect people or businesses from having their property or wealth damaged or destroyed.

insurance agent *n.* insurance company employee who sells insurance and helps purchasers determine what insurance they need to protect their assets.

insurance policy *n.* contract between an insurance company and a person or business being insured that describes the premium(s) to be paid and the insurance company's obligations.

intellectual property *n.* intangible property created using the intellect, such as an invention, book, painting, or music.

interest *n.* payment for using someone else's money; payment received for lending money.

interest rate *n.* money paid for the use of money, expressed as a percentage per unit of time.

Internal Revenue Service *n.* the federal government bureau in charge of taxation.

Internet *n.* the world's largest computer network, connecting millions of users worldwide.

interoffice *adj.* describes something sent from one person to another within the same office, using the office distribution system.

inventory *n.* items on hand to be sold.

investment *n.* something into which one puts money, time, or energy with the hope of gaining profit or satisfaction, in spite of risks.

invoice *n.* an itemized list of goods delivered or services rendered and the amount due; a bill.

ISP *n.* abbreviation for Internet Service Provider; services that provide access to the Internet for subscribers' computers. Some ISPs, such as Microsoft Network or America Online, also provide software for browsing the Internet and chatting with other subscribers, among other services.

kaizen *n.* Japanese word for "continuous improvement"; the philosophy that continually seeking to improve quality will steadily increase profits.

lateral thinking *n.* a way of perceiving that looks for indirect approaches to a problem or obstacle; the opposite of vertical thinking.

lawsuit *n.* attempt to recover a right or claim through legal action.

layaway *n.* store policy allowing a customer to make a down payment on an item to secure it and then make monthly payments on the remaining balance (the store keeps the item until it is fully paid for).

letter of agreement *n.* written agreement between parties regarding a business arrangement; less formal and detailed than a contract and usually used for arrangements of brief duration or rel

letterhead *n.* stationery imprinted with the name, address, phone and fax numbers, logo, etc., of a business.

leveraged *adj.* financed by debt, not equity.

liable *adj.* to be responsible for lawsuits that arise from accidents, unpaid bills, faulty merchandise, or other business problems.

liability *n.* an entry on a balance sheet showing the debts of a business.

liability insurance *n.* insurance that covers the cost of injuries to a customer or damage to property caused by a business's product or service.

license *n.* (1) authorization by law to do some specified thing (2) to grant the right to use the licensor's name on a product or service.

licensee *n.* person granted the right to use the licensor's name on a product or service sold by the licensee.

licensor *n.* person who sells the right to use his or her name or company name to a licensee; unlike the franchisor, the licensor does not attempt to dictate exactly how the licensee does business.

Limited Liability Company (LLC) *n.* a form of business ownership offering the tax advantages of a partnership as well as limited legal liability; this form is not available in all states.

limited partnership *n.* form of partnership in which certain partners have limited investment in a business and therefore limited liability.

logo *n.* short for logotype, a distinctive company trademark or sign.

majority interest *n.* ownership of more stock in a corporation than all other stockholders own together.

manufacture *v.* to make or produce a tangible product.

market *n.* a group of people potentially interested in buying a product or service; any scenario or designated location where trade occurs.

market segment *n.* a group of consumers who have a similar response to a particular type of marketing.

marketing *n.* the development and use of strategies for getting a product or service to the consumer and generating interest in it.

marketing mix *n.* the combination of four factors — product, price, place, and promotion — that communicate a marketing vision to your consumer.

market clearing price *n.* the price at which the amount of a product or service demanded by consumers equals the amount the supplier is willing to sell at that price; the price at which the supply and demand lines cross. Also called "equilibrium price."

markup *n.* an increase in the price of a product to cover expenses and create a profit for the seller.

maturity *n.* the date at which a bond must be redeemed by the company that issued it.

media *n.* *pl.* means of communication (newspapers, radio, television, etc.) that reach the general public, usually including advertising.

memo *n.* short for memorandum, from the Latin word for "to be remembered"; a brief, concise note from one person to another.

mentor *n.* a person who agrees to volunteer time and expertise, and provide emotional support to help another person reach his or her goals.

mission statement *n.* a short, written statement that informs your customers and employees what your business goal is and describes the strategy and tactics you intend to use to meet it.

modem *n.* device that connects a computer to a phone or cable line and translates digital information between them.

monopoly *n.* a market with only one producer; the control of the pricing and distribution of a product or service in a given market as a result of lack of competition.

negotiation *n.* discussion or bargaining in an effort to reach agreement between parties with differing goals.

net *n.* final result; in business, the profit or loss remaining after all costs have been subtracted.

networking *n.* the act of exchanging valuable information and contacts with other businesspeople.

newsgroup *n.* an online discussion group focused on a specific subject.

operating cost *n.* each cost necessary to operate a business, not including cost of goods sold. Operating costs can almost always be divided into USAIIRD: utilities, salaries, advertising, insurance, interest, rent, and depreciation. Operating costs are also called "overhead."

opportunity *n.* a chance or occasion that can be turned to one's advantage.

opportunity cost *n.* the value of what must be given up in order to obtain something else.

optimist *n.* a person who consistently looks on the bright side of situations or outcomes.

overhead *n.* the continuing fixed costs of running a business; the costs a business has to pay to be able to operate.

owner's equity *n.* net worth; the difference between assets and liabilities.

par *adj.* the face value of a bond.

partnership *n.* an association of two or more people in a business enterprise.

patent *n.* an exclusive right, granted by the government, to produce, use, and sell an invention or process.

percentage *n.* literally, "a given part of a hundred"; a number expressed as part of a whole, with the whole represented as 100 percent.

philanthropy *n.* a concern for human and social welfare that is expressed by giving money to charities and foundations.

pilferage *n.* stealing by employees or customers of a business's inventory.

premium *n.* the amount above par for which a bond is trading on the open market; the cost of insurance, usually expressed as a monthly or annual payment by the policyholder to the insurance company.

present value *n.* the amount an investment is worth discounted back to the present.

press release *n.* an announcement sent to the media to generate publicity.

principal *n.* the amount of a debt or loan before interest is added.

product *n.* something that exists in nature, or made by human industry, usually to be sold.

production/distribution structure *n.* the manufacturer-to-wholesaler-to-retailer-to-consumer chain along which a product progresses.

profit *n.* the sum remaining after all costs are deducted from the income of a business.

profit and loss statement *n.* an income statement showing the gain and loss from business transactions and summarizing the net profit or loss.

profit per unit *n.* the selling price minus the cost of goods sold of an item.

profit margin *n.* the percentage of each dollar of revenue that is profit; profit divided by revenue times 100.

progressive tax *n.* a tax that takes a greater percentage of higher incomes than of lower incomes.

projection *n.* a forecast or prediction of financial outcome in the future; business plans include projections of how the entrepreneur expects financial statements to come out.

promissory note *n.* a written promise to pay a certain sum of money on a specified date.

promotion *n.* the development of the popularity and sales of a product or service through advertising and publicity.

proportional tax *n.* a tax that takes the same percentage of all incomes.

prototype *n.* a model or pattern that serves as an example of how a product would look and operate if it were manufactured.

public domain *adj.* free of copyright or patent restrictions.

publicity *n.* free promotion, as opposed to advertising, which is purchased.

quality *n.* the degree of excellence of a product or service.

quota *n.* a restriction imposed by the government on the amount of a specified good that can be imported into that government's country.

rate of return *n.* the return on an investment, expressed as a percentage of the amount invested.

recession *n.* an economic downturn; less employment and business activity.

redeem *v.* to turn in a bond to the issuing corporation at the date of maturity for conversion into cash.

return on investment *n.* profit on an investment, expressed as a percentage.

risk *n.* the chance of loss.

royalty *n.* a share of the proceeds of the sale of a product paid to a person who owns a copyright; also refers to the fee paid to a franchisor or licensor.

sales tax *n.* consumption tax levied on items that are sold by businesses to consumers. States raise revenue through sales tax.

savings account *n.* a bank account in which money is deposited and on which the bank pays interest to the depositor.

self-employment tax *n.* a tax people who work for themselves pay in addition to income tax; includes the Social Security tax obligation for people who are self-employed.

self-esteem *n.* belief in oneself; a good feeling about oneself.

service *n.* intangible work providing time, skills, or expertise in exchange for money.

share *n.* a single unit of stock in a corporation.

shareware *n.* free software available on the Internet; shareware is usually the test or "light" version of the software.

signatory *n.* person signing a contract, thereby legally committing to compliance with the contract.

small claims court *n.* state court where disputes for relatively small amounts of money are settled between complainants who are allowed to represent themselves instead of using attorneys.

socially responsible business *n.* a business venture that expresses the entrepreneur's ethics and core values.

Social Security *n.* a federal government program that pays benefits to retired people and the families of dead or disabled workers.

sole proprietorship *n.* a business owned by one person. The owner receives all profits and is legally liable for all debts or lawsuits arising from the business.

speculative *adj.* very uncertain or risky.

start-up cost *n.* an expense involved in getting a business going; start-up costs are also called the "original investment" in a business.

statistics *n.* facts collected and presented in numerical fashion.

strategy *n.* the plan for how a business intends to outperform its own performance and that of its competition.

stock *n.* an individual's share in the ownership of a corporation, based on how much he or she has invested in the corporation.

supply *n.* a schedule of the quantities that a business will make available to consumers at different prices.

tactics *n.* the practical ways in which a business carries out its strategy.

tariff *n.* a tax imposed by a government on an import designed to make the import more expensive than a similar domestic product and, therefore, less attractive to domestic consumers.

tax *n.* a percentage of a business's gross profit or an individual's income taken by the government to support public services.

tax evasion *n.* deliberate avoidance of the obligation to pay taxes; may lead to penalties or even jail.

tax-exempt *adj.* the condition of an entity that is allowed to produce income sheltered from taxation.

test market *v.* to offer a product or service to a limited, yet representative, segment of consumers in order to receive feedback and improve the product or service, before attempting to place it in a larger market.

trade balance *n.* the difference between the value of a country's imports and its exports.

trademark *n.* any word, name, symbol, or device used by a manufacturer or merchant to distinguish a product.

trade-off *n.* an exchange in which one benefit or advantage is given up in order to gain another.

value pricing *n.* a strategy based on finding the balance between price and quality that will attract the most consumers.

variable cost *n.* any cost that changes based on the volume of units sold; a term sometimes used instead of "cost of goods sold."

venture capital *n.* funds invested in a potentially profitable business enterprise despite risk of loss.

vertical thinking *n.* a type of thought process that "stacks" one idea on top of another; vertical thinking can lead to "concept prisons" because it encourages you to fit new information into existing patterns.

website *n.* an Internet document that can contain sound and graphics, as well as text.

Give a man a fish and you feed him for a day.

Teach a man to fish and you feed him for a lifetime.

—Lao Tzu